Non-State Rules in International Commercial Law

Through further technological developments and increased globalisation, conducting business abroad has become easier, including for Small and Medium Enterprises (SME). However, the legal issues associated with international commerce have not lessened in complexity, including the role of non-state rules.

This book provides a comprehensive analysis of non-state rules in international commercial contracts. Non-state rules have legal authority in the national and international sphere, but the key question is how this legal authority can be understood and established. To answer this question this book examines first what non-state rules are and how their legal authority can be measured, it then analyses how non-state rules are applied in different scenarios, including as the applicable law, as a source of law, or to interpret either the law or the contract. Throughout this analysis three other important questions are also answered: when can non-state rules be applied? when are they applied? and how are they applied? The book concludes with a framework and classification that leads to a deeper understanding of the legal authority of non-state rules.

Providing a transnational perspective on this important topic, this book will appeal to anyone researching international commercial law. It will also be a valuable resource for arbitrators and anyone working in international commercial litigation.

Johanna Hoekstra is a Lecturer in Law at the University of Essex, UK.

Routledge Research in International Commercial Law

Available titles in this series include:

International Commercial and Marine Arbitration
Georgios I. Zekos

International Commercial Arbitration and the Arbitrator's Contract
Emilia Onyema

Jurisdiction and Arbitration Agreements in International Commercial Law
Zheng Sophia Tang

Progressive Commercialization of Airline Governance Culture
Jan Walulik

Economic and Environmental Regulation of International Aviation
From Inter-National to Global Governance
Steven Truxal

Combining Mediation and Arbitration in International Commercial Dispute Resolution
Dilyara Nigmatullina

Non-State Rules in International Commercial Law
Contracts, Legal Authority and Application
Johanna Hoekstra

Non-State Rules in International Commercial Law

Contracts, Legal Authority and Application

Johanna Hoekstra

Routledge
Taylor & Francis Group
LONDON AND NEW YORK

First published 2021
by Routledge
2 Park Square, Milton Park, Abingdon, Oxon OX14 4RN

and by Routledge
605 Third Avenue, New York, NY 10017

Routledge is an imprint of the Taylor & Francis Group, an informa business

British Library Cataloguing-in-Publication Data
A catalogue record for this book is available from the British Library

Library of Congress Cataloging-in-Publication Data
Names: Hoekstra, Johanna, author.
Title: Non-state rules in international commercial law : contracts, legal authority, and application / Johanna Hoekstra.
Description: Milton Park, Abingdon, Oxon ; New York, NY : Routledge, 2021.
| Series: Routledge research in international commercial law | Includes bibliographical references and index.
Identifiers: LCCN 2020044776 (print) | LCCN 2020044777 (ebook) | ISBN 9780367195441 (hardback) | ISBN 9780367220846 (ebook)
Subjects: LCSH: Commercial law. | Export sales contracts. | Conflict of laws--Commercial law. | Contracts (International law) | International commercial arbitration.
Classification: LCC K1005 .H645 2021 (print) | LCC K1005 (ebook) | DDC 346.07--dc23
LC record available at https://lccn.loc.gov/2020044776
LC ebook record available at https://lccn.loc.gov/2020044777

ISBN: 978-0-367-19544-1 (hbk)
ISBN: 978-0-367-74081-8 (pbk)
ISBN: 978-0-367-22084-6 (ebk)

Typeset in Galliard
by Spi Global, India

Contents

Abbreviations

ALI	American Law Institute
CESL	Common European Sales Law
CFR	Common Frame of Reference
CISG	Convention for the International Sales of Goods
CMI	Comité Maritime International
DCFR	Draft Common Frame of Reference
EFTA	European Free Trade Association
EU	European Union
FAA	Federal Arbitration Act
GAFTA	Grain and Free Trade Association
Hague Principles	The Hague Principles on Choice of Law in International Contracts
Hague-Visby Rules	The 1924 International Convention for the Unification of Certain Rules of Law relating to Bills of Lading amended by the 1968 Visby Protocol and the 1979 Special Drawing Rights Protocol
HCCH	Hague Conference of Private International Law
ICC	International Chamber of Commerce
ICJ	International Court of Justice
ICSID	International Centre for Settlement of Investment Disputes
Incoterms	International Commercial Terms
ISDA	International Derivatives and Swaps Association
OAS	Organisation of American States
OHADA	Organisation pour l'Harmonisation en Afrique du Droit des Affaires
NAEGA	North American Export Grain Association
NCCUSL	National Conference of Commissioners on Uniform State Laws (See also ULC)
PLACL	Principles of Latin American Contract Law
PECL	Principles of European Contract Law
Rome I	Rome I Regulation on the Law Applicable to Contractual Obligations
SME	Small and Medium Enterprises

UCC	Uniform Commercial Code
UCP	Uniform Credits & Practices
UCTA	Unfair Contract Terms Act
ULC	Uniform Law Commission (See also NNCCUSL)
UNCITRAL	United Nations Commission on International Trade Law
UNIDROIT	Institution for the Unification of Private Law
ULFIS	Uniform Law on the Formation of Contracts for the International Sales of Goods
ULIS	Uniform Law on the International Sales of Goods
UPICC	UNIDROIT Principles of International Commercial Contract

Acknowledgments

I would like to extend my gratitude to the many people whose help was invaluable along this journey. I would like to thank Professor Olugbenga Bamodu, Professor Christopher Willett, Dr David Holloway, and Dr Youseph Farah for their advice and comments.

A very big thank you to all the wonderful people I met at the University of Essex, who inspired me, and whose friendship I treasure. Especially Tara Van Ho, Sara Hourani, Anil Yilmaz, Diana Guarnizo Peralta, Aysem Diker Van Berg, Apiradee 'Meo' Kongcharoen Springall, Chiara Macchi, Leonardo Valladares Pacheco de Oliveira, Mandy Gray, Liz Harvey, and Laurence Wells. A special thank you to Paulo Henrique Dias Junior, his kindness and generosity will always be remembered.

A very special thank you to some very dear friends for their support, friendship, and advice along the way. Especially Berkin, Ella, and Hülya Ak and Özgür Heval Cinar. Celeste Mohanpersad. Luis Felipe Yanes and Delia Sánchez-del Ángel.

I would also like to extend my thanks to the publication team at Routledge.

Finally, I would like to thank my family, especially my mother Martha Persijn, In loving memory to my father, Uco Hoekstra. In gratitude for their support I would like to dedicate this book to my grandparents, Dr Hayo Lourens Hoekstra and Wilhelmina Catherina Hoekstra-Koopmans.

1 Introduction

Non-state rules in international commercial contracts

1.1 The quest for legal certainty

Advancing technology and furthering economic globalisation have intensified international trade. Information technology helps businesses expand their market share without needing to establish a presence in other countries. Yet, whilst technology and a more intricate infrastructure facilitate international trade, there are still barriers to trading abroad. Small and Medium Enterprises (SME) can be reluctant to offer their services/goods across borders; partly because of the risks that a foreign and unfamiliar legal environment brings. Businesses need to be aware of different judicial procedures and regulations and they will be wary of any extra costs they might incur, for instance because contractual liability extends further than in their home country. This disproportionately affects smaller businesses that have fewer financial resources to mitigate these risks.

Legal harmonisation facilitates international trade; if the law is similar in different countries the legal consequences of doing business abroad are more predictable. Of course, commercial and contract law are not the only laws that affect cross-border trade: tax law, company law, and competition law among others also affect businesses. These areas are often more difficult to harmonise than commercial law as they are more closely connected with states' public policy concerns. Whilst there are harmonisation efforts in these areas the results are (outside of the European Union) more modest.

The harmonisation of international commercial law occurs through international conventions and non-state rules (or soft law). Upon ratification international conventions become part of domestic law. The position of non-state rules is more diffuse and therefore further analysis is needed to understand how these accumulate legal authority. Non-state rules can be uncodified, such as trade usages and general principles, or they can be codified, such as restatements, model laws, and standard contract terms. They are created through spontaneous usage by the merchant community, or purposefully by (international) organisations.

The aim of this book is to improve understanding of how the legal authority of non-state rules in international commercial contracts can be measured. To this end Part 1 considers the general nature of non-state rules and argues that the most important way that the legal authority of non-state rules can be understood is through their ***application***. As such Part 2 assesses the extent to which the parties to the contract can choose non-state rules ***as the applicable law of the contract***. Outside of arbitration, only a few jurisdictions allow for the application of non-state rules as the governing law, but they can usually be included by reference ***in addition*** to a state law. Part 3 then analyses the application of non-state rules ***other than as the governing law of the contract***. This part demonstrates that these rules are applied in various ways; as a source of domestic law, to interpret the contract or the law, and to fill in gaps in the applicable law.

Uncodified non-state rules (trade usages and general principles of law) are often sources of domestic law and are applied as part of the applicable law. In addition, it is shown that while codified non-state rules (such as restatements of law) usually have no standing as a source of law they are frequently used by courts as accepted international commercial practices and principles to interpret both the contract and the law, especially where there are gaps or conflicting laws, or to demonstrate that domestic law proposes the same solution as specific non-states rules. This enhances the legitimacy of domestic law as it shows its compatibility with accepted international commercial practices. Non-state rules are also used to demonstrate that domestic law is divergent from the international majoritarian approach; and in this way non-state rules have a potentially important role to play in furthering discussions on the development of domestic law.

Non-state rules play a key role in resolving international contractual disputes and also contribute to the harmonisation of international commercial law. The main focus of Part 3 is on application of non-state rules in *state courts*. In a way this is most relevant to assessing the legal authority of these rules because of the normative power of courts. By contrast, while arbitration plays a key role in international commerce, one might say that there is less legal authority in what is decided (and in the rules used to decide) because they have no normative power and there is no binding precedent. Nevertheless, arbitration is extremely important in international commerce and the various points made above on non-state rules do apply in arbitration just as they apply in litigation. So, this serves to further augment to at least some degree the authoritative role of non-state rules in international commercial law.

The book concludes that non-state rules assume various roles in the contractual relationship with different degrees of legal authority. They are used as contractual rules and as such their authority comes from the contract. They can be used as the governing law of the contract and their authority derives from private international law. They can be considered sources of domestic law and as such their authority comes from that law. They are used to interpret the law and the contract and derive their authority from their position as general principles and practices of international commercial law.

Non-state rules can thus (depending on the situation) be considered contractual rules; normative practices; rules of law (rules which have a normative value but are not law); or (domestic) law. Non-state rules gain in legal authority through their application, and this application can come in various different forms: sometimes as the governing law of the contract, but more routinely for instance as contractual rules, as a source of domestic law, to interpret the applicable law, and to interpret the contract.

The primary contribution of this book lies in providing greater clarity as to the legal authority of non-state rules. This fills various important gaps. Research on non-state rules frequently focuses on their application as the governing law, both in litigation and arbitration;[1] and whilst this is discussed here, the focus is on what this says about the legal authority of these rules. In addition, this focus on the question of legal authority takes this book beyond the discussion about the governing law of the contract. As indicated above, the book emphasises the various ways in which non-state rules are applied even when the non-state rules are not the governing law of the contract. There is a body of work, which focuses on how non-state rules shape and influence principles of commercial law and how they contribute to the creation of transnational legal orders.[2] There is only a limited focus on the question of the legal authority of non-state rules.[3] Other work covers the use of non-state rules to establish an internationally accepted authoritative commercial law practice against which the authority of domestic law is measured[4], how

1 On arbitration see for instance: 'Gbenga Bamodu, 'Exploring the Interrelationships of Transnational Commercial Law 'the New Lex Mercatoria' and International Commercial Arbitration' (1998) 1 African Journal of International and Comparative Law 37

Gabrielle Kaufmann-Kohler, 'Soft Law in International Arbitration: Codification and Normativity' (2010) Journal of International Dispute Settlement 1,

Larry A. di Matteo, 'Soft law and the principle of fair and equitable decision making in international contract arbitration' (2013) The Chinese Journal of Comparative Law 1,

Michael Pryles, 'Application of the Lex Mercatoria in International Commercial Arbitration' (2008) 31 UNSWLJ 319,

On the applicable law see for instance:

David Oser, The Unidroit Principles of International Commercial Contracts: a Governing Law (Martinus Nijhoff 2008),

Michael Joachim Bonell, 'The Law Governing International Commercial Contracts and the Actual Role of the UNIDROIT Principles' (2018) 23 Uniform Law Review 15,

Larry A. DiMatteo, International Contracting: Law and Practice (Wolter Kluwer Law & Business 2013,

Ralf Michaels, 'Thee Re-statement of Non-State Law: The State, Choice of Law, and the Challenge from Global Legal Pluralism' (2005) 51 Wayne Law Review 1209, and

Symeon C. Symeonides, 'Party Autonomy in International Contracts and the Multiple Ways of Slicing the Apple' (2014) 39 Brooklyn Journal of International Law 1123.

2 See for instance Ralf Michaels 'The UNIDROIT Principles as Global Background Law' (2014) 19 Uniform Law Review 643

Terence C. Halliday and Gregory Shaffer (editors), Transnational Legal Orders, (2015 Cambridge University Press).

3 See for instance: Nils Jansen, *The Making of Legal Authority* (2010) Oxford University Press.

4 Michael Joachim Bonell and Ole Lando, 'Future Prospects of the Unification of Contract Law in Europe and Worldwide' (2013) 18 Uniform Law Review 17

Larry A. DiMatteo, 'The Scholarly Response to the Harmonization of International Sales Law' (2012) 30 Journal of Law & Commerce 1

Ralph Michaels, 'the UNIDROIT Principles as Global Background Law' (2014) 19 Uniform Law Review 643

Hugh Collins, Cosmopolitanism and Transnational Private Law (2012) 8 European Contract Law Review 311.

privately-made law gains authority despite lack of democratic accountability[5], how codified non-state rules become part of the lex mercatoria[6], or how the lex mercatoria develops into sector-specific authoritative legal practices.[7] The analysis in this book contributes to this wider discussion by focusing precisely on the *application* to measure the legal authority of non-state rules.

Improving understanding as to the legal authority of non-state rules is not only an important contribution in relation to these rules but also adds to our understanding of legal harmonisation. The realisation that different legal regimes form a barrier against international trade has led to the creation of a body of transnational commercial law that either lowers or removes these barriers. Non-state rules are key to this development. They contribute towards creating a truly transnational body of commercial law and towards harmonising the principles underlying international commercial law; and to fully understand this role it is necessary to examine how their legal authority is established. There is a significant amount of literature that analyses legal harmonisation and non-state rules, and this work contributes to this literature by focusing the discussion through the lens of legal authority.[8]

The book also furthers scholarship on the important and perennial issue in commercial law of how to improve certainty and predictability for the benefit of contracting parties.[9] So by improving understanding of the legal authority of non-state rules (in particular in relation to when and how they will be applied) this book can contribute to helping the contracting parties

5 A.M Garro, 'Rule-Setting by Private Organisations, Standardisation of Contracts and the Harmonisation of International Sales Law' in Ian F Fletcher, Loukas Mistelis & Marise Cremona (editors) Foundations and Perspectives of International Trade Law (Sweet & Maxwell 2000)

David V. Snyder, 'Private Lawmaking' (2003) 64 Ohio State Journal 371

Günther Teubner, 'Global Bukowina: Legal Pluralism in the World Society' in Günther Teubner (editor), Global Law without a State (1997 Brookfield).

6 Klaus Peter Berger, *The Creeping Codification of the New Lex Mercatoria 2nd Revised Edition* (2010 Wolters Kluwer).

7 Axel Metzger, 'Transnational Law for Transnational Communities: The Emergence of a Lex Mercatoria (or Lex Informatica) for International Creative Communities' (2012) 3 J Intell Prop Info Tech & Elec Com L 361

Leonardo V. P. de Oliveira, Lex sportiva as the contractual governing law (2017) 17 International Sports Law Journal 101.

8 See for instance: Bernardo M. Cremades & Steven L. Plehn, 'The New Lex Mercatoria and the Harmonization of the laws of International Commercial Transactions' (1983–1984) 2 Boston University International Law Journal 317,

Larry A DiMatteo, 'The Scholarly Response to the Harmonization of International Sales Law' (2012) 30 Journal of Law & Commerce 1 and Ian F Fletcher, Loukas Mistelis & Marise Cremona (editors) Foundations and Perspectives of International Trade Law (Sweet & Maxwell 2000).

9 See for instance: Kermit Roosevelt III, 'Certainty vs. Flexibility in the Conflict of laws' (2018) Public Law and Legal Theory Research Paper Series Research Paper No.18-40, 7 and Ingeborg Schwenzer, 'Who Needs a Uniform Contract Law, and why?' (2013) 58 Villanova Law Review 723.

to manage risks, by reference to a clearer understanding as to when particular non-state rules may apply.

The rest of this introductory chapter defines first what an international contract is; discusses several organisations that play a key role in the development of non-state rules; examines the main categories of non-state rules; and finishes by mapping out the overall structure of the remainder of the book.

1.2 International commercial contracts

This book focuses on non-state rules in the context of international commercial contracts. A commercial contract can be defined as a contract *'in which both parties deal with each other in the course of business, whether as merchants or as provider and recipient of financial or other services supplied for business purposes.'*[10] The UNIDROIT Principles of International Commercial Contracts state in their pre-amble that commercial should be interpreted in a broad manner and the term is mainly intended to exclude consumer transactions and applies to both simple transactions such as sale contracts as well as more complex economic transactions such as investment, concession, agency, and lease contracts.[11] Therefore, the term commercial focuses on the capacity in which the contracting parties act.

The notion of internationality is defined in different ways. Defining factors involve differences in nationalities, domicile, residence, or a contract which concerns the interests of international trade.[12] At its broadest, a contract is international when not all elements of the contract belong to the same legal system.[13] This definition is so broad that it can be artificial as the foreign element would not necessarily be intrinsically important to the contract (such as a German national domiciled in France and engaging a contractor located in France to refurbish his house in France, the German nationality has no real effect on the transaction.)

Article 1504 of the French Procedural Code reads that arbitrage is international when it affects the interests of international commerce.[14] The French courts have extrapolated from this, that a contract is international when it affects the interests of international commerce.[15] Also used in France is the judicial criterion: a contract is international when it is attached to two different legal orders.[16] By combining these criteria the definition would thus be: a

10 Roy Goode, *Commercial Law* (Second Edition, Penguin Books 1995) 11.

11 Pre-Amble Comment 2.

12 Michael Joachim Bonell, 'The Unidroit Principles of International Commercial Contracts: towards a new lex mercatoria?' [1997] International Business Law Journal 5.

13 Jean de la Colette, *Les Contrats de Commerce Internationaux* (Third edition, De Boeck Université 1996) 12.

14 Code Procédure Civile, Livre IV L'Arbitrage, Titre II L'Arbitrage International, Article 1504.

15 Pierre-Alain Gourion, Georges Peyrard and Nicolas Soubeyrand, *Droit du Commerce International* (fourth edition, L.G.D.J. Lextenso Editions 2008) 168.

16 Ibid, 169.

contract that is attached to at least two different legal orders and that affects the interests of international commerce.

Place of business is often used to determine whether the contract is international. The English Unfair Contract Terms Act (UCTA) states that Article 26 on international supply contracts is applicable to contracts made by parties whose places of businesses are in territories of different states.[17] The Convention for the International Sale of Goods (CISG) defines an international contract as: *(1) This Convention applies to contracts of sale of goods between parties whose places of business are in different States.* This reflects the place of business criterion used in the UCTA.

Other legal instruments have a wider definition whereby place of business is only one of the possible criteria. The Inter-American Convention on the Law Applicable to International Commercial Contracts defines internationality as: *a contract is international if the parties thereto have their habitual residence or establishment in different State Parties, or if the contract has objective ties with more than one state party.* The Hague Principles of Choice of Law in International Commercial Contracts state in Article 1(2): *a contract is international unless each party has its establishment in the same State and the relationship of the parties and all other relevant elements, regardless of the law chosen, are connected only with that state.*

For the purpose of this book, it is not necessary to make a choice between the different criteria to determine when a contract is international, but it is important to keep in mind that diverging definitions exist in different jurisdictions.

1.3 Key organisations

This section offers a brief introduction to the key organisations that draft non-state rules. The main international organisations are UNIDROIT, UNCITRAL, and the Hague Conference on Private International Law.

UNIDROIT (the International Institute for the Unification of Private Law) is located in Rome, Italy. It was founded in 1926 as an auxiliary organ of the League of Nations and after the demise of the latter it was re-established in 1940 as an intergovernmental organisation. It has 63 member states. UNIDROIT states that its purpose is: '*to study needs and methods for modernising, harmonising and co-ordinating private and in particular commercial law as between States and groups of States and to formulate uniform law instruments, principles and rules to achieve those objectives.*'[18] Since its establishment, it has developed numerous instruments in the wider area of commercial law, such as international conventions, restatements of law (including the UNIDROIT Principles of International Commercial Contracts), model laws, and guides.

17 Unfair Contract Terms Act 1977, Article 26 http://www.legislation.gov.uk/ukpga/1977/50/section/26.

18 UNIDROIT https://www.unidroit.org/about-unidroit/overview.

The Hague Conference on Private International Law (HCCH) uses the tagline: 'The World Organisation for Cross-border Co-operation in Civil and Commercial Matters.'[19] It was first convened in 1893 by Tobias Asser and established as a permanent international organisation in 1951. It has 83 members: 82 states and the EU. Non-member states can ratify instruments promulgated by the Hague Conference. HCCH is focused on the development of private international law instruments, mainly international conventions. In commercial law they developed conventions on the international sale of goods, agency, and securities and the Principles on Choice of Law in International Commercial Contracts.

The United Nations Commission on International Trade Law (UNCITRAL) is '*the core legal body of the United Nations system in the field of international trade law.*'[20] It is a subsidiary body of the United Nations and it was established in 1966 and has 60 full members. The membership rotates between the member states of the UN who are elected for terms of six years. Other states participate as observer states and have voting rights. UNCITRAL contributes to the harmonisation of international commercial law through the creation of international conventions, model laws, model contracts, rules, and guidelines.

Regional organisations contribute to the development of non-state rules. The EU focuses mainly on consumer contracts and not on commercial contracts. The most significant impact of the EU on international commercial law is the Europeanisation of private international law. Several private initiatives have filled this gap by developing non-state rules for international (commercial) contracts in the European context, partly with the goal that these could serve as a foundation for an eventual European contract law instrument. An example is the Principles of European Contract Law, which were developed by the Lando Commission.[21]

A key regional organisation is OHADA (Organisation pour l'Harmonisation en Afrique du Droit des Affaires) that was founded in 1993 to harmonise business law in Africa.[22] It has 17 member states across West and Central Africa. Whilst membership is open to all African states its focus is upon francophone countries which have legal systems based on the French legal system.

OHADA harmonises the law through the development of Uniform Law Acts which are implemented by the Member States. There are currently nine uniform acts covering areas of company law, financial law, contract law, arbitration, and commercial law. The Uniform Acts are supplemented with case law collections, legal opinions, guidelines etc. OHADA set up a court that

19 The Hague Conference on Private International Law: https://www.hcch.net/en/home.

20 UNCITRAL: https://uncitral.un.org/en/about.

21 The Commission on European Contract Law founded in 1982 and named after its chairman, Professor Ole Lando.

22 OHADA https://www.ohada.org/index.php/en/.

ensures its laws are applied and interpreted in a consistent way as this leads to greater legal harmonisation

Trade associations play a key role in the development of non-state rules. The International Chamber of Commerce (ICC) describes itself as *'the world business organization, enabling business to secure peace, prosperity and opportunity for all.'*[23] The ICC plays a key part in the development of non-state rules. The two most well known set of rules it has produced are the INCOTERMS and the Uniform Customs & Practice for Documentary Credits (UCP). The ICC also produces numerous model contracts (clauses), arbitration rules, and uniform rules in international commerce.

There are numerous (international) trade associations that develop contract terms, model contracts, and guidelines, which can all be considered as non-state rules. These organisations often have in-house dispute resolution mechanisms and rules (in the form of ADR and arbitration.) Examples include the Grain and Feed Trade Association, the International Bottled Water Association, the International Cotton Association, and the International Wool Textile Organisation.

1.4 Categories of non-state rules: uncodified

Non-state rules in international commercial law are not a singular entity. They have different origins, functions, and objectives. The first division is between codified and uncodified non-state rules as there are some fundamental differences between the two categories. First, uncodified rules are often recognised as a source in domestic law whereas codified non-state rules are usually not. Codified non-state rules often derive their legal authority at least partly from being connected with uncodified non-state rules: they are used to interpret uncodified non-state rules. Second, their origin is different. Trade associations and international organisations create codified rules. Uncodified non-state rules are spontaneous creations by the merchant community, which are later affirmed by courts and arbitral tribunals. Third and most obviously, they are set up differently. Codified non-state rules are written down, certain, and precise, and drafted/distributed by an organisation/group. Uncodified rules are unwritten, their content is difficult to determine, and their interpretation is diffuse. No single organisation or group can claim responsibility for their administration.

Uncodified non-state rules can be divided into two main categories: trade usages and general principles of law. The following paragraphs will briefly explore each category.

Trade usages, customs, and practices are characterised by their spontaneous creation from within the merchant community. In contractual relations custom, trade usages, and practices can assume different roles:

23 ICC : https://iccwbo.org/about-us/.

- *to define jargon, clarify ambiguities and explain technical terms*
- *to add terms to the contract*
- *to allow commercial meanings to control contrary lay definitions.*[24]

General principles of law are the second category of uncodified non-state rules. General principles of law exist on different levels of law. The concept exists in international law as the general principles recognised as a source of law by the International Court of Justice (ICJ).[25] These are intended for state-to-state relations. In principle a private party cannot be found liable for violation of general principles of law as meant by article 38.[26] Therefore, general principles in international commerce cannot be equated with general principles of law under article 38 and should be considered as a distinct concept.

General principles of law also exist in domestic legislations. They are the general principles underlying the national law. These principles are not necessarily the same as those recognised in public international law. Not all domestic law principles are internationally accepted and therefore cannot be considered as international principles of commercial law. An example is good faith in the pre-contractual phase, which is a general principle in civil law but not in English common law.[27] There are thus different types of general principles. The first are general principles of law common to most nations, the second general principles of domestic law. A third type would be general principles of EU law as recognised by the European Court of Justice (ECJ).[28]

General principles of international/transnational commercial law are a hybrid of principles that are derived from public international law and domestic laws and which are applicable in international commercial transactions between private parties. General principles in international commerce transcend individual legal systems and have a transnational applicability. Examples of general principles of international commercial law are 'pacta sunt servanda' and 'clausula rebus sic stantibus.'

1.5 Categories of non-state rules: codified

Codified non-state rules are drafted by international organisations, trade associations, or private groups and can be divided in model laws, restatements of law, model contract clauses, and guides and opinions. They can be

24 Harold J Berman, 'Towards an Integrative Jurisprudence: Politics, Morality, History' (1988) 76 California Law Review 779, 784.

25 Statute of the International Court of Justice Article 38: The Court, whose function is to decide in accordance with international law such disputes as are submitted to it, shall apply: […]
c. the general principles of law recognized by civilized nations […].

26 Giudetta Cordero-Moss, 'The Transnational Law of Contracts: What It Can and What It Cannot Achieve' in Todd Weiler and Freya Baetens (editors), *New Directions in International Economic Law: In Memoriam Thomas Wälde*, (Martinus Nijhoff 2011), 61–63.

27 Ibid.

28 See for instance the webpage of the EU: http://eur-lex.europa.eu/legal-content/EN/TXT/?uri=URISERV:l14533.

aimed at national legislators (model laws, restatements of law, guidelines), at the contracting parties (restatements of law, model clauses, guidelines) or at courts (restatements of law, guidelines).

International organisations develop model laws, which are made available to states, usually accompanied by implementation guidelines. States adopt the model laws (possibly with changes). Model laws are different from conventions which only permit a small number of reservations (if any) to be made and are then ratified in their entirety whereas model laws can be adapted at will by the state. A successful example is the Model Law on International Arbitration as legislation based on this model law has been adopted by 83 states.[29] Other successful model laws are the UNCITRAL Model Law on Electronic Commerce,[30] the UNCITRAL Model Law on Electronic Signatures,[31] the UNCITRAL Model Law on Cross-Border Insolvency,[32] and the UNIDROIT Model Law on leasing.[33]

Model laws also exist within (federal) jurisdictions. In the United States the NCCUSL/ULC promotes increased legal uniformity through the development of model laws.[34] Their most prominent work is the Uniform Commercial Code (UCC), which has the goal to harmonise the law on commercial transactions in the USA. Another example is the Uniform Electronic Transactions Act, which was adopted by 47 US states.

Model contracts and clauses are elaborated by international organisations or by trade associations. Model contracts are also called standard contracts although this name can cause confusion with standard adhesion contracts. The first are drafted by an outside source whereas the second type are drafted in-house and contain the standard terms and conditions of the particular company.[35] The standard contract discussed here is the model contract. Model contracts extend to the whole contract, part of the contract,

29 For full list of states see: http://www.uncitral.org/uncitral/en/uncitral_texts/arbitration/1985Model_arbitration_status.html.

30 Legislation based on this model law has been adopted by 64 states. http://www.uncitral.org/uncitral/en/uncitral_texts/electronic_commerce/1996Model_status.html.

31 Legislation based on this model law has been adopted by 32 states. http://www.uncitral.org/uncitral/en/uncitral_texts/electronic_commerce/2001Model_status.html.

32 Legislation based on this model law has been adopted by 40 states. http://www.uncitral.org/uncitral/en/uncitral_texts/insolvency/1997Model_status.html.

33 http://www.unidroit.org/instruments/leasing/model-law.

34 The National Conference of Commissioners on Uniform State Laws (NCCUSL) is also known as the Uniform Law Commission (ULC) and was established in 1892. Its goal is to provide states with 'non-partisan, well-conceived, and well drafted legislation that brings clarity and stability to critical areas of state statutory law.'

35 Clive M Schmitthoff, 'The Unification or Harmonisation of Law by Means of Standard Contracts and General Conditions' (1986) 17 International & Comparative Law Quarterly 551, 551.

or individual contractual terms.[36] Parties can adopt model contracts in their entirety or adapt them to fit their specific needs.

The most well known international organisations that design model contracts for international commerce are UNCITRAL and the ICC. The ICC has a specialised commission dedicated to the development of model contracts.[37] Examples include contracts on commercial agency, franchising, mergers, sale of goods, licencing, and turnkey transactions.

Trade associations are important players in this area. Trade Associations draft model contracts specifically for their branch. An example of such an organisation is the ISDA (International Swaps and Derivatives Association), which creates legal definitions of contractual terms and model contracts.[38] Other examples are FIDIC (International Federation of Consulting Engineers) which designs model contracts for civil engineers, the JCT (Joint Contracts Tribunal) which drafts model building contracts, and BIMCO (Baltic and International Maritime Council), which creates model charter-parties.[39] Model contracts elaborated by trade associations can be biased towards the seller or service provider as these form the membership of the association.[40] They are thus considered less neutral than those model clauses drafted by the ICC, UNCITRAL, or other organisations that have a broader membership basis and mission.

The Incoterms (an acronym for International Commercial Terms) are developed by the ICC based on existing trade terms. The Incoterms were first published in 1923 and are updated frequently. The latest version (the Incoterms 2020) was published in September 2019. The ICC did not invent these trade terms and therefore defining them is not restricted to the ICC. The contract should specify that the included trade term is an Incoterm and which version should be applied.

Throughout the years the ICC has developed new trade terms, either based on existing ones or on the perceived need for these in international commerce whereas other terms are omitted in the newer versions because they are not used frequently. Incoterms omitted in the 2010 update were DES (Delivery Ex Ship) and DDU (Delivery Duty Unpaid). In the 2020 version Delivery At Terminal was removed. It is of course still possible to include these terms in a contract, but the parties would need to make sure to refer to the earlier version of the Incoterms to ensure a predictable interpretation. Usage of the Incoterms is widespread.

36 Ibid, 556.

37 The ICC Commission on Commercial Law and Practice (CLP).

38 ISDA http://www2.isda.org/.

39 FIDIC: http://fidic.org/
JCT https://www.jctltd.co.uk/
BIMCO: https://www.bimco.org/.

40 Clive M Schmitthoff, 'The Unification or Harmonisation of Law by Means of Standard Contracts and General Conditions' (1986) 17 International & Comparative Law Quarterly 551,553.

Trade terms divide the responsibilities between the buyer and the seller with regards to transportation of goods and transfer of risk.[41] Each trade term is shortened to three letters. The Incoterms are traditionally divided in three or four categories (the first two are often placed together) that represent increasing responsibilities for the seller:

- Ex- works (place of delivery). The buyer collects the goods at the named place and arranges for transport from there. The obligation of the seller is to make the goods available at the place of delivery, which is usually the premises of the seller.
- F terms: FCA (Free Carrier place of delivery) FAS (Free Alongside Ship), and FOB (Free on Board). The seller delivers the goods to the first carrier at the named place (FCA), to the dock alongside the named ship (FAS), or on board the ship (FOB)
- C terms: CFR (Cost and Freight), CIF (Cost, Insurance, and Freight), CPT (Carriage Paid To), and CIP (Carriage and Insurance Paid To). Under these C terms the seller is responsible for shipping the goods to the named destination. The seller assumes the costs associated with the carriage of goods. Under CIF and CIP, the seller also assumes the responsibility and the costs for insuring the goods.
- D terms: DPU (Delivery at Place Unloaded), DAP (Delivery At Place), and DDP (Delivery Duty Paid). The seller takes responsibility to deliver the goods at the named place unloaded (DPU), at the named place ready for unloading (DAP), or to the named place including all imports/ duties paid for (DDP).[42]

The 2020 version of the Incoterms changed the categorisation. It places the terms in two categories: those can be used for any type of transportation (EXW, FCA, CPT, CIP, DPU, DAP, DDP) and those that are only for carriage by ship (FOB, FAS, CFR, and CIF.)

The Uniform Customs and Practice (UCP) are developed by the ICC. They were first published in 1933. They are a set of contractual terms aimed at standardising letters of credits. The ICC Banking Commission revises them regularly.[43] The UCP 600 is the latest version and was published

41 The parties can of course adapt the Incoterms if they wish to do so.

42 There are other trade terms, but these do not fall under the ICC Incoterms. An example is FIS (Free In Store) where the seller assumes all costs and responsibilities including unloading the goods at the premise of the buyer.

43 The ICC Banking Commission also issues guides and supplements to the UCP. Among these are the International Standard Banking Practice (ISBP) and the eUCP.

The ISBP are *'a checklist of back practices worldwide for checking documents under the UCP'* according to the ICC (http://www.iccwbo.org/About-ICC/Policy-Commissions/Banking/Task-forces/International-Standard-Banking-Practice-(ISBP)/).

In 2002 the ICC Banking Commission developed the eUCP: The Uniform Customs and Practice for Documentary Credits for Electronic Presentation. They refer back to the UCP and are not intended as a standalone instrument. They merely facilitate the electronic presentation of the documents for the documentary credit. The eUCP declare in article 2e: *'a Credit subject to the eUCP ("eUCP credit") is also subject to the UCP without express incorporation of the UCP.'*

in 2007. The UCP are '*technical, complete, regularly updated and lead to diverging jurisprudence.*'[44] The latter is because they are applied in different jurisdictions. The UCP are not comprehensive and therefore they need to be supplemented by the applicable law.

The UCP were developed out of existing practices in documentary credit and thus have a customary basis. Their acceptance was not immediately widespread because the first version of the UCP did not consider the laws and practices of some important financial hubs like the UK and the US where bankers consequently continued to use their own practices.[45] Subsequent versions of the UCP remedied this and the UCP have achieved world wide acceptance.[46]

Restatements of law are drafted by international organisations. They are codified non-state rules that offer principles and rules for contractual relations. They put in mind a model law in their design, but instead of being aimed at states they are aimed at the contracting partners. The concept resembles that of the restatements of law drafted by the American Law Institute (ALI).[47] They consist of principles and rules that restate existing law and usages whilst at the same time adapting these to the needs of international commerce. The number of restatements is small although their impact is significant. The most prominent ones are the UNIDROIT Principles of International Commercial Contracts (UPICC), the Principles of European Contract Law (PECL,) and the Principles of Latin American Contract Law (PLACL).[48]

Guides and legal opinions are a fourth category of codified non-state rules. These include best practice guides, interpretation advice, arbitral case law digests, legal opinions, and other similar type documents. They are written by international organisations, trade branch associations, study groups, scholars, think thanks, or (groups of) individual (s.)

1.6 Structure of the remainder of the book

In order to understand the legal authority of non-state rules in international commercial contracts this book answers certain core questions: what is the

44 Pierre-Alain Gourion, Georges Peyrard and Nicolas Soubeyrand, *Droit du Commerce International* (Fourth edition, L.G.D.J. Lextenso Editions 2008) 94.

45 Hans van Houtte, *The Laws of International Trade* (Sweet & Maxwell 1995) 265.

46 Ibid, 266.

47 The American Law Institute (ALI) is, in its own words, '*the leading, independent organisation in the United States producing scholarly work to clarify, modernize, and otherwise improve the law.*' ALI was founded in 1923 and is composed of 3,000 elected members who are judges, legal scholars, and lawyers. Their most well known works are the Restatements of Law. These are treatises that extract general principles of law from current case law. They are not binding, but they are highly persuasive.

48 The Principles of Asian Contract Law are currently under development. See for instance: Jungjoon Ka, 'Introduction to PACL' in (2014) Tony Angelo, Luca Castellani &Yves-Louis Sage (editors) Contributions to the Study of International Trade/ADR in the South Pacific 55
Shiyuan Han, 'Principles of Asian Contract Law: An Endeavor of Regional Harmonization of Contract Law in East Asia (2013) 58 Villanova Law Review 589.

nature of non-state rules and what does this mean in terms of how we should measure their legal authority? Having concluded that the legal authority of non-state rules should be measured by reference to their application, the book asks in what circumstances they can be applied as the governing law of the contract; and in what other ways they can be applied. The book is divided into three parts that address these questions in turn. Each of these parts consists of three chapters.

Part one (chapters 2, 3 and 4) explores the nature of non-state rules. The aim of this part is to first define what non-state rules are and explain what their place is in international commercial law; and second to consider how the legal authority of non-state rules can be understood and measured. To these ends chapter 2 explores the characteristics of non-state rules and their relationship with the lex mercatoria, before beginning to examine the concept of legal authority in relation to non-state rules. It explores whether law has legitimacy beyond the state; how that legitimacy can be understood; and how the concept of legal authority can be understood in relation to non-state rules. Crucially it introduces the idea that the legal authority of non-state rules is heavily dependent on their acceptance in the business and legal communities; which in turn means that key to understanding their authority must be their application. Chapter 3 takes a broader approach to the question of non-state rules. Whereas chapter 2 focused on defining these rules; chapter 3 focuses on the wider role that non-state rules have in both international commercial law and transnational commercial law. It does this through first exploring the place of non-state rules in international commercial law, before discussing legal harmonisation in international commercial law and the contribution of non-state rules to this process. Chapter 3 thus complements chapter 2 by ensuring an understanding of the wider context in which non-state rules function. Legal harmonisation being a crucial function of non-state rules, is key to creating an understanding of the functioning of non-state rules in this context. Non-state rules can only contribute to harmonisation if they are used by the business community and by courts. This usage includes when they are applied. Through this application they gain legitimacy, and this enhances their role in international commercial law. This in turn makes them more authoritative which makes it more likely that courts will apply them. Legal harmonisation is thus both caused and strengthened through applying non-state rules.

Chapter 4 narrows the focus to consider the different roles that non-state rules have within the contract and their status as a source of law. This brings Part 1 to a close with the conclusion that the legal authority of non-state rules can be determined in several ways: first through understanding the different concepts of what a source of law is (origin, process of how they were created, reason why the rule was created, and substance of the rule); and second through understanding how they can gain in legal authority (through support by the business community and legal professionals and their application in state courts and arbitral tribunals). Amongst these factors, it is argued that *application* is of overriding importance. This is because application demonstrates how non-state rules are used, how frequently they are used, in what manner they are applied, how their origin and substance is understood by legal professionals, and the support they have from the business community and legal professionals.

After establishing that the application of non-state rules is key to understanding their legal authority the second part of the book analyses the circumstances in which non-state rules are applied. This part focuses on the agency of the contracting parties to include non-state rules in the choice of law clause as well as the agency of the courts and tribunals to apply non-state rules as the governing law. Chapter 5 starts with an analysis of how non-state rules could be applied as the governing law and then discusses party autonomy in international commercial contracts and the agency of the parties to choose non-state rules as the applicable law of the contract. It concludes that this is usually not possible in litigation, although the parties may choose to include non-state rules by reference in supplement to the applicable law. Chapter 6 analyses in more detail the links between private international law and non-state rules. The purpose is to understand why private international law generally does not allow for their usage as the applicable law and whether there are any exceptions to this overall rule. Chapter 7 examines the agency of the parties and tribunals to choose non-state rules in international arbitration and how courts deal with the enforcement of arbitral awards where non-state rules are the applicable law. This chapter confirms that in arbitration, the parties and the tribunal can usually choose non-state rules as the governing law. The conclusion from these chapters is that within private international law there is very limited scope to use non-state rules as the governing law of the contract and that the reasons for this are linked to the fundamental principles underlying private international law even though these reasons are not necessarily compelling. Things are substantially different in international commercial arbitration where the parties and the tribunal have considerably more agency to use non-state rules as the governing law. Based on arbitration laws that allows for this usage, courts are then for the most part willing to enforce an award, based on non-state rules.

Part three examines the application of non-state rules in ways *other than as the governing law of the contract*. It focuses on the application of non-state rules in addition to or as part of the applicable domestic law. It analyses how different categories of non-state rules are applied; notably trade usages, accepted principles and practices of international commercial law, and codified non-state rules. Chapter 8 considers the application of non-state rules through the applicable domestic law. It focuses on the application of trade usages, which are considered as a source of law in most jurisdictions. Chapter 9 focuses on how courts use non-state rules as international commercial practices and principles. This can be to interpret domestic law, international conventions, or the contract. Non-state rules are also used as a point of reference to show that domestic law is either in line with internationally accepted practices or differs significantly from this. Chapter 10 analyses how courts apply codified non-state rules as an expression or reflection of the lex mercatoria, general principles of law, or trade usages. The court/tribunal applies codified non-state rules given their coherency, consistency, and completeness. Furthermore, they are easy to uncover as they are written down. This solves the difficulties of finding the concrete substance of the lex mercatoria. Codified non-state rules therefore play an authoritative role in defining the lex mercatoria.

Overall Part 3 concludes that non-state rules play a key role in international commercial contracts and are regularly applied in state courts as either a source of law or to interpret the contract and the law. Non-state rules gain in legal authority through regular application as a source of law, accepted commercial law practices, and as a reference point for interpreting the law and the contract. Courts use them as a reference point against which the suitability of domestic law in relation to international commerce is measured. Codified non-state rules especially gain in legal authority through their application as an expression/reflection of uncodified non-state rules. Their substantive quality, ease of access, and the concrete solutions they propose lead to a more consistent approach to the application of non-state rules.

Finally, the concluding chapter draws upon the previous chapters to conclude as to how the legal authority of non-state rules in international commercial contracts can be measured and understood. It concludes that non-state rules fulfil several roles and that the legal authority differs depending on the role. They may have legal authority as contractual provisions, as the applicable law of the contract, as sources of domestic law, and as accepted commercial law practices. They can be employed as contractual rules and derive their authority from the contract; they can be the governing law of the contract and derive their authority from private international law; they can be considered sources of domestic law and derive their authority from domestic law; they can be used to interpret the law and the contract and derive their authority from being considered general principles and practices of international commercial law. They are law; rules of law; contractual rules, and/or normative practices depending on the situation. Overall, considering the range of important ways in which non-state rules can be applied, they are undoubtedly of significant legal authority.

Part 1

The nature of non-state rules and how to measure their legal authority

2 Defining non-state rules

2.1 Introduction

This chapter seeks to improve understanding of the fundamental nature of non-state rules and starts the discussion on how to measure their legal authority. The first half of the chapter examines the characteristics of non-state rules and explores how they are linked with the lex mercatoria. The second half of the chapter starts exploring the concept of legal authority in relation to non-state rules. Domestic law gets its legitimacy from the state, which also enforces the law. This is different for non-state rules, which are characterised by their voluntary nature. As such it is argued, the key to understanding the legal authority of non-state rules is to understand the transnational framework that gives these rules legitimacy; and that this in turn means that their legal authority is heavily dependent upon the support that they have from the merchant community, legal professionals, arbitral tribunals, and courts. The key to understanding that support is through analysing the application of non-state rules.

By way of further introduction, there are a few important points to make about terminology. Non-state rules are also called 'soft law'. However, this term is mainly used in public international law. This makes the term less adequate for use in international commercial law as the understanding of soft law in international commercial law is not necessarily the same as in public international law. 'Non-state rules' is a more neutral concept as it does not imply that its elements all qualify as law. The word 'rules' is comprehensive enough to apply to all rules, including those whose status as a source of law is more debatable.

The phrase 'non-state' indicates the origin of the rules. They emanate from an origin other than a state legislator. State should be read in a broad way and includes regional and municipal authorities. Some non-state rules are spontaneous creations that emerge from the merchant community whereas others are created deliberately by organisations. The commonality as to their origin is that it lies outside the realm of the state. Therefore, 'non-state 'is the common denominator that unifies these rules. Non-state does not necessarily mean that there is no connection with the state, as these rules do not exist in a vacuum. They can be supported by state authorities in their usage and application through for instance their acceptance as a source of law.

2.2 Characteristics of non-state rules

Non-state rules are a diverse group of rules, instruments, and norms that on first sight do not have a great deal in common except that they all aim to facilitate international commerce. Legislations differentiate between different types of non-state rules. As an example, the Uniform Commercial Code (UCC) stipulates that the court, regardless of whether the parties have included them in the contract, should apply trade usages, but it only allows the UNIDROIT Principles of International Commercial Contracts to be applied as contractual rules at the request of the parties.

According to Abbot and Snidal '*The realm of soft law begins once legal arrangements are weakened along one or more of the dimensions of obligation, precision, and delegation*.'[1] This article was written in the context of public international law but these three dimensions can define non-state rules in international commercial law.

The first dimension is obligation.[2] The obligation of non-state rules is overall weaker than that of state law although it is not absent. Trade usages for instance will be applied unless the parties contract out of them. Moreover, as the contract can be considered to have the quality of law between the parties[3], contractual provisions (which may include non-state rules) can cancel variable rules of the applicable domestic law. It is hence, not so that non-state rules have no obligatory force, whether that is through law or through the contract, but that overall, this force is weaker and based on the consent of the parties. Non-state rules must be contracted into or can be contracted out of depending on their status in domestic law. Therefore, ultimately the parties control their application.

The second dimension from Abbott and Snidal's model is precision. Uncodified non-state rules are imprecise. Their exact content is, unwritten, flexible, and not easy to establish. On the other hand, codified non-state rules are precise and their content is clear as they are written down and extensive commentary exists on how they should be applied and interpreted.

The final dimension is delegation. Non-state rules are not initiated by the state. This does not mean that states have no role in the creation of non-state rules as international organisations are financed by states. Furthermore, states can push for the creation of new rules or for the revising of current ones by

1 Kenneth W Abbott and Duncan Snidal, 'Hard and Soft Law in International Governance' (2000) 54 International Organization 421,422.

2 Parts of this analysis appeared first in Johanna Hoekstra, 'The Normative Influence of the UNIDROIT Principles of International Commercial Law on Courts' (2019) 23 The Vindobona Journal of International Commercial Law and Arbitration 54.

3 Jacques Ghestin, 'La notion de contrat' (1990) 12 Periodicals Archive Online 7,10
See also : Article 1134 of the French Civil Code : 'Les conventions légalement formées tiennent lieu de loi à ceux les ont faits.'

instigating or financing a project. However, the involvement of the state is indirect, and the state delegates the creation of the instruments to others. In most cases non-state rules are either spontaneous creations by the merchant community or are created through a private initiative by an (international) organisation.

In conclusion, following Abbot and Snidal's characterisation, non-state rules are *legal arrangements* that are weakened along one or more of the dimensions of *obligation*, *precision*, and *delegation*. Non-state rules are weakened along at least two of these dimensions. All non-state rules are weakened along the dimension of delegation, as they are not created by a state, whereas codified non-state rules create weak obligations as they usually need to be contracted into and uncodified non-state rules are less precise.

Non-state rules serve several functions. They are aimed at states, courts, and businesses. For businesses they can serve to provide a neutral law of the contract, contribute to drafting the contract, and ensure the contract is suitable for international transactions. For states they can serve as a model for harmonising the law, for shaping the law, and ensuring the law is fit for international transactions. For courts they contribute to a transnational interpretation of the law, ensure that the law is applied in a predictable manner for international transactions, and provide the court with further tools to understand the intentions of the parties. Block-Lieb identifies three important functions of non-state rules: gap filling, socialising, and advocacy.[4] They fill gaps in the law by building on existing legal instruments, advising on interpretation, and through providing additional rules. They socialise companies, states, and individuals by helping to develop a common legal language across time and space. They advocate the need for legal harmonisation and the creation of new laws through demonstrating possible ways forward.

2.3 Defining the (new) lex mercatoria

Non-state rules cannot be equated with the lex mercatoria, however the two concepts are intrinsically linked and to understand this link a more in-depth discussion of the lex mercatoria is necessary. It is important to remember that there are (at least) two leges mercatoriae that are referred to in academic discussions. The first is the ancient lex mercatoria, which dates from at least the early Middle-Ages and, whose origins can be linked back even further to Roman law and the old maritime codes such as the Sea Law of Rhodes (Lex Rhodia) which emerged around 800 BC.[5] It can be defined as '*a body of rules*

4 Susan Block-Lieb, 'Soft and Hard Strategies: the Role of Business in the Crafting of International Commercial Law' (2019) 40 Michigan Journal of International Law 433, 473.

5 Harold J Berman, The Law of International Commercial Transactions (Lex Mercatoria), (1987) 2 Emory Journal of International Dispute Resolution 235, 238
Although it can be argued that the ancient shipping rolls are separate from the lex mercatoria that developed through year markets and fairs and focused mainly on land trade.

and principles relating to merchants and mercantile transactions, distinct from the ordinary law of the land. Possessed of a certain uniformity in its essential features, it yet differed on minor points from place to place.'[6] From the 7th-9th century onwards in Europe merchants were considered a distinct class and formed merchant courts on year markets and fairs where they resolved their own disputes according to their own rules with little outside interference.[7]

The second lex mercatoria is the new lex mercatoria that emerged in the middle of the 20th century and is considered as a revival or continuation of the medieval lex mercatoria.

The term lex mercatoria is used interchangeably by many scholars to refer to both leges mercatoriae. This is often done for practical reasons but also for principled ones. Using the term lex mercatoria for both emphasises the continuity between the two. Although the lex mercatoria was less visible in the 17th-19th century it did not disappear completely.[8] There is thus only one lex mercatoria, which changed and developed over the centuries.

The lex mercatoria mainly emerged because of the rise in year markets, the creation of guild houses, the revival of the study of Roman law, and the increase in commerce after the fall of the Western Roman Empire.[9] The concept of a transnational law different from more local regulations has roots in Roman law where the ius gentium had specific rules that governed relations between Roman citizens and non-Romans. The lex mercatoria governed a special class of people (merchants) in a specific place (such as a market/fair/town/port), it was administered by merchant courts, and it was more relevant to the needs of international commerce than local laws & customs.[10] Temporary merchant courts existed on markets and fairs, administered by merchants themselves whereas more permanent courts developed around guild houses focusing on the specific trade its members specialized in. The medieval lex mercatoria consisted mainly of the practices of trade guilds, customs, usages, and principles taken from previous decisions of merchant courts.[11]

There is a tendency to romanticise the medieval lex mercatoria as a unified body of law, which was applied consistently throughout Europe.[12] Although

6 William Mitchell, *An Essay on the Early History of the Law Merchant* (Cambridge University Press 1904) 10.

7 Ibid, 25.

8 Harold J Berman, The Law of International Commercial Transactions (Lex Mercatoria) (1987) 2 Emory Journal of International Dispute Resolution 235, 299.

9 William Mitchell, *An Essay on the Early History of the Law Merchant* (Cambridge University Press 1904) 22 and Harold J Berman, The Law of International Commercial Transactions (Lex Mercatoria) (1987) 2 Emory Journal of International Dispute Resolution 235, 240.

10 Ralf Michaels, 'The Re-statement of Non-State Law: The State, Choice of Law, and the Challenge from Global Legal Pluralism' (2005) 51 Wayne Law Review 1209, 1231.

11 Klaus P Berger, 'The New Law Merchant and the Global Market Place' (2000) 4 International Arbitration Law Review 92.

12 Roy Goode, 'Usage and its Reception in Transnational Commercial Law' in Jacob S Ziegel and Shalow Lerner (editors), *New Developments in International Commercial and Consumer Law, proceedings of the 8th Bienal Conference of the International Academy of Commercial and Consumer Law* (Hart Publishing1998) 7.

there is consensus that some form of the lex mercatoria existed, its coherence and extensiveness is disputed.[13] The lex mercatoria was not a complete and uniform body of law, but consisted of different sets of rules with strong regional differences.[14] Some describe the medieval lex mercatoria as a North Italian concept, which spread from there to the rest of Europe, but never achieved any real unification across the different areas.[15] Others state that the differences between customs were minor, and that it is thus possible to speak of a common lex mercatoria.[16] Given the customary nature of the lex mercatoria, there is limited textual evidence that has survived and it is difficult to come to any firm conclusions regarding the coherence and universality of the lex mercatoria. The term lex mercatoria is used historically which means that there was an early awareness of its existence. One of the earlier references to the lex mercatoria can be found in the Little Red Book of Bristol, which was published in the 13th century.[17]

The lex mercatoria slowly disappeared as unified national laws emerged with the rise of the nation state. The lex mercatoria was codified in civil law systems, whereas in England the lex mercatoria became a matter for the courts and was consequently absorbed in the common law.[18] The absorption of the lex mercatoria in national laws made the latter better suited for (international) commerce, but ultimately contributed to the loss of the universal character of commercial law.[19] The lex mercatoria did not disappear, but its presence diminished considerably and it was no longer applied independently but through the domestic court system.[20]

The concept of the lex mercatoria was revived in the second half of the 20th century. This renewal came through merchants, ship owners, insurers,

13 Emily Kadens argues against the existence of a coherent and unified medieval lex mercatoria on the ground that the evidence for such a legal system is flimsy. Looking at court decisions, texts written on merchants during that period, and other material, Kadens concludes that there most probably was not a lex mercatoria in the sense that is understood now. She notes that there was no real reason for the existence of an extensive lex mercatoria because commerce was usually done face to face and thus gave rise to less disputes, merchants used brokers and local agents when travelling to foreign cities who would inform them of local customs and laws. (Emily Kadens, 'The Myth of the Customary Law Merchant' (2012) 90 Texas Law Review 1153.

14 Roy Goode, 'Usage and its Reception in Transnational Commercial Law' in Jacob S Ziegel and Shalow Lerner (editors), *New Developments in International Commercial and Consumer Law, proceedings of the 8th Bienal Conference of the International Academy of Commercial and Consumer Law* (Hart Publishing1998) 7.

15 William Mitchell, *An Essay on the Early History of the Law Merchant* (Cambridge University Press 1904) 7.

16 Ibid.

17 Little Red Book of Bristol: https://archive.org/details/littleredbookbr02enggoog.

18 Lord Mansfield in the case of *Pillans and Rose v. van Mierop and Hopkins* [1765] 3 Burr 1663 (QB) '*rules of the law merchant are questions of law to be decided by the courts rather than matters of custom to be proven by the parties and such rules apply to all persons.*'

19 Harold J Berman, The Law of International Commercial Transactions (Lex Mercatoria) (1987) 2 Emory Journal of International Dispute Resolution 235, 243.

20 Ibid, 299–300.

and bankers who were confronted with more complex legal questions due to the increase in international trade, and who wished to increase predictability through legal harmonisation.[21] This issue generated interest from the scholarly community. The starting point of the study of the new lex mercatoria is an article written by professor Berthold Goldman in 1956 where he discusses the nationality of the Suez Canal Company, and argues that the Company was not of a specific nationality due to its organisation and global presence, and that it belonged to a transnational legal order and is subject to the international legal order.[22]

This idea was further developed in the 1960s by authors such as Goldstaijn, Fragistas, and Goldman in France, and Clive Schmitthoff in the UK and led to a theory of the new lex mercatoria.[23] The concept of this new lex mercatoria originates in the community of scholars and is based on their observations of mercantile practices in the 20th century. Goldman saw standard contract terms and the emergence of arbitration as important drivers behind the development of the new lex mercatoria.[24]

The new lex mercatoria is a spill over effect from globalisation, which entrenched party autonomy and furthered private law making.[25]

Is it possible in today's fragmented world for a unified lex mercatoria to exist? Due to diverse legal systems and different understandings of contract law it is difficult to speak of a universal lex mercatoria. One of the reasons why it is unlikely that a truly global lex mercatoria exists is economic disparity.[26] The development of the lex mercatoria is mainly restricted to developed liberal market states that have a significant amount of international trade. Merchants from nations that have less cross-border trade, because of a lack of economic development and/or state restrictions on international trade, are not involved in shaping the lex mercatoria in a meaningful way because of power disparity. This means that the lex mercatoria might be something which they participate in or have imposed on them, but they are not equal

21 Ibid, 243.

22 This article appeared in the newspaper Le Monde on the 4th of October 1956. An English translation and a scan of the original article can be found at: http://www.trans-lex.org/9/.

23 Klaus Peter Berger, 'Berthold Goldman and the Dijon School: The rebirth of the Lex Mercatoria' http://www.trans-lex.org/000001.

See also for instance: Clive M Schmitthoff, 'The Unification of the Law of International Trade' (1964 Handelshögskolan Göteburg, Skrifter) reproduced in Chia-Jui Cheng (editor), Clive M Schmitthoff, *Select Essays on International Trade* (1988 Marinus Nijhoff Publishers) 170

Berthold Goldman, 'Frontières du Droit et Lex Mercatoria' (1964) Archives du Philosophie du Droit.

24 Berthold Goldman, 'The Applicable Law: General Principles of Law- Lex Mercatoria' in J.D.M Lew (editor) ' Contemporary Problems in Arbitration' (1987 Springer) 113.

25 Ross Cranston, 'A Theory for International Commercial Law?' (2006) http://biblio.juridicas.unam.mx/libros/5/2332/18.pdf 253,261.

26 Gunther Teubner, 'Global Bukowina: Legal Pluralism in the World Society' in Gunther Teubner (editor), Global Law without a State (1997 Brookfield) 19.

co-creators. Thus, it is not truly the product of the global merchant community. The differences in legal culture also make it difficult to have one universal lex mercatoria. Therefore, there is no global and unified group of merchants that speak with one voice. Perhaps, it is thus better to speak of the lex mercatoria as a global phenomenon whose precise place, content, and uniformity differs between trades, regions, and communities.

Sceptics of the lex mercatoria might argue that the lex mercatoria cannot exist because only the state can create or enforce law.[27] This might have some validity as most judicial power rests with the nation state, but does not do justice to a cosmopolitan and globalised world that consists of fragmented communities and regions where more informal forms of law making exist both inside and outside international commerce. The law can have force if people believe it has force. If a majority of merchants treat the lex mercatoria as law, even when adhering to it goes against their personal interests, this means that the lex mercatoria is real no matter whether it is endorsed by the state.[28]

There are several key issues that determine how we understand the lex mercatoria. The first key issue, which was discussed in the previous paragraphs, is whether the lex mercatoria exists. The second issue is understanding what the lex mercatoria is. Is the lex mercatoria a distinct legal order or is it part of an existing legal order (domestic or international)?

Berger analyses three separate theories on the perception of the lex mercatoria. The first sees the lex mercatoria as a mass of rules, which can be used to supplement the applicable law, the second defines the lex mercatoria as an autonomous law, and the third sees the lex mercatoria as an independent legal system.[29] The third view confirms '*the existence of transnational rules made up of usages and principles which would constitute a true juridical order specific to the operators of international commerce.*'[30]

The second theory is that of the lex mercatoria as an autonomous law. Goldman suggests that the lex mercatoria is an independent legal order, which is dependent upon national legal orders for its implementation.[31] A major difference between the medieval lex mercatoria and the new lex mercatoria is that the first operated independently of national/regional laws, whereas now domestic law has final jurisdiction over international commercial transactions.[32] The concept and the role of the state is drastically different from the Middle Ages, especially in how it exercises control over its territory and its role in the administration of private law. The role of the lex

27 Klaus Peter Berger, *The Creeping Codification of the Lex Mercatoria* (Kluwer Law International 1999) 102.

28 Ibid, 106.

29 Ibid 40.

30 Louis Marques, *International Uniform Commercial Law: towards a progressive consciousness* (Ashgate Aldershot 2005) 11.

31 Berthold Goldman, 'Lex Mercatoria: Lecture' *Forum Internationale 3*, (Kluwer 1983) 22/23.

32 Clive Schmitthoff, 'The Unification of the Law of International Trade' in Clive Schmitthoff, The *Sources of the Law of International Trade* (Frederick A. Praeger 1964).

mercatoria changed as the role of the state changed. It is an autonomous law, but it is not a completely independent legal system. In 1924 the North Dakota Supreme Court stated that:

> the law merchant is a system of law that does not rest exclusively on the institutions and local customs of any particular country, but consists of certain principles of equity and usages of trade which general convenience and a common sense of justice have established to regulate the dealings of merchants and mariners in all the commercial countries of the civilised world.[33]

The first view of the lex mercatoria is in line with traditional legal doctrine, which considers the lex mercatoria as *'professional norms, social rules, customs, usages, contractual obligations, intra-organisation or inter-organisational agreements, arbitration awards – but not law.'*[34] This theory emphasises that law is the expression of the will of states.[35] In this theory the absence of a unified and independent merchant community combined with the lack of an opinio iuris make it difficult to justify that the lex mercatoria is (customary) law.[36]

Berger forges the three approaches together by describing the lex mercatoria as *'the totality of international trade usages which has the character of an independent legal system that derives its justification from acknowledgement by domestic laws'*[37] The lex mercatoria is autonomous in its development, but is connected to domestic legal systems which determine when it can be applied. Businesses are at the core of the development of the lex mercatoria but the domestic law of that state determines its legitimacy within a specific state.

2.4 The content of the lex mercatoria

The next key issue is defining the substance of the lex mercatoria. There are again three main hypotheses. In the first the lex mercatoria encompasses the whole of transnational commercial law. This view is probably the least popular. Lando identified 8 elements of the lex mercatoria:

- Public international law aspects
- Uniform laws

33 *Bank of Conway v. Stary et al* 51 N.D. 399, 200 N.W. 505 (1924).

34 Günther Teubner, 'Breaking Frames: Economic Globalization and the Emergence of *lex mercatoria*' (2002) 5 European Journal of Social Theory 199, 206.

35 Harold J Berman, The Law of International Commercial Transactions (Lex Mercatoria) (1987) 2 Emory Journal of International Dispute Resolution 235, 304.

36 Gunther Teubner, 'Global Bukowina: Legal Pluralism in the World Society' in Gunther Teubner (editor), *Global Law without a State* (Brookfield 1997) 9.

37 Klaus Peter Berger, *The Creeping Codification of the Lex Mercatoria* (Kluwer Law International 1999) 40.

- General principles of law
- Rules of international organisations
- Uncodified customs and usages
- Codified customs and usages
- Standard-form contracts
- Reported arbitral awards.[38]

This thus means that all transnational commercial rules, public international law, and arbitral awards should be considered lex mercatoria. Dalhuisen also includes elements of EU law and domestic law in his classification. Following his work, in order of importance, the lex mercatoria consists of:

- Fundamental basic principles like pacta sunt servanda
- Custom and practices of a mandatory nature including proprietary restrictions
- Uniform substantive treaty law of a mandatory nature such as certain EU laws
- Mandatory general principles such as good faith
- Contractual terms including the applicable law
- Directory customs and practices
- Uniform treaty rules of a directory nature like the CISG
- Directory general principles of particular legal structures.[39]

The lex mercatoria would thus consist of most elements of international commercial law and constitutes a legal system that can be ordered and hierarchised.

The intermediary view identifies the lex mercatoria as all non-state rules. This would include usages and practices, general principles, model contracts, restatements of laws, codified usages, arbitral awards, but not public international law or international conventions.[40]

The most restricted definition reduces the lex mercatoria to uncodified non-state rules. It omits codified non-state rules: *'none of these norms qualify as lex or even ius, and many of them are not mercatoriae. For example, although the UNIDROIT Principles are limited to international 'commercial' contracts, neither the Principles of European Contract Law nor the credit card association rules are so limited.'*[41] The lex mercatoria should thus be restricted to: *'what Roman lawyers described as ius non scriptum and thus [...] that*

38 Ole Lando, 'The Lex Mercatoria in International Commercial Arbitration' (1985) 34 International & Comparative Law Quarterly 747, 748.

39 Jan Dalhuisen, *On Transnational and Comparative Commercial, Financial and Trade Law Volume I, - The New Lex Mercatoria and its Sources* (Hart Publishing 2001) 169–171.

40 Roy Goode, 'Usage and Its Reception in Transnational Commercial Law' (1997) 46 International & Comparative Law Quarterly 2.

41 Symeon C Symeonides, 'Party Autonomy and Private-Law Making in Private Law: The Lex Mercatoria that Isn't' published in *Liber Amicorum Konstantinos D Kerameus* (Sakkoulas/Kluwer Press 2006) 6.

part of transnational commercial law which consists of the unwritten customs and usages of merchants.'[42] The essence of the new lex mercatoria as being *'uncodified, non-statutory, and non-conventional.'*[43]

Within this approach there is a sub-discussion on whether general principles of law should be included. The lex mercatoria would in that view, be confined to the practices, usages, and customs exclusive to international commerce.[44] The inclusion of general principles is questioned because they vary between jurisdictions as does their interpretation and they are thus not truly uniform.[45]

General principles of law can originate within the international legal order or within the domestic legal order. They do not originate within the practices of the merchant community. At the same time, it can be considered that the general principles of international commercial law are different to these two concepts. They might start as public international law or domestic law, but they can develop into common principles applicable to the practices of international commerce. Merchants would expect courts to interpret their contract in light of principles such as reasonableness and good faith. The value that the business community attaches to these principles would warrant their inclusion in the lex mercatoria.

Standard contracts and conditions do not have a customary origin, yet Goldman proposes these could be included in the lex mercatoria because they originate within the business community.[46] This serves as an illustration that although there might be three broad theories on the substance of the lex mercatoria, within these three theories there are also different viewpoints on what should be included.

In conclusion there are three key issues that shape our understanding of the lex mercatoria. The first is whether the lex mercatoria can exist. The second is whether it is a distinct legal order. The third issue is establishing the substance of the lex mercatoria. There is no consensus on any of these issues. Berger notes that a worldwide survey amongst legal practitioners found that the vast majority would not recommend choosing the lex mercatoria as the applicable law as it is not well defined.[47] Defining the lex mercatoria is thus

42 Roy Goode, Herbert Kronke, Ewan McKendrick and Jeffrey Wool, *Transnational Commercial Law: Text, Cases and Materials* (Oxford University Press 2007) 6.

43 Roy Goode, 'Usage and Its Reception in Transnational Commercial Law' (1997) 46 International & Comparative Law Quarterly 2.

44 This view is for instance espoused by Goode et all who write that general principles of (international) law should be seen as a separate source within transnational commercial law: Roy Goode, Herbert Kronke, Ewan McKendrick and Jeffrey Wool, *Transnational Commercial Law: Text, Cases and Materials* (Oxford University Press 2007) 6 and 50.

45 Jan Ramberg, *International Commercial Transactions* (ICC Kluwer Law International Norstedts Juridik AB 1998) 21.

46 Berthold Goldman, 'Lex Mercatoria: Lecture', *Forum Internationale 3*, (Kluwer 1983), 5/6.

47 Klaus Peter Berger, 'The New Law Merchant and The Global Market Place: a 21st Century View of Transnational Commercial Law' in Klaus Peter Berger (Editor), *The Practice of Transnational Law* (Kluwer Law International 2001) 6.

not only of theoretical importance, but also of practical importance because it solves the unpredictability that prevents its usage. For this purpose, the first two issues are mainly of academic interest whilst the question of the actual content of the lex mercatoria is also of practical interest. Businesses will not be as interested in theoretical debates on the existence of the lex mercatoria, and whether it should be classified as an autonomous system. They do want to know what they can expect if they use the lex mercatoria or if the court/arbitral tribunal applies it, and therefore it is important to have a workable definition of its contents.

If one adheres to the wider views of what the lex mercatoria consists of this moves it further away from the medieval lex mercatoria. In the lex mercatoria the object (the regulation of international commerce), and the origin (customary) are important: it is '*an ensemble of general principles and legal rules growing out of a process of spontaneous, institutional law making.*'[48] If the lex mercatoria is equivalent to all transnational commercial law or even to just all non-state rules (including codified) it means that custom is no longer its primary origin. It means that the lex mercatoria can be deliberately created by states and (international) organisations and the merchant community will no longer determine the content. Thus, by adopting the wider approach one changes the nature of the lex mercatoria.

If one sees the new lex mercatoria as a continuation of the medieval lex mercatoria it would be logical to take the medieval lex mercatoria as a starting point. Mitchell defines 5 characteristics of the medieval lex mercatoria:

- Transnationality
- Custom as the primary source
- A spirit of equity
- Self-administered by merchants
- Speedy and informal procedures.[49]

If one would define the lex mercatoria according to the above criteria the closest definition is that of an unwritten law which is spontaneously created and is formed by the customs, trade usages and practices of merchants, as well as by the general principles of transnational commercial law and that through its usage gains in legal authority. The concept of non-state rules is thus broader than that of the lex mercatoria as it encompasses a wider range of sources (including codified non-state rules). Whilst the lex mercatoria consists of non-state rules, not all non-state rules can be considered lex mercatoria.

48 Ibid.

49 William Mitchell, *An Essay on the Early History of the Law Merchant* (Cambridge University Press 1904) 13.

2.5 Understanding legal authority

After having defined the concept of non-state rules it is important to begin formulating how legal authority can be understood in relation to non-state rules. What makes non-state rules more than simple social norms or guidelines that businesses might adhere to, but which carry no legal obligation? How can we establish whether rules have legal authority? If the source of the legal authority of domestic law is the state, then this would not apply to non-state rules, which have a different origin. This and the following sections provide some tentative analysis as to the ways that the legal authority of non-state rules can be established. Ultimately the argument is that the legal authority of non-state rules depends significantly on their acceptance by the business and legal communities; and that this in turn depends to a significant degree on the extent to which these rules are applied. The following sections indicate why this aspect is crucial to measuring how non-state rules acquire legal authority.

First, there is a need to create an understanding of how legal authority is attributed to a rule. How do we establish whether a rule is a source of law? Bonnecase defines a source of law as: '*the imposed and predetermined forms that borrow concepts of behaviour from society to impose themselves as the rule of law.*'[50] Mistelis defines it as '*the sovereign authority by which a legal rule is applied and the origin of such rules*' as well as '*the manifestation and substance of the principles and rules of law.*'[51] Thus, a source of law is both the origin (where it comes from) as well as the result (the specific rule). Oppetit clarifies that there are two types of sources: formal (statutory law and case law) and material (doctrine/jurisprudence).[52] Formal sources are a technical process through which law is created whereas material sources affect what laws are created (the substance).

Combining these reflections, it emerges that a source of law is the origin (where it comes from), the technique (how it became law), the reason (why it became law), and the result (the substance of the law). Thus, if as an

50 As quoted in G Legrand, 'La Notion de Droit en France au 19eme siècle' (1921) 23 Revue Néo-Scolastique de Philosophie 436.

51 Loukas Mistelis, 'Is Harmonisation a Necessary Evil? The Future of Harmonisation and New Sources of International Trade' in Ian F Fletcher, Loukas Mistelis and Marise Cremona (editors), *Foundations and Perspectives of International Trade Law*, (Sweet & Maxwell 2000) 10.

52 Bruno Oppetit, 'Le Droit International Privé, Droit Savant' (1992) 234 Droit Savant recueil Cours de l'académie de DIP de la Haye 331

Doctrine should be seen in the context of civil law. It refers to legal scholarship, which together forms a framework on how the law should be interpreted, it is both prescriptive and descriptive. Doctrine is a primary or secondary source of law depending on the jurisdiction and can be regularly quoted in court. Doctrine becomes more important if there is less statutory law available.

Legal doctrine in the common law refers to a fundamental set of principles underlying the law. It proceeds more from case law than from legal scholarship. Although there are similarities it needs to be kept in mind that civil law and common law have a different approach to the concept of doctrine.

example one takes (international) trade usages, their origin is their spontaneous creation in commercial relations by the merchant community; the technique is their regular and consistent usage by that merchant community and the enforcement of these usages in courts; the reason is to facilitate (international) commerce and the belief that the merchant community should be allowed to self-organise; and the end result is the actual content of these trade usages. Of course, the process is not clearly separated in practice, but this serves as an adequate example to understand the diverse aspects of the notion of a source of law.

Within the state there is a hierarchy whereby the higher rules (the constitution) provide legitimacy for the lower ones which makes it easier to understand where their legal authority comes from.[53] Ultimately, the state decides this legitimacy. The political process determines what the law is and those that apply the law carry out the will of the state. The government can implement what legislation it wants, regardless of whether this legislation is based on rational arguments or a legal need.[54] Its authority comes from the legitimacy provided by the state.

The legal authority of non-state rules can be asserted through the state. The state can recognise non-state rules as a source of law, it can sanction their application by courts, and it can allow for the parties to the contract to use them. Whilst non-state rules are not created by the state, they can still gain legal authority through their acceptance by the state. The notion that law can only be called law if its source is a sovereign is ahistorical and there always have been laws that do not meet this criterion.[55] Today's understanding of law is based on 19th century concepts of statehood where the nation state is the focal point of all authority.[56] A rule cannot be excluded as being law '*purely on the ground that on the basis of a theory the sources of law are exhaustive and thus conclusive, and any other instance does not have the necessary competence to legislate.*'[57]

Legal authority is not exclusively the product of the state and the legitimacy of rules can be asserted without the sanction of the state. Historically, legislative texts written by non-state actors had strong legal authority: '*European private law has long been developed on the basis of texts that were largely independent of political domination. the Decretum Gratiana as well as the Saxon Mirror were written by actors outside of the political, governmental sphere of sovereigns and the authority of the Roman Corpus Iruis Civilis*

53 Günther Teubner, 'Breaking Frames: Economic Globalization and the Emergence of Lex Mercatoria' (2002) 5 European Journal of Social Theory 199, 206.

54 Nils Jansen, *The Making of Legal Authority* (2010) Oxford University Press, 1.

55 Friedrich K Juenger, 'American Conflicts Scholarship and the New Law Merchant' (1995) 28 Vanderbilt Journal of Transnational Law 487, 490.

56 Gunther Teubner, 'Global Bukowina: Legal Pluralism in the World Society' in Gunther Teubner (editor), *Global Law without a State* (1997 Brookfield) 9.

57 David Oser, *The Unidroit Principles of International Commercial Contracts: a Governing Law* (Martinus Nijhoff 2008) 122.

resulted from its recognition by the legal profession.'[58] The state does not exist in a vacuum and exists alongside different orders, social, legal, political, at different levels, including international.[59]

Legal pluralism is not a 21st century concept. If compared with 19th century ideas of statehood and law this might seem that way, but this does not do justice to a past where multiple laws and norms have always co-existed and governed different communities or different situations, even within one single territorial unit. It is inappropriate to disallow the qualification of a rule as law on the ground that non-state rules are not the law of the land. Foreign law is not the law of the land and yet its inherent quality as law would not be questioned.[60]

The exact status of law changes between times and places. In France case law has recognized that the lex mercatoria possesses the quality of law.[61] This means that the lex mercatoria has legal authority, but it does not mean that the lex mercatoria would now be a permissible choice of law in court litigation. There is consequently not one sole reality when it comes to establishing whether something is (a source of) law.[62] The status of a source of law shifts between situations as it depends on the jurisdiction, the applicable law, and the specific facts of the case.

2.6 Measuring the legal authority of non-state rules

If a source of law is determined by the origin of the source, the process through which it was established, the reason why it came into existence, and the substantive result then to understand how non-state rules acquire legal authority, the same four lenses could be applied. The four lenses that measure whether a rule is a source of law in domestic law can be used to determine whether non-state rules have the quality of a source of law. This alone is not enough to measure the legal authority of non-state rules, but it forms a starting point to establishing this authority.

Non-state rules can have legal authority within the state and within the transnational sphere. Understanding the legal authority in the domestic sphere is straightforward. It would be understood and measured in the same

58 Nils Jansen, *The Making of Legal Authority* (2010 Oxford University Press) 41.

59 Ralf Michaels & Nils Jansen, 'Private Law Beyond the State – Europeanization, Globalization, Privatization (2006) 54 American Journal of Comparative Law 843, 889.

60 David Oser, *The Unidroit Principles of International Commercial Contracts: a Governing Law* (Martinus Nijhoff 2008) 122.

61 *Valenciana de Cementos Portland SA v. Primary Coal Inc* (1991) Cour de Cassation Civile, 1991 Bulletin Civil 1 No. 1354

An arbitral award was challenged on the grounds that the arbitrator overstepped his mission by acting as amiable compositeur without the authority to do so through applying the lex mercatoria. The court of cassation denied the appeal on the grounds that the lex mercatoria is law, and therefore the arbitrator had not acted as amiable compositeur.

62 Ralf Michaels, 'The Re-statement of Non-State Law: The State, Choice of Law, and the Challenge from Global Legal Pluralism' (2005)*51 Wayne Law Review* 1209, 1238.

way as any state law is. So, if trade usages are considered a source of domestic law then they get their authority from that recognition. This would not differ from any other law. More challenging is to understand the legal authority of non-state rules beyond the state.

First, it is important to understand that the international business community consists of different stakeholders such as merchants, legal professionals, and arbitrators. There is no final arbiter whereas the state often has that ultimate authority in an instrument (constitution) and institutions (the national government and the courts.)

The first criterion is thus origin. The legislative authority of state law is there from the start; the political process from which it is developed empowers the rule as law. The legislative authority of non-state rules is always posteriori; the rule comes into existence first and through subsequent usage and application it can achieve authority.[63]

If the law receives its legitimacy from the forum, which initiated or sanctioned it, then the same would hold true for non-state rules. Non-state rules are transnational or international in origin. Their origin lies in international organisations, trade associations, and the practices between merchants. They do not emerge from the nation state and they exist in parallel with the state. These same entities that originated the rules can (partly) affirm their legitimacy as sources of law.

Non-state rules can have an organisational or customary origin. They can thus be deliberately created by organisations or emerge through usage by the business community. The standing of the organisation could help determine the legitimacy of the rule. Some institutions like UNIDROIT have broad international support that gives them legitimacy. Trade associations might not have that same international recognition, but they have the support of (parts of) the business community. Codified non-state rules represent the commitment of the scholars and the institutions promulgating these rules.[64] Whereas trade associations are suspected of acting mainly in their own interests, international organisations and groups of scholars are considered neutral, serving legal harmonisation for principled reasons, which adds to the perception of their authority.[65]

Yet, the support of the business community also gives legitimacy to rules, which serve that same community. The Incoterms, the finance contract terms of the ICC (such as the UCP600 and the Uniform Rules for Demand Guarantee (URDG)), and the contract terms emitted by trade associations are widely used in the business community. They are used far more frequently than the UPICC and the PECL for instance. These standard terms are drafted by organisations that represent the business community. Frequency of usage is also explained by the fact that these contract terms are intended for specific

63 Roy Goode, 'Usage and Its Reception in Transnational Commercial Law' (1997) 46 International & Comparative Law Quarterly 3.

64 Ibid.

65 Nils Jansen, *The Making of Legal Authority* (2010 Oxford University Press) 41.

contracts (such as documentary credits) or for specific parts of the contracts (such as passage of risk). Their smaller scope means that the effect of including these in the contract is more predictable than using a restatement of law as the governing law.[66]

Other non-state rules are private initiatives which are supported by legal professionals and the scholarly community but do not have the same institutional support. This diminishes the legal authority they could lay claim too, as the support of an institution adds legitimacy to the instrument because of its perceived transcendence. It is more than the work of a single author or a group of authors, but it is impersonal and bypasses the individual. Private initiatives need to emphasise professional excellence and neutrality to encourage usage, which in turn can add to their legal authority.

The second lens ties in with the first one: the process through which the rule came into existence. Codified non-state rules are purposefully drafted. This can either be through trade associations in which stakeholders have an important say in how the rules should be shaped and where they are accepted in accordance with the rules of the association, or it can be through an international organisation where they are drafted by experts and approved by the organisation. It can also be a private initiative whereby a group of individuals draft the non-state rules. Merchants create uncodified non-state rules through regular and consistent practice of certain usages.

The third lens is the reason why the instrument came into existence. International organisations and trade associations will justify the choices that they make on why they are creating a certain instrument. This could be to save the international business community money[67], to solve confusion between existing terms, which have different interpretations[68], to lower barriers to international contracting[69], to provide rules into an international area in which there are none[70], or to modernise existing usages.[71] Of course, for uncodified non-state rules there are no formal justifications. They come into

66 Henry Deed Gabriel, 'the Use of Soft Law in the Creation of Legal Norms in International Commercial Law: How Successful Has it Been?' (2019) 40 Michigan Journal of International Law 413,426.

67 It is estimated that the Aircraft Protocol to the Cape Town Convention saves the industry $4 billion yearly in borrowing cost (see: Roy Goode, 'Contract and Commercial Law: The Logic and Limits of Harmonisation' (2003) 7 Electronic Journal of Comparative Law).

68 The Incoterms were drafted out of pre-existing trade terms which were interpreted differently depending on the port.

69 The UNIDROIT Principles were designed to create a neutral law of the contract. See for instance: Michael Joachim Bonell, An International Restatement of Contract Law: the UNIDROIT Principles of International Commercial Contracts (2nd edition, Transnational Publishers 1997).

70 For instance, the early 20th century Warsaw Convention on carriage by air (see: Alexander N Sack, 'International Unification of Private Law Rules on Air Transportation and the Warsaw Convention' (1933) 4 Air Law Review 345).

71 The UCP600 were created out of existing banking practises with the aim to modernise these to be more fit for 20th century banking practices (see for instance: Hang Yen Low, UCP 600: the new rules on documentary compliance (2010) 52 International Journal of Law and Management 193.

existence because merchants start using them (trade usages) or courts start applying them (general legal principles.) The users deem that these are practices and principles that are beneficial for international commerce.

The fourth lens is the content of the instrument. It should not be the origin of the rule, which characterizes its legal value, but its substance.[72] The authority of state law comes from the legislative force that enacts it; the content of the law is of secondary importance. It is not binding because of the rationality of its arguments but because it is the result of a binding political process.[73] On the other hand, non-state rules derive their authority not from the authoritative force but from the rationality behind the argument: non ratione imperii, sed imperio rationis. The argument has to persuade the users. Courts can refer to legal analyses that consider and comment on the specific rule. It would be difficult to decide whose opinions should carry the most value in this determination. Arbitrators? Judges? Scholars? Merchants? Lawyers? This is ambiguous.

The above four lenses: origin, process, reason, and content can thus help unpack the nature of non-state rules and begin to determine their legal authority. This forms the start to the process of understanding the legal position of non-state rules. Whilst this first step is crucial, these lenses also fall short of measuring the legal authority of these rules in the transnational sphere. The reason is that within the state it is the institutional framework that legitimates the laws. The procedures ensure accountability from the state. Legal procedures immediately confer legitimacy on the laws they create. Without these procedures the law functions to enhance the arbitrary powers of the state without any political accountability.[74] This is not the same for the processes through which non-state rules are created. The organisations and people that created the rules cannot give them legitimacy. There needs to be an outside factor that legitimizes them This institutional framework does not exist in the transnational sphere but there are major stakeholders. There are first the institutions, international organisations, and trade associations. The discussion above on origin already discussed how these contribute to establishing that legal authority. The second group is businesses. The business community creates rules (either through spontaneous usage or trade associations) and more importantly uses these rules. The final major players are the formal dispute resolution mechanisms: arbitral tribunals and courts. These recognise the legal authority of these rules through applying them in disputes.

Thus, in addition to the four lenses (origin, procedure, reason, and substance) that are used to determine whether something can be considered a source of law, the second step is to understand how we can measure the legal authority of non-state rules in the transnational sphere, where two additional issues are key: support (from the business community and legal professionals);

72 David Oser, *The Unidroit Principles of International Commercial Contracts: A Governing Law* (Martinus Nijhoff 2008) 120.

73 Nils Jansen, *The Making of Legal Authority* (2010 Oxford University Press) 86.

74 Jan Klabbers, the Undesirability of Soft Law (1998) 67 Nordic Journal of International Law 381, 387/391.

and (more generally but also indicative of support by the business legal worlds) *application* (by courts and tribunals).

The first issue to understand is how support can be determined. The support of the business community and other stakeholders such as legal professionals can partly be understood through perception and use of non-state rules. It is not just the intrinsic quality of a norm that defines whether something is law, but how it is perceived by the community.[75] The drafters of an instrument can present and position this in such a way that there is a perceived legal authority to it from the start which in turn engenders further support and usage. Law has a *'generally perceived legitimate authority'* by which is meant what the average citizens believes to be law and what they adhere to because they believe this to be morally right.[76] People, institutions and states recognise the authority of tradition, the authority of expertise, and the authority of moral claims.[77] Creating a link between non-state rules and existing law and principles can enhance the legitimacy of the former. Claiming an instrument is based on existing legal principles and/or trade usages shows that non-state rules fit into the greater legal framework, that they are not newly invented, but are a continuation of an older tradition. This creates support from the business community that already uses (and even trusts) those existing principles and trade usages.

On the other hand, by juxtaposing itself as being different from domestic law non-state rules can also gain legitimacy from users. If non-state rules are not different in form and procedure from domestic law, then they no longer represent an alternative option and there is no reason why the parties to the contract should favour them over state law.[78] The attractiveness of non-state rules lies in providing efficiency, flexibility, and clarity. The rules are a product of the market and find a balance between optimising a just solution and the cost of that solution (both in terms of time and money), whereby state laws are not concerned with procedural costs and finding that balance between costs and administering justice.[79] The differences between non-state rules and state law thus contribute to creating business support for non-state rules.

To enhance perception the form in which something is presented is important. If an instrument presents itself as authoritative then this helps it being perceived as authoritative. The document should in appearance be authoritative, coherent, and easy to apply, and it should mimic legal codifications.[80] For

75 Thomas Schultz, *Transnational Legality: Stateless Law and International Arbitration* (Oxford University Press 2014) 16/17.

76 Ibid, 30.

77 Rodney Bruce Hall & Thomas J Biersteker, 'The Emergence of Private Authority in the International System' in Rodney Bruce Hall & Thomas J Biersteker (editors) 'The Emergence of Private Authority in Global Governance (CUP 2002) 5.

78 Ralf Michaels, 'The True Lex Mercatoria: Law Beyond the State' (2007) 14 Ind J Global Legal Stud 447, 462.

79 Gillian K Hadfield, Privatizing Commercial Law: Lessons from the Middle and Digital Ages , (2000) Working Paper No.195, 40/41.

80 Nils Jansen, *The Making of Legal Authority* (2010 Oxford University Press) 106.

instance, the commentary on the UPICC does not justify the choices the drafters made, it is an explanation of the rules and they do not reveal which part of the Principles are descriptive of the current majoritarian approach and which part is prescriptive and the commentary presents the UPICC as the law as it ought to be.[81] The UPICC thus present themselves in authoritative fashion. Legal authority resides where the participants in the legal process believe it resides, if non-state rules are perceived to have authority then they have authority.

The next step is to establish how the support of the instrument can be measured in practice. This is not necessarily easy. The business world is heterogeneous, private, and, fragmentary. One step is how non-state rules are perceived by other organisations that have legitimacy, either because they are trade associations or established international organisations. For instance, the International Trade Centre's Model Contract for the International Commercial Sale of Goods states that: *'Questions relating to this contract that are not settled by the provisions contained in the contract shall be governed by the United Nations Convention on Contracts for the International Sale of Goods (…). Questions not covered by the CISG shall be governed by the UNIDROIT Principles of International Commercial Contracts (….)'*[82] UNCITRAL lists a number of instruments on their website which they did not elaborate, but which they do endorse.[83] The other side is true as well. If the business community deliberately excludes an instrument, then this shows a lack of support. Model contracts developed by trade associations regularly exclude the application of international conventions.[84] The CISG is regularly excluded from international contracts, although the exact extent is unclear because there is no comprehensive data available.[85] Some of the reasons are lack of familiarity with the CISG and a positive bias towards domestic law.[86] Such an

81 Ibid, 70.

82 The International Trade Centre is a subsidiary organisation of the WTO and UNCTAD (United Nations Conference on Trade and Development). Its mission is to '*to foster inclusive and sustainable growth and development through trade and international business development.*'
http://www.intracen.org/itc/about/mission-and-objectives/
International Trade Centre, Model Contracts for Small Firms, Model Contract for International Commercial Sales of Goods,
http://www.intracen.org/uploadedFiles/intracenorg/Content/Exporters/Exporting_Better/Templates_of_contracts/3%20International%20Commercial%20Sale%20of%20Goods.pdf.

83 Examples are The Hague Principles on Choice of Law, the UNIDROIT Principles in International Commercial Contracts, UCP, Incoterms, and the International Standby Practices.
http://www.uncitral.org/uncitral/en/other_organizations_texts.html.

84 See for example
GAFTA model contract, clause 28
http://www.gafta.com/write/MediaUploads/Contracts/2016/1_2016.pdf
NAEGA model contract, clause 27
http://naega.org/images/naegacontract.pdf.

85 Ingeborg Schwenzer and Pascal Hachem, 'the CISG- Successes and Pitfalls' (2009) 57 The American Journal of Comparative Law 457,463.

86 Charles R Calleros, 'Towards Harmonization and Certainty in Choice of Law Rules for International Contracts: Should the U.S. Adopt the Equivalent of Rome I?' (2010) 28 Wisconsin International Law Journal 639, 642.

exclusion, shows a lack of support in the business community as they see no advantage to using the rules.

The authority of legal texts is determined from within the legal system by the participants of that system.[87] These participants assign authority to the texts with how they use these and how they interpret them.[88] The law is not stagnant, the law needs interpretation, and there are gaps in the law. Legal professionals, including lawyers and judges therefore need to advance the law, and they partly determine what the law is and how it is used. To do so they can have recourse to non-state rules, and this usage contributes to their legitimacy. After all, legal professionals make the choice of which arguments to use and which sources they base these arguments on. It is not enough for a text to declare itself an authority (like the UPICC and PECL do in their pre-amble) but also for it to be used as such: *'Indeed the corpus iuris did not become the legal basis for the ius ccommune because an Emperor or a Prince had declared it binding, but for the only reason that learned lawyers used it as the standard textual reference within their legal discourse, first in Italy and later in most other European countries.'*[89] When legal professionals decide to use a specific rule they add to its legitimacy.

The above gives some indication on how support can thus be understood through perception and usage, but it is also clear that it is difficult to measure as there is only limited data available. It is unknown how often businesses use non-state rules. We know that trade associations (which are supported by businesses) create them and that trade usages play a prominent role in certain trades (especially commodity trades.) It is more difficult to measure how often non-state rules are included in contracts (no reliable data exists on this.)

There is one key way that usage of non-state rules can be gauged: this is through their application by courts and tribunals. Application can measure the support and perception of non-state rules in the international business community and among legal professionals. The difficulty lies in the fact that non-state rules are applied more frequently in arbitration but that as arbitral awards are usually not published the exact extent of application is not known. If non-state rules are applied at the request of the parties, this helps to understand the level of support these rules have among the business community. If non-state rules are applied without inclusion in the contract this contributes to understanding their legal authority beyond contractual rules.

Application cannot only help gain a better understanding of the perception and usage of non-state rules, but it also influences their legitimacy and legal authority. The legislative authority of state law is there from the start; the political process through which it is developed empowers the text as law. Non-state rules acquire legitimacy and legal authority posteriori, after they have been developed.[90] Partly through their usage and support by the com-

87 Nils Jansen, *The Making of Legal Authority* (2010 Oxford University Press) 20.
88 Ibid, 44.
89 Ibid, 28.
90 Ibid, 41.

munity and partly through application and thus recognition by courts and arbitral tribunals. If they are applied by courts, then they become more than voluntary guidelines and gain authoritative force.

2.7 Conclusion: understanding non-state rules

This chapter examined first what non-state rules are and why they cannot be equated with the lex mercatoria. Whilst the two are not the same they are linked. The lex mercatoria consists of those non-state rules, which have a customary and uncodified origin. There are multiple theories on what the (new) lex mercatoria is. The most appropriate theory is to define the lex mercatoria along the same characteristics as the medieval lex mercatoria. This means that the lex mercatoria is unwritten and consists of those usages, practices, and principles developed within the merchant community.

Non-state rules, is a wider concept and includes codified rules as well as those rules whose origins are not strongly linked to the merchant community. They are defined as those legal norms that aim to regulate international commerce and that have been weakened along one or more of the dimensions of obligation, precision, and delegation following Abbot and Snidal's theory.[91]

After establishing what non-state rules are, the second half of the chapter began to develop a picture of how the legal authority of non-state rules can be understood: the core issue for this book. It discussed how sources of law are seen through four lenses: origin, procedure, reason, and substance. However, these lenses are not enough to understand whether a rule is a voluntary guideline or whether it has legal force. For that it is necessary to understand the framework that can give it legitimacy. That legitimacy and legal authority exists in the domestic sphere and in the transnational sphere. The legal authority within the domestic sphere comes from the state and by extension the state's institutions, including its courts. Legal authority in the transnational sphere can be measured through how non-state rules are approached by the key stakeholders: the business community, legal professionals, arbitral tribunals, and courts. It is necessary to understand the support non-state rules have from these stakeholders through perception, usage, and application. The latter is key, because if they are applied by courts they become more than voluntary guidelines, they now create obligations on the parties and thus have a form of legal authority.

Following this discussion of the definition of non-state rules and an initial exploration of how their legal authority can be measured, the next chapter approaches non-state rules from the perspective of legal harmonisation. Non-state rules play a key role in the harmonisation of international commercial law and their legal authority cannot be truly understood without exploring this role.

91 Kenneth W Abbott and Duncan Snidal 'Hard and Soft Law in International Governance' (2000) 54 International Organization 421.

3 The place of non-state rules in international commercial law

3.1 Introduction

This chapter examines the place that non-state rules occupy in international commercial law. The starting point is to understand the differences between international commercial law and transnational commercial law and what place non-state rules occupy within those concepts. This discussion is closely linked to the harmonisation of law. Non-state rules play a key part in this process and make a significant contribution to the harmonisation of international commercial law. To understand the legal authority of non-state rules, it is thus not only necessary to know their place in international commercial law but also how they contribute to legal harmonisation. Understanding this contribution sheds light on the support that non-state rules have in the business community. This support is one of the key factors to understanding the authority of non-state rules as chapter 2 established. Non-state rules represent a bottom up type harmonisation, that means that they are not imposed by the state but rather flow from the merchant community itself, which decides to use them. The consistent and repeated usage of non-state rules creates common legal principles and a common framework of understanding between merchants. This enhances their application in courts and in turn this application influences their legal authority. Non-state rules can only contribute to harmonisation if they are used by the international business community, by states, and by courts. The more important the role of non-state rules in harmonisation, the more likely that they will be applied, which then furthers legal harmonisation and through these processes non-state rules gain in legal authority.

3.2 International commercial law and transnational commercial law

The regulation of international commerce occurs on two different levels. The first is the international public law level where regulations are made through international organisations, including principally the World Trade Organisation, the World Bank, and the International Monetary Fund, as well as through bilateral and multilateral trade agreements. This area is commonly known as ***international economic law***. Its goal is to organise the legal rules of the economy on a global and regional level through, for instance, tariff and custom regulations, and import and export agreements. The regulatory framework is aimed at the obligations of the state. Therefore, international economic law affects businesses indirectly.

The second level of organisation is that which is generally referred to as ***international commercial law***. This concerns private law regulations in international trade and is applicable directly to businesses and other commercial private actors. It consists mainly of domestic law regulations; it is administered through the state.

Typically, the term international trade law is used synonymously with international economic law.[1] However, in the UK international trade law is regularly used as a synonym for international commercial law or to incorporate both international commercial law and international economic law.[2] This means that within the UK context it is possible to find texts referring to international trade law but discussing international commercial law.[3]

Overall, international economic law is public law whereas international commercial law is considered private law. This dichotomy is more nuanced when looking at the subject areas in more detail. Certain public aspects of company law, fiscal law, competition and intellectual property law could be included in the definition of international commercial law.[4] There is no consensus on whether these subjects should be included within commercial law or should be seen as completely separate. Whilst the international contract contains a link to all these areas it is debatable how far that linkage should be extended to determine the exact boundaries of international commercial law. The boundaries between public law and private law are fading and this leads to further convergence between international economic law and international commercial law.[5]

Contract law regulates the rights and obligations between the parties. Yet, the contract does not exist in a vacuum and obligations emanating from the contract extend beyond private law. These include fiscal obligations, obligations with regards to money laundering, fraud, corruption, import and export restrictions, as well as increasing human rights obligations for businesses, including non-financial reporting and due diligence on company and

1 Jan Hendrik Dalhuisen, *On Transnational and Comparative Commercial, Financial and Trade Law* (third edition, Hart Publishing 2007) 2.

2 Ibid.

3 See for instance: Indira Carr & Peter Stone, *International Trade Law* (sixth edition, Routledge 2017) and Carole Murray, David Holloway, Daren Timson-Hunt & Giles Dixon, *Schmitthoff: the Law and Practice of International Trade* (12th edition Sweet & Maxwell 2012).

4 Pierre-Alain Gourion, Georges Peyrard and Nicolas Soubeyrand, *Droit du Commerce International*, (fourth edition, L.G.D.J. Lextenso Editions 2008) 86.

5 Klaus Peter Berger, *The Creeping Codification of the Lex Mercatoria* (Kluwer Law International 1999)160.

supply chain activities.[6] These elements all influence the international transactions between companies. Thus, it can be concluded that '*international commercial transactions are the interchange between public and private law*'[7]

International commercial law is a branch of domestic law. There is no overarching international legislative body. Each state drafts and administers its own international commercial law. International commercial law is thus properly described as the domestic law that regulates international commerce.

The term international law is often used to refer exclusively to public international law. Textbooks titled 'international law' frequently focus only on public international law.[8] Jessup wrote that the term international law is misleading when referring to international private law regulations, as the term seems to refer exclusively to interstate relations.[9] Therefore, the perception of the term international does not necessarily match with the domestic law substance of international commercial law. However, as the aim of the subject is international, it is justified to use this term even if it can create some confusion.

International commercial law can be classified as a sub-branch of commercial law. Commercial law is defined as '*the law relating to the facilitation and regulation of commerce*'[10] and as '*the totality of the law's response to mercantile disputes, encompassing all these principles, rules and statutory provisions of whatever kind and from whatever source, which bear on private law rights and obligations of parties to commercial actions.*'[11] International commercial law is then properly defined as the sub-branch of commercial law that regulates

6 See for instance the UN Guiding Principles on Business and Human Rights (2011)
See for a discussion on this subject: Denis G Arnold, 'Corporations and Human Rights Obligations' (2016) 1 Business and Human Rights Journal 255
Claire Methven O'Brien and Sumithra Dhanarajan, 'The Corporate Responsibility to Respect Human Rights: A Status Review' (2015) National University of Singapore, Faculty of Law Working Paper Series, Working Paper 2015/005
Examples of legislation include:
The UK Modern Slavery Act 2015
The EU Non-Financial Reporting Directive (Directive 2014/95/EU)
The French Due Diligence Law (La loi n°2017-399 Relative au Devoir de Vigilance des Sociétés Mères et Entreprises Donneuses d'Ordre).

7 Loukas Mistelis, 'Is Harmonisation a Necessary Evil? The Future of Harmonisation and New Sources of International Trade' in Ian F Fletcher, Loukas Mistelis and Marise Cremona (editors) *Foundations and Perspectives of International Trade Law,* (Sweet & Maxwell 2000) 5.

8 See for instance: Malcolm Evans, *International Law*, (Oxford University Press 2018), Malcolm Shaw, *International Law* (Cambridge University Press 2017), Antonio Cassese, *International Law* (Oxford University Press 2015), Jan Klabbers, *International Law,* (Cambridge University Press 2017).

9 Quoted in Roy Goode, 'Usage and Its Reception in Transnational Commercial Law' (1997) 46 International & Comparative Law Quarterly 2.

10 Nicholas H D Foster, 'Comparative Commercial Law: Rules or Context?' in Esin Örucü and David Nelken (Editors) *Comparative Law, A Handbook* (Hart Publishing 2007) 263.

11 Roy Goode, Herbert Kronke, Ewan McKendrick and Jeffrey Wool, *Transnational Commercial Law: Text, Cases and Materials* (Oxford University Press 2007) 4.

and facilitates international private commercial transactions and includes international elements next to domestic elements.

The term transnational commercial law is also regularly used to further distinguish between domestic international commercial law and the international aspects of international commercial law. The term transnational mainly became known through the works of Jessup who considered this more appropriate than the term international because of the way the latter is often used synonymously with public international law.[12] He defined this as: *'all law which regulates actions or events that transcend national frontiers.'*[13] Transnational law is thus more inclusive than international law as it refers to a wider range of international legal interactions. Others took this definition and refined it such as Lalive who defines transnational law as between international law and domestic law and consisting of substantive rules rather than solely procedural rules like private international law.[14]

Yet, transnational commercial law cannot be used as a synonym to international commercial law. They are different concepts. According to Goode transnational commercial law is more properly defined as *'… not particular to or the product of any one legal system but represents a convergence of rules drawn from several legal systems or even a collection of rules which are entirely anational and have their force by virtue of international usage and its observance by the merchant community. In other words, it is the rules, not merely the actions or events that cross-national boundaries.'*[15] Mistelis defines transnational commercial law as follows: *'the corpus of law resulting from the harmonisation or convergence of national laws, whether by international convention, conscious or unconscious judicial parallelism, uniform rules for specific types of contract and international restatements of principles of contract law.'*[16]

If one follows these definitions, transnational commercial law consists solely of those legal elements that are transnational/international in origin, whereas international commercial law includes both these elements as well as domestic sources of law. Transnational commercial law is therefore the part of international commercial law that is international in origin and objective. Transnational commercial law is not a supranational law but exists in parallel to the nation state. It is intertwined with the state, as it is ultimately dependent on the state for enforcement.

12 Olugbenga Bamodu, 'Extra-national Legal Principles in the Global Village: a Conceptual Examination of Transnational Law' (2001) 4 International Arbitration Law Review 7, 7.

13 As quoted in Roy Goode, Herbert Kronke, Ewan McKendrick and Jeffrey Wool, *Transnational Commercial Law: Text, Cases and Materials* (Oxford University Press 2007) 4.

14 Jean-Flavien Lalive, 'Contracts between a State or a State Agency and a Foreign Company' (1964) 13 International and Comparative Law Quarterly 987, 1008–1009.

15 Roy Goode, Herbert Kronke, Ewan McKendrick and Jeffrey Wool, *Transnational Commercial Law: Text, Cases and Materials* (Oxford University Press 2007) 4.

16 Loukas Mistelis, 'Is Harmonisation a Necessary Evil? The Future of Harmonisation and New Sources of International Trade' in Ian F Fletcher, Loukas Mistelis and Marise Cremona (editors), *Foundations and Perspectives of International Trade Law*, (Sweet & Maxwell 2000) 10.

To summarise the above, the conclusion is that international commercial law is a branch of domestic law. It is different from international economic law, which regulates relations between states, as it concerns private contractual relations. It mainly consists of private law but is connected to public law and international economic law and is a branch of commercial law. Each jurisdiction has its own international commercial law. Its objective is international, and it includes elements of both domestic law and international elements. Those international elements together are grouped under the term transnational commercial law.

3.3 The effects of diverging legal systems

The natural effect of trade is to create a mutual need between states: states become dependent on one another for the export and import of products and monies.[17] In the same vein, it also creates a mutual need between businesses. Businesses strive to grow and at some point, will often wish to expand beyond state borders to enlarge their market share and get access to new products, services, and markets. Trading abroad brings legal uncertainty, as businesses will operate under another legal system with which they will be less familiar. Especially for SME, which for financial reasons have less access to legal counsel and other expertise, this unpredictability can be a deterrent to conducting business abroad. For instance, 39% of EU businesses that sell online but that do not sell cross-border, mention diverging contract laws as one of the obstacles to trading abroad.[18]

Within an international contract the parties can insert a choice of law clause to indicate the applicable law to the contract. One of the possibilities would be the domestic law of either party. This has the advantage of being familiar to one of the parties and if the execution of the contract (partly) takes place in that legal system it can be hoped the law provides suitable solutions for the dispute. There are also disadvantages. One of the parties is confronted with a legal system with which they are not familiar and could incur additional costs for translations and specialised legal counsel. Furthermore, psychologically a party might feel more comfortable with their own domestic law (regardless of whether there is a legal reason to choose it) and the choice can make the relation between the parties feel more uneven. In contracts between a private company and a state or state agency the company might question the neutrality of the state law. Therefore, parties might be reluctant to give the other party the advantage of using their own domestic law. If the parties have equal bargaining power this can lead to an impasse.

17 Charles-Louis de Secondat Montesquieu, *De l'Esprit des Lois Livre XX, Chapitre 2, De l'Esprit du Commerce* http://classiques.uqac.ca/classiques/montesquieu/de_esprit_des_lois/partie_4/de_esprit_des_lois_4.html 24.

18 European Commission, 'A Digital single market strategy for Europe' (2015) Com 192 of 6th May 2015.

In the case of unequal bargaining power, the stronger party can impose their choice of law and (potentially) leave the other party at a disadvantage.

The other option is to choose the law of a third country. Choosing a neutral law places the parties on an equal footing. The parties are equally unfamiliar with the law and this affects predictability. The outcome of a dispute might be different from the intentions of the parties. Furthermore, if the applicable law has no connection at all with the contract, then problems could arise if the agreement contains concepts that are known in the legal system where the contract was performed but not in the applicable law. An example is a floating charge, which does not exist in every legal system. Therefore, the neutral law might not be the best fit for the contract.

If the parties cannot agree on a choice of law, the contract will be silent on this issue. This leads to additional legal uncertainty, as then the forum that is seized will apply its private international law to decide whether they have jurisdiction and if they do what the applicable law is. A unified private international law can help to reduce legal uncertainty with regards to determining the applicable law. As procedural law it does not unify the law substantively and therefore the uncertainty as to the content and the interpretation of the applicable law remains.

In 1949 Mario Matteucci, the then Secretary General of UNIDROIT, wrote that private international law is not sufficient to solve problems coming out of the differences between legal systems and that '*unification of private international law and international unification of private law*' are both needed.[19] There is a need to develop a unified international commercial law, a true transnational commercial law: '*International trade needs a real jus commune mercatorum, a material law that can govern international relations.*'[20] This is more suited to the needs of business than transposing domestic law solutions to an international context.[21]

Domestic commercial law is tailored to transactions that take place within the legal framework of that state and some provisions are less suited to international transactions. The UCC contains a perfect tender rule.[22] This means that the goods should conform exactly to the contract. If they do not conform, the buyer can return the goods to the seller. This rule is less practical in the international context. If the merchandise does not conform exactly to

19 Mario Matteucci, 'Prospects of International Unification of Law from a European Viewpoint' (1949) 10 Louisiana Law Review 15, 16.

20 Klaus Peter Berger, 'Lex Mercatoria doctrine and the UNIDROIT principles of international commercial contracts' (1997) 28 Law and Policy in International Business 943, 958

Quoting from: *Progressive Codification of the Law of International Trade* United Nations Documents A/CN.9/L.19 (1970).

21 Loukas Mistelis, 'Is Harmonisation a Necessary Evil the Future of Harmonisation and New Sources of International Trade' in Ian F Fletcher, Loukas Mistelis and Marise Cremona (editors) *Foundations and Perspectives of International Trade Law* (Sweet & Maxwell 2000) 20.

22 UCC § 2-601 Buyer's Rights on Improper Delivery.

the contract and the buyer sends it back this causes more significant logistic problems. The merchandise needs to be taken on a potentially long and difficult journey across borders and through customs with all the associated costs, delays, and risks. Therefore, the CISG has no perfect tender rule and the buyer can only refuse the merchandise if the non-conformity is of such severity that it can be considered a fundamental breach of the contract. In case of minor differences between the goods that were delivered and that which was contractually agreed the buyer cannot refuse to accept the merchandise but can claim damages.[23] Therefore, the buyer is compensated for his loss, the goods are put to use, and the additional costs for the seller are kept to a minimum. This pragmatism is more suited to the realities of international commerce.

The need for a truly transnational international commercial law has regularly been expressed over the decades. In 1979 Schmitthoff wrote

> No branch of law suffers as much from the division of the world into many national legal systems as commercial law. That division is a serious obstacle to the international exchange of goods and services. On the international level – as in the home market - businessmen want to supply goods to their customers and make sure that they receive the purchase price, they want to build factories and installations, establish a proper distribution network for their goods or services, in brief, they want to get on with the business. But they do not wish to get entangled in legal snares, such as those created by the diversity of national laws.[24]

Dalhuisen writes: '*At least in the area of professional dealings the formation and operation of transnational law may be considered the national and unavoidable consequence of the internationalisation of the flow of goods, persons, services, knowledge, capital, payments and assets.*'[25] Orlandi states that '*foreign traders often fear municipal laws as they can hide dangerous traps for the success of their businesses.*'[26] Eleanor Fox writes that '*Disharmonies of law and procedure are costly and bothersome.*'[27] Michael Kabik discusses how: '*International trade has been hindered by a myriad of distinct domestic laws governing the sale of goods.*[28]'

23 CISG Article 46 (2) and 74.

24 Clive M Schmitthoff, 'American and European Commercial Law' (1979) 6 Journal of Legislation 44, 44.

25 Jan Hendrik Dalhuisen, *On Transnational and Comparative Commercial, Financial and Trade Law* (Third edition, Hart Publishing 2007) 5.

26 Chiara Giovannucci Orlandi, 'Procedural Law Issues and Uniform Law Conventions' (2000) 5 Uniform Law Review 23, 23.

27 Eleanor M Fox 'Harmonization of Law and Procedures in a Globalized world' (1991) 60 Antitrust Law Journal 593, 593.

28 Michael Kabik, 'Through the Looking-Glass: International Trade in the 'Wonderland' of the United Nations Conventions of the International Sales of Goods' (1992) 9 International Tax and Business Lawyer 408, 409.

More intense international trade leads to a further need for harmonised law.[29] These considerations all lead to the starting point that legal harmonisation is beneficial for businesses and trade.

Although the need for a harmonised law is thus regularly discussed and affirmed, the question is whether diverging laws really do hamper international trade. There is some evidence that diverging laws lead to higher transactions costs and this leads to higher prices and therefore this affects the economy.[30] To measure whether diverging laws have a strong negative effect on international trade more extensive empirical research is necessary.[31]

Section 2.6 discussed that the CISG is regularly excluded from international contracts, although the exact extent is unclear. Furthermore, courts do not always apply the CISG even when it has not been excluded. This has especially been the case in the US.[32] However, there is evidence that this is changing. A Westlaw database search in 2006 fielded around 48 decisions in the US involving the CISG whereby two-thirds of these decisions stemmed from the preceding 5 years.[33] Repeating the same database research in July 2015, 185 decisions are found. The same database search in February 2020 finds 281 cases so in the past 14 years the number of cases referring to the CISG has risen significantly. The rising number of cases indicates further acceptance and entrenchment of the CISG within the US.

The above discussion of the CISG shows a certain reluctance towards the use of harmonised international commercial law. It also shows that, as the instrument becomes more well known the usage increases. This thus supports the importance of uncertainty avoidance in international commercial law. There is an assumption that a harmonised international commercial law is needed to increase predictability, but there is a lack of empirical evidence to support or denounce this assumption.

Not all businesses have the same need for a harmonised international commercial law. Professor Schwenzer identified three distinct groups:[34]

29 Franco Ferrari, 'Le Champ d'Application des << Principes pour les Contrats Commerciaux Internationaux>> élaborés par UNIDROIT' (1995) 47 Revue Internationale de Droit Comparé 985, 986/987.

30 Jan M Smits, 'European Private Law: A Plea for a Spontaneous Legal Order' in Deirdre M Curtin, Jan M Smits et al. (editors) *European Integration and Law: Four Contributions to Celebrate the 25th Anniversary of Maastricht University's Faculty of Law* (Antwerp-Oxford 2006) 70.

31 Ibid, 70.

32 Franco Ferrari, 'Homeward Trend and Lex Forism in International Sales Law' [2009] International Business Law Journal 333,336/337

Francesco G Mazzotta, 'Why Do Some American Courts Fail to get it Right?' (2005) 3 Loyola University Chicago International Review 85.

33 Karen Halverson Cross, 'Parol Evidence under the CISG: The 'Homeward Trend' Reconsidered' (2007) 68 Ohio State Law Journal 133

Some of these decisions concern appeals.

34 Ingeborg Schwenzer, 'Who Needs a Uniform Contract Law, and why?' (2013) 58 Villanova Law Review 723, 723–725.

Group 1:

- Parties are from different countries but share the same language
- Parties have similar legal systems (common law countries, France/French speaking African countries)
- The parties will choose the law of one of their own countries, or will opt for a third country with a similar legal system
- The outcome in court would be predictable for the parties and they will not feel the need for a unified law. They are sufficiently at ease in both systems to make either law a viable option.

Group 2:

- One of the parties has stronger bargaining power
- The stronger party determines the choice of law. If the stronger party allows the weaker party to determine the applicable law for strategic reasons, such as with a view to long-term cooperation, it still maintains agency with regards to the decision.
- Litigation outcome is predictable for the stronger party and this party would thus not feel the need for a uniform law
- Uniform law could be beneficial for the weaker party or parties. The law will then be same regardless of which domestic law is applied, as substantively these are similar. A uniform commercial law would increase predictability and legal certainty for the parties.

Group 3:

- Parties come from countries with different legal systems and languages and have equal bargaining power.
- The preferred choice is the law of a third country – a neutral law
- This choice leads to several problems such as linguistic issues (parties already do might not share the same language and the third country law is in another language) and a weak knowledge of the law which could potential disadvantage one or more of the parties.
- This leads to additional legal and translation costs
- The outcome is unpredictable for the parties so for this group there is a stronger need for a harmonised law.

3.4 The harmonisation of international commercial law

The terms harmonisation and unification are often used interchangeably even though they are not necessarily the same thing. Schmitthoff suggests that these are two distinct concepts that function differently: unification means that a new unified law replaces existing national laws, whereas harmonisation is aimed at harmonising the underlying principles of national laws.[35] UNCITRAL describes harmonisation as '*the process through which domestic laws may be modified to enhance predictability in cross-border commercial transactions* and unification as '*the adoption by states of a common legal standard governing particular aspects of international business transactions.*'[36] UNCITRAL gives model laws as an example of legal harmonisation and international conventions as an example of legal unification whilst acknowledging that the two concepts are closely related in practice.[37]

Unification can refer to uniformity of sources (the laws are the same) and uniformity of results (the laws are applied in the same way). There are no supranational courts in international commercial law that can apply the law in an authoritative manner. As the sources are applied in domestic courts from different legal systems uniformity should be understood as uniformity of sources.[38] Unification of law leads to the creation of transnational commercial law whereas the harmonisation of law ensures that the (international) commercial laws of various states become progressively more similar in nature, principles, and rules. Transnational commercial law is only aimed at international transactions. Domestic commercial law is aimed at all transactions. Therefore, harmonisation of international commercial law leads to further similarity between commercial laws (both domestic and international) whereas transnational commercial law is the uniform body of law that exists in parallel to the state.

The emphasis on harmonising international commercial law through the creation of transnational commercial law leads to a further division between domestic contracts and international contracts as the law is harmonised for international transactions. Within one state different laws are applicable to domestic contracts and international contracts. If commercial law is harmonised for all transactions, then the law will be the same across both domestic and international transactions. This is not necessarily more desirable as international trade has different requirements from domestic trade.

Even if the concepts of unification and harmonisation are distinguishable, they are also inevitably linked. For instance, if an international convention (uniform law) is ratified it will in turn influence domestic law as the convention is applied within the national legal system (leading to harmonisation of law). Therefore, this book uses the term harmonisation for ease of reading but means both harmonisation and unification.

35 Clive M Schmitthoff, 'American and European Commercial Law' (1979) 6 Journal of Legislation 44, 45.

36 http://www.uncitral.org/uncitral/en/about/origin_faq.html.

37 Ibid.

38 Camilla Baasch Andersen, 'Uniformity in the CISG in the First Decade of its Application' in Ian F Fletcher, Loukas Mistelis and Marise Cremona (editors) *Foundations and Perspectives of International Trade Law*, (Sweet & Maxwell 2000) 291.

3.5 Legal harmonisation through international conventions

Legal unification can occur through international conventions. Upon ratification, there is a direct obligation on the state to implement the convention. The part of the law that is covered by the convention is then uniform across ratifying states. It does not matter which participating state's law is applicable to the contract because substantively the laws are the same. The application of conventions is not perturbed by the elements of domestic law that can interfere with the application of a foreign law or non-state rules. Conventions therefore create certainty and foreseeability for the contracting parties.

Those perturbing elements are mainly international public policy and mandatory laws. International public policy (also called international public order) refers to the cornerstone principles of the legal system that are that fundamental to its functioning, that a court will not enforce any arbitral award or decision from a foreign court or apply those provisions of the applicable foreign law that run contrary to this. International public policy is distinct from domestic public policy, which has a wider scope and includes mandatory rules. Mandatory laws (also known as lois de police) are those laws that are perceived '*as so essential for the political, social and, economical organisation of the state that they determine their field of application without taking into account the conflicts of law.*'[39]

By ratifying a convention, a state gives up a small amount of its sovereignty. The impact on sovereignty from ratifying a treaty is three-fold: it diminishes the authority to enact laws, it diminishes the authority of executive branches to design, implement and enforce legislations, and it can diminish the authority of the court to interpret the law.[40] In commercial law conventions, the loss of sovereignty is minimal: these conventions can often be contracted out of by the parties, they are only applicable to a specific set of transactions, they mainly replace variable rules of commercial law, they are applied/interpreted by domestic courts, and there is no overarching international body that oversees their implementation and application.

There are drawbacks to unification through international conventions. They are '*very difficult to achieve and rather clumsy in operation.*'[41] Drafting a convention involves different stakeholders and negotiations take a long time. It is consequently an expensive process.

The changes the instrument brings are also not necessarily those that the drafters set out to achieve. Peter Hall identifies three types of policy changes:

39 This is the definition of Professor Phocion Francescakis which is used in the commentary on article 3 of the French civil code.

40 Susan Block-Lieb, 'Soft and Hard Strategies: the Role of Business in the Crafting of International Commercial Law' (2019) 40 Michigan Journal of International Law 433, 467.

41 Konrad Zweigert and Heinz Kötz, *An introduction to comparative law* (*Tony* Weir tr, third edition, Oxford University Press 1998) 25.

- First order: characteristics of incrementalism
- Second order: strategic changes
- Third order: a paradigm shift.[42]

International conventions could theoretically belong to any of these categories, yet in practice are likely to be changes of the first order. Conventions are usually drafted along the lines of lowest common denominator policy; that is to say, the bottom line on which the stakeholders can find agreement. States prefer transnational laws to resemble national laws. If international commercial law resembles domestic commercial law this reduces transaction costs for the contracting parties in that particular jurisdiction. They would thus not need to spend additional funds to familiarise themselves with a transnational legal instrument that does not resemble their own legislation. This encourages international trade and enhances the economy. Furthermore, it confirms a state's leading position in international commerce.[43] States would thus strive towards changes of the first order even if changes of the second or third order would be more effective in accomplishing uniformity.

The draft convention is defined by the prior law, as there is a need to accommodate existing domestic rules.[44] The convention does not begin as a tabula rasa; the starting point is formed by the various domestic legal systems of the states involved in drafting the convention. Drafters (and ultimately governments) need to compromise to find agreement. The final text is often an uneasy compromise between the different solutions proposed by states that seek to impose rules that resemble their own laws.[45] This often leads to general and minimalist provisions.

The application of the convention will lack uniformity because it leaves room for divergent interpretations. Thus, whilst a change of the second or third order might be needed to attain a desirable degree of uniformity, the result will often not surpass a change of the first order. This means that the investment of time and money into drafting a convention might be disproportionate in comparison to the achieved results.

Conventions do not form a comprehensive legal framework. Conventions cover a specific area in the field of international commercial law such as factoring, financing mobile equipment, carriage of goods by sea etc. Even within that area, they leave gaps. For instance, the CISG covers the international sale of goods, but excludes certain types of sales such as, sales by auction, sales on execution, and sales of stocks, shares, investment securities,

42 Peter A Hall, 'Policy Paradigms, Social Learning, and the State: The Case of Economic Policy Making in Britain' (1993) 25 Comparative Politics 275, 279.

43 Clayton P Gillette & Robert E Scott, 'The Political Economy of International Sales Law' (2005) International Review of Law and Economics 446, 467.

44 Henry Deeb Gabriel, 'The Advantages of Soft Law in International Commercial Law: the role of UNIDROIT, UNCITRAL, and The Hague Conference' (2008) 34 Brooke Journal of International Law 655,661/662.

45 Marco Torsello, 'Reservations to International Uniform Commercial Law Conventions' (2000) 5 Uniform Law Review 85, 86.

negotiable instruments, money, ships, vessels, and electricity.[46] The CISG also does not cover certain issues that are central to contracting such as validity of the contract and therefore the applicable law remains important. These gaps usually occur because the drafters concur that the legal positions are too far apart to make a compromise feasible, these are areas of greater public policy interest and state sovereignty concerns, or these are areas in which there is already a strong national law that states are unlikely to wish to displace.[47] Records of negotiations for the CISG show that the diverging approaches between states to international contracting, led to leaving out controversial issues on which there was no consensus.[48]

Once a convention is drafted, it needs to be ratified by enough states to enter into force. It can take years before a convention gets the required number of signatures. Sometimes this momentum is never achieved, and a convention fails to enter into force. Even if a state has been an active participant in the drafting process, it does not necessarily mean that this state will ratify it.[49]

Examples of conventions in commercial law that have failed to enter into force are for example:

The 1980 United Nations Convention on International Multimodal Transport of Goods: one ratification.[50]
The 1983 Convention on Agency in the International Sales of Goods: five parties.[51]
The 1986 Convention on the Law Applicable to Contracts for the International Sale of Goods: two parties.[52]
The 1988 United Nations Convention on International Bills of Exchange and International Promissory Notes: five parties.[53]
The 2001 United Nations Conventions on the Assignment of Receivables in International Trade: one ratification.[54]

46 CISG Article 2.
47 Marco Torsello, 'Reservations to International Uniform Commercial Law Conventions' (2000) 5 *Uniform Law Review* 85.
48 Keith Loken, 'A New Global Initiative on Contract Law in Uncitral: Right Project, Right Forum?' (2013) 58 Villanova Law Review 509, 513.
49 An example is the Inter-American Convention on the Law Applicable to International Contracts (1994). The United States were actively involved in drafting the document, but they never ratified it.
50 https://treaties.un.org/doc/Treaties/1980/05/19800524%2006-13%20PM/Ch_XI_E_1.pdf.
51 http://www.unidroit.org/fr/lo-marchandises/ol-agency-en-2.
52 http://www.hcch.net/index_en.php?act=conventions.text&cid=61.
53 http://www.uncitral.org/uncitral/en/uncitral_texts/payments/1988Convention_bills_promissory.html.
54 http://www.uncitral.org/uncitral/en/uncitral_texts/security/2001Convention_receivables.html.

The 2009 UNIDROIT Convention on Substantive Rules for Intermediated Securities: zero parties.[55]

These conventions could still enter into force, but especially for the older ones this is unlikely as new developments have out-dated some of the provisions and the momentum for ratification has passed.

Other conventions enter into force, but only receive a few ratifications. If an instrument is only in vigour in a small number of states, its contribution to establishing global security and predictability for merchants is limited. Examples are:

The 1964 Convention Relating to a Uniform Law on the International Sales of Goods (ULIS) (entered into force in 1972): currently in force in three countries.[56]
The 1964 Convention relating to a Uniform Law on the Formation of Contracts for the International Sales of Goods (ULFIS) (entered into force in 1972): currently in force in two countries.[57]
The 1970 International Convention on Travel Contracts (entered into force in 1976): currently in force in seven countries.[58]
The 1971 Convention on the Recognition and Enforcement of Foreign Judgments in Civil and Commercial Matters (entered into force in 1979): currently in force in four countries.[59]
The 1978 Convention on the Law Applicable to Agencies (entered into force in 1992): currently in force in four states.[60]
The 1985 Convention on the Law Applicable to Trusts and their Recognition (entered into force in 1992): currently in force in five countries.[61]
The 1988 UNIDROIT Convention on International Factoring: nine parties[62]
The 1988 UNIDROIT Convention on International Financial Leasing: ten parties.[63]
The 1994 Inter-American Convention on the Law Applicable to International Contracts two parties.[64]

This is not to say that conventions cannot be successful. Some conventions have attracted a large number of signatories:

55 http://www.unidroit.org/status.
56 http://www.unidroit.org/instruments/international-sales/international-sales-ulis-1964.
57 http://www.unidroit.org/status-ulfc-1964.
58 http://www.unidroit.org/instruments/transport/ccv.
59 http://www.hcch.net/index_en.php?act=conventions.text&cid=78.
60 http://www.hcch.net/index_en.php?act=conventions.text&cid=89.
61 http://www.hcch.net/index_en.php?act=conventions.text&cid=59.
62 http://www.unidroit.org/instruments/factoring.
63 http://www.unidroit.org/fr/leasing-ol-2/leasing-anglais.
64 http://www.oas.org/juridico/english/treaties/b-56.html.

The 1924 International Convention for the Unification of Certain Rules of Law relating to Bills of Lading (Hague Rules) or The Hague Rules and the 1969 Protocol (Hague-Visby Rules): 90 parties.[65]

The 1929 Convention for the Unification of Certain Rules Relating to International Carriage by Air (Warsaw Convention): 152 parties.[66]

The 1958 New York Convention on the Recognition of Foreign Arbitral Awards (entered into force in 1958): 164 parties.[67]

The 1974 Convention on the Limitation Period in International Sale of Goods (as amended by the protocol of 1980): 30 parties.[68]

The 1980 Convention on the Contracts for the International Sale of Goods (entered into force in 1988): 94 parties.[69]

The 1999 Convention for the Unification of Certain Rules for International Carriage by Air (Montreal Convention): 136 parties.[70]

The 2001 Cape Town Convention on International Interests in Mobile Equipment (entered into force in 2006): 80 parties.[71]

A final drawback is that once a convention has entered into force it can ossify and the provisions could become out-dated. Once a convention has entered into force amending it is difficult, even if changing circumstances make this desirable. Amending the provisions requires the same process of ratification that the original convention did. It is not certain all participating states will ratify the amending protocol. The 1924 Brussels convention on Carriage of Goods by Sea was amended in 1968 and in 1979 with additional protocols.[72] Some of the countries that signed the 1924 convention did not sign both or either of the additional protocols. This means that there are diverging rules in force, whereby in some states the 1924 convention is applicable without the protocols and in other states, the 1924 convention is applicable along with the 1968 protocol and/or the 1979 protocol. This hinders legal harmonisation.

3.6 Legal harmonisation through non-state rules

Edlund differentiates between three types of harmonisation:

65 http://www.comitemaritime.org/The-1924-Bills-of-Lading-Convention-and-its-1968-and-1979-Protocols-Hague-Visby- Rules/0,2799,19932,00.html.

66 http://www.icao.int/secretariat/legal/List%20of%20Parties/WC-HP_EN.pdf.

67 http://www.uncitral.org/uncitral/en/uncitral_texts/arbitration/NYConvention.html.

68 http://www.uncitral.org/uncitral/en/uncitral_texts/sale_goods/1974Convention_status.html.

69 http://www.uncitral.org/uncitral/en/uncitral_texts/sale_goods/1980CISG.html.

70 http://www.icao.int/secretariat/legal/List%20of%20Parties/Mtl99_EN.pdf.

71 http://www.unidroit.org/instruments/security-interests/cape-town-convention.

72 The 1924 International Convention for the Unification of Certain Rules of Law relating to Bills of Lading amended by the 1968 Visby Protocol and the 1979 Special Drawing Rights Protocol are collectively known as The Hague-Visby Rules.

- Direct approach (purposeful legislation designed and enforced by legislators)
- Indirect approach (harmonisation is not the intended goal, but it can be a by-product)
- Party-autonomy approach (bottom-up approach, the parties themselves agree to use transnational rules)[73]

Harmonisation can thus be top down or bottom up. The direct approach is reflected in international conventions. They are drafted on purpose with the goal to unify the law. The second approach occurs for instance with the creation of standard terms and conditions by trade associations. They are not created on purpose to harmonise the law, but they can nonetheless contribute to this process. The third approach originates in the merchant community. Harmonisation through non-state rules could occur through the indirect approach (standard terms for instance) and the party autonomy approach (trade usages for example.)

Non-state rules are not drafted with the goal to be ratified by states. This leaves the drafters free to come up with the 'best' solution instead of the 'most acceptable' solution. The risks of lowest common denominator policy and minimal harmonisation are more easily avoided. Non-state rules are less expensive to draft. There is no need to organise a plenary conference and there is less need for extensive negotiations that are necessary to get states to agree to become a signatory. Non-state rules are more flexible and can accommodate different legal traditions more easily.[74]

There are instances when non-state rules are more effective in attracting support than conventions. UNCITRAL developed a convention for the use of Electronic Communications in International Contracts.[75] This entered into force in 2013 and is ratified by eighteen states. UNCITRAL also developed model laws on Electronic Commerce[76] and Electronic Signatures.[77] 74 and 33 jurisdictions respectively have adopted these model laws. The scope of the instruments differs, but the convention builds upon the model laws

73 Hans H Edlund, 'The Concept of Unification and Harmonization' in Morten M Fogt (editor), *Unification and Harmonization of International Commercial Law: Interaction or Deharmonization?* (Wolters Kluwer Law & Business 2012) 11.

74 Henry Deeb Gabriel, 'The UNIDROIT Principles of International Commercial Contracts: An American Perspective on the Principles and Their Use' (2012) 17 Uniform Law Review 507, 526.

75 UN Convention on the Use of Electronic Communications in International Contracts (2005)
For full text see: http://www.uncitral.org/pdf/english/texts/electcom/06-57452_Ebook.pdf.

76 For full text see: http://www.uncitral.org/pdf/english/texts/electcom/05-89450_Ebook.pdf.

77 For full text see: http://www.uncitral.org/pdf/english/texts/electcom/ml-elecsig-e.pdf.

(which were published earlier) and provides updates to these.[78] Therefore, the three instruments are closely intertwined, yet the model laws have been more successful at attracting state support than the convention.

Non-state rules contribute in different ways to the harmonisation of law. Harmonisation can be achieved through the state, courts, and end users (such as businesses). States adopt model laws and through their implementation in domestic law, these bring harmonisation. Model contracts, trade usages, restatements of law, guidelines, and standard terms and conditions focus on merchants, legal professionals, and courts. The agency is on these stakeholders to use the non-state rules and through their usage, non-state rules become a bridge between different legal systems.

Harmonisation of law and the lex mercatoria are relatively unrelated: harmonisation is the drawing together of state laws whereas the lex mercatoria is a separate legal system that applies to international commerce.[79] If one sees the lex mercatoria as an independent legal system, then this would exist independently of any national laws, and would have no influence on these; at least not more than a foreign state law would. It would be a uniform law but not one that has a harmonising effect on domestic commercial law. However, as the lex mercatoria does not exist in a vacuum and is (at least sometimes) applied in state courts there is a link between the lex mercatoria and domestic international commercial law. In the long term, this link could lead to harmonisation of the underlying legal principles. This can create a more similar understanding of the law between states, courts, legal professionals, businesses, and legal scholars, which in turn could lead to more uniform laws.

Whilst the above discussion might seem in favour of harmonisation through non-state rules, it is not to say that this is always the best option. This harmonisation is weaker than through international conventions because the usage of non-state rules is voluntary, and their application in courts is more modest. They are applied mainly in arbitration and as arbitral awards are usually confidential and are not binding precedents, the contribution of non-state rules to the harmonisation of law is weakened. Conventions have the advantage that they are not hindered by mandatory rules of domestic law and the limits imposed by international public policy. In some areas, like property law, that require absolute certainty, conventions are a better method of achieving unification, whereas in areas that are deeply rooted in national traditions, the chances of a convention being successful are minimal and other methods of harmonisation should be used.[80]

78 *'The Convention is intended to strengthen the harmonisation of the rules regarding electronic commerce and foster uniformity in the domestic enactment of UNCITRAL model laws relating to electronic commerce, as well as to update and complement certain provisions of those model laws in light of recent practice.'*
http://www.uncitral.org/uncitral/en/uncitral_texts/electronic_commerce/2005Convention.html.

79 Lord Justice Mustill, 'Contemporary Problems in International Commercial Arbitration: A Response' (1989) 17 International Business Lawyer 161,162.

80 Herbert Kronke, 'International Uniform Commercial Law Conventions: advantages, disadvantages, criteria for choice' (2000) 5 Uniform Law Review 13, 20.

Non-state rules and international conventions are closely linked. In a state where a convention is not ratified it would be considered a non-state rule. Schaffer and Pollack divide the interaction between soft law or non-state rules and hard law, which would include domestic law and ratified conventions in three theories.[81]

- Legal positivist view: hard law and soft law co-exist next to each other. Hard law has a binding nature and is the preferred option. Soft law is not formally binding but can in the long-term lead to hard law.
- Rationalist view: soft law and hard law are chosen for different situations. The preference is not always for hard law as it depends on the situation. Hard law and soft law can work together.
- Constructivist approach: the law facilitates interactions that create links. Soft law can work better to build up these links because it has a more bottom up approach than hard law.[82]

The legal positivist approach favours international conventions as the primary means of harmonisation and sees non-state rules as complimentary, but not as a full viable alternative to hard law. Domestic (and conventional) law is binding and non-state rules could form an inspiration or a first step for developing hard law. Non-state rules are the 'next best option' if a hard law agreement is not (yet) possible. An example is model laws, which are soft law, but they are used to develop domestic law, which is binding.

The rational approach sees non-state rules and hard law as alternatives whereby some situations favour use of the one, and other situations use of the other. This approach would support the interaction of hard law and soft law where they build on one another. An example is the CISG, which is hard law, and the CISG Advisory Council, which is a private initiative that drafts opinions on how the CISG should be interpreted in order to achieve more uniformity.[83] These opinions are not binding but can be considered as influential. Non-state rules thus build on existing hard law. Travaux préparatoires, guidelines, and practices precede the creation of hard law or build further upon an existing legal instrument. In this view, conventions should deliberately leave room for the development of custom, which can fill in the gaps of the instrument.[84] General and ambiguous articles are a strength, because they allow the convention to organically develop beyond the original text. The usages and customs that develop out of the convention can

81 Gregory C Schaffer and Mark A Pollack, 'Hard vs Soft Law: Alternatives, Complements and Antagonists in International Governance' (2010) 94 Minnesota Law Review 706, 707.

82 Ibid.

83 See: http://www.cisgac.com/.

84 Clive M Schmitthoff, 'The Unification or Harmonisation of Law by Means of Standard Contracts and General Conditions' (1986) 17 International & Comparative Law Quarterly 551, 569.

inspire the drafters of future legal instruments who will then incorporate existing usages in their works.

The constructivist approach is the most bottom-up approach (whereas the legal positivist view is the most top down) and would favour the building of a common legal culture in international commerce through the use of non-state rules by the business community. This common legal culture would create general principles and usages of international commerce, which then influence domestic law. This common legal culture could influence how new laws are drafted and how courts apply the law. This method of interaction will ultimately lead to stronger harmonisation as it unifies the principles underlying the law and not just the concrete rules. It is a more gradual approach and it will take far longer to see any harmonising effects.

The relationship between hard law and soft law is always varying and the interaction between the two mainly depends on the interaction between the power and interests of the actors.[85] In international commerce, these actors include the state, the business community, arbitrators, and legal professionals. Although the state undoubtedly has the most power it does not necessarily have the most vested interest, and therefore the state is content to leave considerable agency to the other actors in the process. States can facilitate the use of soft law by allowing for its usage (whether out of lack of interest or for other reasons) and merchants can use their agency to create and use non-state rules. Organisations can create and promote non-state rules. Arbitrators (and sometimes state courts) can apply non-state rules. Researchers and legal professionals can propagate the use of different types of law, including non-state rules. These actors thus all have an influence on the creation, development, and the use of non-state rules and how these are used vis à vis hard law.

3.7 Conclusion: the role of non-state rules in the harmonisation of international commercial law

To understand the place of non-state rules in international commercial law it is crucial to understand how they contribute to legal harmonisation. This helps to understand their legal authority because a) it leads to a fuller understanding of the nature of non-state rules and b) it sheds further light upon their usage and application. Harmonisation contributes to more uniformity between domestic international commercial laws and their underlying principles. One of the methods for achieving this harmonisation is the creation of uniform law. The resulting uniform law is transnational commercial law. Thus, it could be said that legal harmonisation is focused on international commercial laws (that is to say the domestic international commercial law of each state) so these develop in the same direction. Unification is focused on

85 Gregory C Schaffer and Mark A Pollack, 'Hard vs Soft Law: Alternatives, Complements and Antagonists in International Governance' (2010) 94 Minnesota Law Review 706, 799.

transnational commercial law, a uniform law that is the same across different states. In practice the two terms are often used interchangeably.

Harmonisation of international commercial law should lead to more legal security in international commerce. The need for this is sometimes questioned, as there is a lack of empirical evidence that diverging laws hamper international trade, however many governments, scholars, and international organisations are convinced of this necessity. International conventions are not displaced by mandatory laws and thus lead to more uniformity than non-state rules do. They are expensive to draft and are often based on lowest common denominator policy. Harmonisation through non-state rules is cheaper and more flexible. However, they lead to less uniformity because of their voluntary nature, which means they are applied less frequently and less consistently. They are applied mainly in arbitration and as arbitral awards are confidential this hampers their contribution to legal harmonisation.

Harmonisation through non-state rules is bottom-up and the agency to use them is with the international business community (including businesses and arbitrators) as well as the courts that apply them. This chapter demonstrated that support and application are necessary for non-state rules to contribute to harmonisation. If they are not used frequently and consistently then their contribution is limited. This would impact their perceived authority, as it is precisely that usage and application that provides legitimacy to non-state rules in the transnational legal sphere. This would then become a self-perpetuating cycle where they are not applied frequently because they are not perceived as having legal authority and therefore do not contribute to legal harmonisation which in turn again impacts how their authority is perceived. Thus, usage and application are key to enhance the contribution of non-state rules to legal harmonisation and through this contribution, enhance their legal authority. As their usage is voluntary this leads to an understanding of the support that they have within the international business community and this contributes to understanding their legal authority.

4 The roles of non-state rules in the contractual relationship

4.1 Introduction

This chapter analyses the role of non-state rules within the contractual relationship; and how in this context we can measure authority through application. Whereas chapter 3 focused on the broader role of non-state rules in international commercial law, this chapter focuses more narrowly on the type of legal authority that can be attributed to categories of non-state rules. Non-state rules are a diverse group of sources and the first part of this chapter establishes how non-state rules can be classified. The second part then examines the different types of non-state rules respectively; international conventions, uncodified non-state rules (trade usages and general principles of law), codified non-state rules in the form of model laws, model contract terms and clauses, guidelines and opinions, and finally, restatements of law. It analyses for each of these categories how they function as a source of law and their role within the contract and how this influences their legal authority. This discussion is necessary because of the diffuse standing of non-state rules as a source of law. The discussion is even more pertinent as codified non-state rules are a relatively recent development and their role as a legal source is not (yet) clear.

This chapter forms the conclusion to Part 1 and demonstrates further how the application of non-state rules is the most important way in which their legal authority can be established. This is because non-state rules are not static entities that derive their authority from their existence within an established legal framework like state law. Rather, their legal authority is far more situation dependent and changes through time and space. This chapter shows that how non-state rules are applied in relation to the contract determines how their legal authority in a specific situation can be measured. It examines how specific non-state rules have legal authority either directly because of their status as a source of law in a specific jurisdiction, because they are used as contractual rules, or finally because they have become accepted international commercial practices and principles.

4.2 Classifying sources of international and transnational commercial law

Goode discusses how a traditional hierarchy of sources of transnational commercial law would be first international conventions, then trade usages, and in the last place restatements of law.[1] However, this hierarchy is more diffuse in practice: for instance when a ratified convention is expressly excluded from the contract whereas a restatement of law is incorporated, the latter takes precedence over the first.[2] Where sources of law fit in the hierarchy also depends on the jurisdiction. In common law jurisdictions scholarly contributions are secondary sources of law (if sources at all) whereas in Germany they are considered primary sources of law.[3] Therefore enumerating sources of international commercial law should not be done in a strict hierarchy as the practice is more dynamic and differs depending on the situation, the contract, and the jurisdiction. Although establishing a hierarchy of sources would not be beneficial, classifying sources of transnational commercial law is necessary to understand the place and nature of non-state rules:

'When the distinction between law and other social norms disappears, when every social actor who is creating social norms and who has the power to execute them is treated as a legislator, when the validity of positive law goes side by side with other types of legitimate validity (for example, factual acceptance by a majority), and, finally, when negotiating processes between various social actors make valid law – then it makes no more sense to speak of 'the law', and one has to give up the principles of equal adjudication and of the democratic legitimacy of legislation.'[4]

An attempt should be made to distinguish between law and social norms. The first can be enforced. The second cannot be.[5] In order to define the legal authority of non-state rules it is hence necessary to analyse their role as a source of law.

Below is a first classification based on the distinction between international commercial law and transnational commercial law:

- International commercial law (domestic legislation, international conventions once ratified and entered into force)

1 Roy Goode, 'Usage and its Reception in Transnational Commercial Law' in Jacob S Ziegel and Shalow Lerner (editors), *New Developments in International Commercial and Consumer Law, proceedings of the 8th Bienal Conference of the International Academy of Commercial and Consumer Law* (Hart Publishing 1998) 6.

2 Ibid.

3 Larry A DiMatteo, 'The Scholarly Response to the Harmonization of International Sales Law' (2012) 30 Journal of Law & Commerce 1,3.

4 Klaus Günther, 'Legal Pluralism or Uniform Concept of Law: Globalisation as a Problem of Legal Theory' (2008) http://www.helsinki.fi/nofo/NoFo5Gunther.pdf 13.

5 Although some laws are also social norms and vice versa.

- Transnational commercial law. This includes non-state rules (custom, trade usages and practices, general principles of law, restatements of law, model laws, model contracts, model contract terms) and international conventions.

The first type of sources has the state as origin or as enactor. Even if the state was not involved in making the rules, the state will need to ratify the legislation before it becomes part of domestic law. The second type is not ratified or enacted by the state. It represents a bottom-up approach of legislation whereas the first category represents a top-down approach. They can be qualified as material sources rather than formal sources.[6] There is a cross over between these categories and some rules can be recognised as a source of domestic law and can also be a source of transnational commercial law (such as trade usages and conventions.)

To further classify non-state rules Busseuil distinguishes between 'sources négociées' (international conventions), spontaneous sources (such as trade usages), and 'sources réflechies' (such as the UPICC and PECL).[7] He thus divides non-state rules into three categories: international conventions, uncodified non-state rules, and codified non-state rules. The next sections of this chapter follow these three categories.

4.3 International conventions

A convention becomes binding on a state if it is ratified and has entered into force. The convention would then be a source of law in that state. In any state which has not ratified it, the convention is a non-state rule and its legal authority would be ascertained in the same way as that of other non-state rules.

International Conventions are not supranational law; at least not if supranational is defined as law issued by a (legislative) body above the state level. They do not have a direct effect like EU Regulations and there is no independent body overseeing how they are applied. Their application and interpretation are a matter for domestic courts. Courts tend to be parochial in their interpretation of international conventions. Baasch Andersen comments that of the 500 cases she read that concerned the application of the CISG only two referred to international case law.[8]

There are two types of international commercial law conventions. The first type harmonises procedural law; mainly private international law. The second

6 Bruno Oppetit, 'Le Droit International Privé, Droit Savant' (1992) 234 Droit Savant recueil Cours de l'académie de DIP de la Haye 331. See section 2.5.

7 Guillaume Busseuil, 'L'Avenir des Principes Unidroit Relatifs aux Contrats de Commerce International et des Principes Européens du Droit du Contrat : du Droit Mou ou Droit Dur ?' [2004] Centre de Droit Civil des Affaires et du Contentieux Economique 1 http://www.glose.org/CEDCACE4.pdf Last accessed: 27 February 2016.

8 Camilla Baasch Andersen, 'Uniformity in the CISG in the First Decade of its Application' in Ian F Fletcher, Loukas Mistelis and Marise Cremona (editors) *Foundations and Perspectives of International Trade Law*, (Sweet & Maxwell 2000) 296.

type harmonises substantive commercial law. Substantive law conventions can be divided in different categories. Most fall in the categories of international sales, carriage of goods, or international financing.

The Hague Conference of Private International Law (HCCH) promulgates conventions that harmonise conflicts of law. An example is the Convention on the Law Applicable to the International Sale of Goods of 1955.[9] On a regional level the EU has done significant work to harmonise private international law. International contract conflicts were regulated by the Brussels Convention on the Jurisdiction and the Enforcement of Judgments in Civil and Commercial Matters (which harmonised conflicts of jurisdiction) and the Rome Convention on the Law Applicable to Contractual Obligations (which harmonised conflicts of law).[10] The corresponding Brussels I Regulation and Rome I Regulation have replaced these.[11] In 1988 the Lugano Convention was signed. This is the analogue of the Brussels Convention and extended the regime to EFTA member states. The EU, Iceland, Switzerland, and Norway signed a new updated Lugano Convention in 2007.[12]

9 The Hague Convention of 15 June 1955 on the Law Applicable to International Sales of Goods

Official text: http://www.hcch.net/index_en.php?act=conventions.text&cid=31 (only available in French)

Another example is: The Hague Convention of 30 June 2005 on Choice of Court Agreements.

Official text: https://www.hcch.net/en/instruments/conventions/full-text/?cid=98.

10 Convention on Jurisdiction and the Enforcement of Judgments in Civil and Commercial Matters of 27 September 1968 (Brussels Convention).

http://www.consilium.europa.eu/en/documents-publications/agreements-conventions/agreement/?aid=1968001

Convention on the Law Applicable to Contractual Obligations of 19 June 1980 (Rome Convention).

http://eur-lex.europa.eu/legal-content/EN/TXT/?uri=uriserv:l33109.

11 Council Regulation (EC) No 44/2001 of 22 December 2000 on Jurisdiction, recognition and enforcement of judgments in civil and commercial matters (Brussels I).

http://eur-lex.europa.eu/legal-content/EN/TXT/?uri=URISERV:l33054

And the updated version: Regulation (EU) No 1215/2012 of the European Parliament and of the Council of 12 December 2012 on jurisdiction and the recognition and enforcement of judgments in civil and commercial matters (Brussels I recast).

http://eur-lex.europa.eu/legal-content/EN/TXT/HTML/?uri=CELEX:32012R1215&from=EN

Regulation (EC) No 593/2008 of the European Parliament and of the Council of 17 June 2008 on the law applicable to contractual obligations (Rome I)

http://eur-lex.europa.eu/legal-content/EN/TXT/?uri=CELEX:32008R0593

The Brussels Convention and the Rome Convention are still applicable in the overseas territories of the European Union member states and in Denmark which has not enacted the Rome I and Brussels I Regulations because of its opt-in status in the area of freedom, security and justice.

12 Strengthening cooperation with Switzerland, Norway, and Iceland: The Lugano Convention (2007)

http://eur-lex.europa.eu/legal-content/EN/TXT/?uri=URISERV:l16029.

In this category should be mentioned the Convention on the Recognition and Enforcement of Foreign Arbitral Awards.[13] This convention, which is commonly known as the New York Convention, has 165 members.[14] This makes it one of the most successful conventions in the wider area of international commerce.

The second category is that of substantive commercial law conventions. The first type of substantive law convention regulates international sales. The CISG is the most successful in this area and as of July 2020 it has 94 contracting states.[15] These include the USA, France, Australia, Russia, and China. Notable absentees are the United Kingdom and India.[16] New countries keep acceding to the CISG. In 2019 these included for instance Laos,[17] Liechtenstein[18], and the Democratic People's Republic of Korea[19] and in 2020 Portugal.[20] The CISG affected approximately 66% of global commerce in 2005.[21] In 2009 this percentage had gone up to 70%-80%.[22] The 'sister convention' of the CISG is the 1974 Convention on the Limitation Period in the International Sale of Goods[23] and has 30 ratifications as of January 2020.[24]

13 For the full text in English see: http://www.newyorkconvention.org/english.

14 For a full list of contracting states see: http://www.newyorkconvention.org/countries.

15 For a full list of members please see: http://www.cisg.law.pace.edu/cisg/countries/cntries.html.

16 On why the UK is not a member see for instance: Sally Moss, 'Why the United Kingdom Has Not Ratified the CISG' (2005) 25 Journal of Law and Commerce 483.

17 United Nations Information Series, the Lao People's Democratic Republic accedes to United Nations Convention on Contracts for the International Sale of Goods (25 September 2019). http://www.unis.unvienna.org/unis/en/pressrels/2019/unisl280.html.

18 UNCITRAL, Liechtenstein accedes to the UN Convention on Contracts for the International Sale of Goods (7 May 2019). https://uncitral.un.org/en/news/liechtenstein-accedes-un-convention-contracts-international-sale-goods-cisg.

19 UNCITRAL Coordination Committee for Australia, *North Korea joins the CISG* (14 April 2019) https://uncca.org.au/2019/04/14/north-korea-joins-the-cisg/.

20 United Nations Information Series, Portugal accedes to United Nations Convention on Contracts for the International Sale of Goods (24 September 2020). https://unis.unvienna.org/unis/en/pressrels/2020/unisl305.html
Presidência do Conselho de Ministros Decreto No. 5/20 (7 August 2020) https://dre.pt/application/file/a/139804918.

21 Franco Ferrari, *Le Contrat de Vente International, Applicabilité et Application de la Convention de Vienne sur les Contrats de Vente Internationale de Marchandises* (second edition, Helling & Lichtenhahn 2000).

22 Ingeborg Schwenzer and Pascal Hachem, 'The CISG- Successes and Pitfalls' (2009) 57 American Journal of Comparative Law 457,457.

23 For the full text see: http://www.uncitral.org/uncitral/en/uncitral_texts/sale_goods/1974Convention_status.html.

24 http://www.uncitral.org/uncitral/en/uncitral_texts/sale_goods/1974Convention_status.html.

The CISG received a positive reception as evidenced by the number of ratifications; it is a *'gem of a future amalgamation of all sales law.'*[25] Zweigert & Kotz call it *'the greatest achievement of UNCITRAL.'*[26] The adoption of the CISG is *'the most profound evidence of the move towards the unification of contract law.'*[27]

Criticism has also been levelled against the CISG. It is too general, and it gives too much room for different interpretations, which leads to diverging case law.[28] The CISG is not comprehensive because it leaves out certain types of sales and some legal issues that are integral to contract law are not covered.[29] Whilst this is true, this type of criticism conveniently overlooks that there are also shortcomings in domestic law..[30] This criticism is also not limited to the CISG and applies to conventions in general as was discussed in Section 3.5. Conventions are born out of compromises between legal systems and are formed by the lowest common denominator on which a majority of participants could agree.

Another type of substantive convention regulates the carriage of goods contract. For carriage of goods by sea the relevant conventions are The Hague-Visby Rules, the Hamburg Convention of 1978, and the Rotterdam Rules of 2010. The Hague-Visby rules are the most prominent and most ratified. They find their origin in the International Convention for the Unification of Certain Rules of Law Relating to Bills of Lading drafted by the Comité Maritime International (CMI).[31]

These so-called Hague Rules were amended in 1968 with a first protocol (Visby) and in 1979 with a second protocol (regarding Special Drawing Rights). As the title of the convention suggests The Hague-Visby Rules cover only carriages of goods under a bill of lading. The Rules have been widely adopted (covering the vast majority of sea trade volume) although

25 Louis Marques, International *Uniform Commercial Law: towards a progressive consciousness (*Ashgate, Aldershot 2005) 2.

26 Konrad Zweigert and Heinz Kötz, *An introduction to comparative law* (Tony Weir tr, third edition, Oxford University Press 1998) 27.

27 Larry A DiMatteo, *International Contracting: Law and Practice* (Wolter Kluwer Law & Business 2013) 235.

28 Jan M Smits, 'Convergence of Private Law in Europe' in Esin Örucü and David Nelken (Editors) *Comparative Law, A Handbook* (Hart Publishing 2007) 224.

29 CISG Article 2
For an analysis on legal issues which are excluded from the CISG see:
Stefan Kröll, 'Selected Problems Concerning the CISG's Scope of Application' (2005–2006) 25 Journal of Law and Commerce 39.
These include pre-contractual negotiations and capacity.

30 José Angelo Estrella Faria, Future Directions of Legal Harmonisation and Law Reform: Stormy Seas or Prosperous Voyage? (2009) 14 *Uniform Law Review* 5, 9.

31 The 1924 Bills of Lading Convention and its 1968 and 1979 Protocols (Hague-Visby Rules). http://www.comitemaritime.org/The-1924-Bills-of-Lading-Convention-and-its-1968-and-1979-Protocols-Hague-Visby-Rules/0,2799,19932,00.html.

not all contracting states have adopted the protocols.[32] Participating states include France, USA, UK, Turkey, Japan, and Italy. The Hague-Visby rules are mandatory and cannot be avoided by including a choice of law clause for a non-contracting state. For instance, in the UK the Carriage of Goods by Sea Act of 1971 gives article X of The Hague-Visby Rules the quality of mandatory law.[33] The Hague-Visby rules are applicable if the bill of lading has been emitted in a contracting state or if the transport begins in a contracting state. They can also be contracted into through the inclusion of a paramount clause in the contract.

The United Nations Convention on the Carriage of Goods by Sea (Hamburg Rules) has not enjoyed the same success as The Hague-Visby rules.[34] They are largely ignored by the larger maritime economies as they are deemed more favourable to the shipper and less so to the carrier. They have attracted 34 ratifications from mainly low tonnage countries.[35]

The Rotterdam Rules are to establish a uniform, updated, and comprehensive regime.[36] They are so far ratified by five states (Spain, Togo, Cameroon, Benin, and the Republic of the Congo (Brazzaville)) and will not enter into force until ratified by at least 20 countries.[37] Those countries that ratify the convention should renounce The Hague-Visby Rules and Hamburg rules if they are signatory to either when the Rotterdam Rules come into force. The hope is that the Rotterdam rules will become the leading convention on carriage of goods by sea, but this is of course dependent on the amount of ratifications it will receive.

There are also numerous conventions for carriage of goods by other means of transportation. These include the Budapest Convention on Carriage of

32 For a full list of countries and their accession to carriage of goods by sea conventions: Hill Dickinson, *Cargo Conventions: Comparing Hague, Hague/Visby, and Hamburg Rules, Shipping at a Glance Guide 1.* http://www.hilldickinson.com/pdf/Cargo%20conventions.pdf.

33 Carriage of Goods by Sea Act 1971 and Carriage of Goods by Sea Act 1992.

34 United Nations Convention on the Carriage of Goods by Sea (The Hamburg Rules) 30 March 1978. http://www.uncitral.org/uncitral/en/uncitral_texts/transport_goods/Hamburg_rules.html.

35 http://www.uncitral.org/uncitral/en/uncitral_texts/transport_goods/Hamburg_status.html.

36 The United Nations Convention on Contracts for the International Carriage of Goods Wholly or Partly by Sea of 11 December 2008 (Rotterdam Rules). http://www.uncitral.org/uncitral/en/uncitral_texts/transport_goods/2008rotterdam_rules.html.

37 For the current status of the Rotterdam Rules: https://uncitral.un.org/en/texts/transportgoods/conventions/rotterdam_rules/status.

Goods by Rivers,[38] the Convention concerning International Carriage by Rail supplemented by the Vilnius Rules,[39] the Warsaw Convention on Carriage of Goods by Air,[40] the Montreal Convention on Carriage of Goods by Air,[41] and the Geneva Convention on Transportation of Goods by Road.[42] The United Nations Convention on International Multimodal Transport of

38 Budapest Convention on the Contract for the Carriage of Goods by Inland Waterway (CMNI) 22 June 2001

This is a regional convention for the European Continent and has so far been ratified by 15 states and entered into force on 1 April 2005

Full text: http://www.unece.org/fileadmin/DAM/trans/main/sc3/cmniconf/cmni.pdf.

39 Convention concerning International Carriage by Rail (COTIF) of 9 May 1980, as amended by the Vilnius Protocol of 3 June 1999

This convention is applicable in Europe, the Maghreb, and Middle East between states that have ratified the convention

The Intergovernmental Organisation for International Carriage by Rail (OTIF) was set up to establish international rail carriage legislation through uniform laws.

Full text of the convention: http://www.otif.org/en/about-otif/conventions-cotif.html.

40 The Convention for the Unification of Certain Rules Relating to International Carriage by Air of 12 October 1929 (Warsaw Convention.) This convention is applicable to both carriages of goods and persons. It was amended by The Hague Protocol of 1955. The Warsaw convention has been ratified by 152 states and The Hague protocol by 137 states. This was followed by the Guadalajara Convention in 1961 (84 contracting states), Guatemala Protocol of 1971 which has never entered into force and the Montreal Protocols 1, 2, 3 4, in 1975. Of these protocols 1,2 and 4 have entered into force (respectively with 48, 49, and 53 members)

For the full text in English see: http://www.vayama.com/pdf/warsawConvention.pdf.

41 Convention for the Unification of Certain Rules for International Carriage by Air of 28 May 1999 (Montreal Convention)

The development of the Montreal Convention occurred for much the same reasons as the Rotterdam Rules. It was felt that the Warsaw Convention and subsequent amendments needed to be modernised and unified. The Montreal Convention draws upon the Warsaw Conventions and its protocols and unifies these into a new instrument. The Convention has been successful with 133 contracting states:

http://www.icao.int/secretariat/legal/List%20of%20Parties/Mtl99_EN.pdf.

Currently the Warsaw Convention (+ protocols) and the Montreal Conventions co-exist. The Montreal Convention takes precedence between contracting states if both are ratified.

For full text see: http://www.jus.uio.no/lm/air.carriage.unification.convention.montreal.1999/.

42 Convention on the Contract for the International Carriage of Goods by Road of 19 May 1956(CMR) (Geneva Convention) this has been ratified by 55 (mainly European) states:

https://treaties.un.org/Pages/ViewDetails.aspx?src=TREATY&mtdsg_no=XI-B-11&chapter=11&lang=en

For the full text see:

http://www.jus.uio.no/lm/un.cmr.road.carriage.contract.convention.1956.amended.protocol.1978/doc.html.

Goods of 1980 has not entered into force.[43] Conventions that regulate carriage of goods are the most successful category of international conventions. This has especially been the case for carriage of goods by sea and air. The need for harmonisation was clear earlier than in other areas of international commercial law. European countries are strongly represented in carriage of goods by rivers and terrestrial transports. This is explained by the geography of the European continent: many small countries combined with a highly developed economy, which means transportation of a high volume of goods and peoples across borders.

A third category of conventions regulates international financing. Examples are the UNIDROIT Convention on International Factoring and the UNIDROIT Convention on International Financial Leasing of 1988.[44] These are in force in respectively nine and ten countries. UNIDROIT also drafted the Convention on International Interests in Mobile Equipment of 2001 (Cape Town Convention), which has 80 contracting states.[45]

The above are the most prominent examples of conventions in international commerce.[46] If conventions are not in force or not in force in a particular state, they are not binding law. In those cases, they can be considered non-state rules as they have an international origin, their substance regulates international private relations between merchants, and they are weakened

43 For the full text of the convention see: http://www.jus.uio.no/lm/un.multimodal.transport.1980/doc.html

It will enter into force upon ratification by 30 states. Given the date of the convention this is unlikely to happen.

44 UNIDROIT Convention on International Factoring of 1988.

http://www.unidroit.org/instruments/factoring

UNIDROIT Convention on International Financial Leasing of 1988.

http://www.unidroit.org/fr/leasing-ol-2/leasing-anglais.

45 Convention on International Interests in Mobile Equipment of 2001.

http://www.unidroit.org/instruments/security-interests/cape-town-convention

The Cape Town Convention has four protocols. The Aircraft protocol, which has 77 contracting states, is in force. The Rail Protocol, the Mining and Agricultural and Construction Equipment, and the Space Protocol are not yet in force.

46 Some other examples

The UN Convention on the Use of Electronic Communications in International Contracts (2005)- entered into force in 2013 and has 7 parties

The UN Convention on the Assignment of Receivables in International Trade (2001) – has one ratification and has not entered into force

The UN Convention on International Bills of Exchange and International Promissory Notes (1988) – has 5 parties and has not entered into force

The UN Convention on Independent Guarantees and Stand-by Letters of Credit (1995) – entered into force in 2000 and has 8 parties

The UN Convention on the Liability of Operators of Transport Terminals in International Trade (1991) – has 4 parties and has not entered into force

UNIDROIT Convention on Agency in the International Sale of Goods (1983) – 4 ratifications and has not entered into force.

along the lines of obligation and delegation, following Abbott and Snidal's model.[47]

4.4 Uncodified non-state rules

Uncodified non-state rules consist of trade usages and general principles of law. Trade usages are characterised by their spontaneous creation within the business community and their adaptability to the needs of that community. The differences between custom, usages, and practices are not always clear. In contemporary commercial law literature, the terms are used interchangeably whereas in practice there is a tendency towards using the term trade usage[48]

Custom is the practice of an authority and usages are the practice of a trade.[49] Customary law as defined by the ICJ contains two important elements: the repeated and consistent practice and the opinio iuris.[50] The common law test is that for a custom to be recognised it needs to be legal, notorious, certain, reasonable, universal, obligatory, and ancient or immemorial.[51] This is a high threshold to meet. In practice, custom in international trade does not always meet that threshold. It is more flexible, transient and adaptable, partly because of its close association with trade usages.

Custom is normative: parties follow the custom because they believe it should be followed. Without this sense of obligation, it cannot be considered custom. This is not the same with trade usages. Parties do not need to believe that the usage is legally binding for it to be enforceable; they only need to adhere to it.

The UCC states that '*a usage of trade is any practice or method of dealing having such regularity of observance in a place, vocation, or trade as to justify an expectation that it will be observed with respect to the transaction in question.*'[52] It does not state that a sense of obligation is necessary. This was confirmed in *Chase Manhattan Bank v. May* where the court stated that usages do not need to meet the standard of custom.[53] This is why trade usages are favoured in modern legislation as there is no need to prove a sense of obligation, but only to prove the actual practice itself. It can be difficult to distinguish between a usage followed out of courtesy or out of a sense of legal

47 Kenneth W Abbott and Duncan Snidal, 'Hard and Soft Law in International Governance' (2000) 54 International Organization 421,422.

48 Roy Goode, 'Usage and its Reception in Transnational Commercial Law' in Jacob S Ziegel and Shalow Lerner (editors), *New Developments in International Commercial and Consumer Law, proceedings of the 8th Bienal Conference of the International Academy of Commercial and Consumer Law* (Hart Publishing1998) 9.

49 Ibid, 9.

50 *The Republic of Nicaragua v. The United States of America* (1986) International Court of Justice.

51 Jim C Chen, 'Code, Custom, and Contract: The Uniform Commercial Code as Law Merchant' (1992) 27 Texas International Journal 91, 98.

52 UCC § 1-303. Course of Performance, Course of Dealing, and Usage of Trade.

53 *Chase Manhattan Bank v. Milton May* (1962) 311 F.2d 117 (3d Cir.).

obligation.[54] Therefore, if there is no need to prove this sense of obligation it lessens the burden of proof. A trade usage thus has binding force regardless of whether the parties recognise this obligation Non-respect of a trade usage is seen as non-respect of a contractual term.[55] Trade usages are applicable in a specific locality or a specific trade and they go beyond the individual contractual relationship and can therefore not be equated with course of dealing.

Practices have a weaker obligation than trade usages. Practices can be associated with the individual contracting parties. In that case, practices are the equivalent of course of dealing and they are binding within the specific relationship. Another explanation is that a practice is a beginning trade usage. The pattern is emerging but is not yet firmly established. A practice is new trade usage, which has not yet acquired obligatory force.[56] Under that definition a practice would not create any legal obligations for the parties unless this has been implied through course of dealing or if the practice is explicitly included in the contract.

Schmitthoff synthesises these differences by describing a gradual process whereby custom is started as practices that are followed by a few businesses which then become general usages within that trade or locality, and which over time may develop into custom.[57] Trade usages and practices are more restricted in time and space than custom, which is more universal and has deeper historical roots, as evidenced by the common law test. It should be kept in mind that these three terms are often used interchangeably in theoretical writing and in practice.[58] As the legislative preference is for the concept of trade usages and in practice custom in international commerce is often equated to trade usages, this book uses the term trade usages as the point of reference and only uses custom when a distinction between the two should be made. Domestic law recognises trade usages (custom, practices...)

54 Roy Goode, 'Usage and its Reception in Transnational Commercial Law' in Jacob S Ziegel and Shalow Lerner (editors), *New Developments in International Commercial and Consumer Law, proceedings of the 8th Bienal Conference of the International Academy of Commercial and Consumer Law* (Hart Publishing 1998) 11.

55 Alejandro M Garro 'Rule-Setting by Private Organisations, Standardisation of Contracts and the Harmonisation of International Sales Law' in Ian F Fletcher, Loukas Mistelis and Marise Cremona (editors), *Foundations and Perspectives of International Trade Law* (Sweet & Maxwell 2000) 314.

56 Roy Goode, 'Usage and Its Reception in Transnational Commercial Law' (1997) 46 International & Comparative Law Quarterly 4,4.

57 Clive M Schmitthoff, 'The Unification or Harmonisation of Law by Means of Standard Contracts and General Conditions' (1986) 17 International & Comparative Law Quarterly 551, 554.

58 *Hellbusch v. Rheinholdt* 550 P.2d 1199 (1976):*'the terms `usage' and `custom' are commonly used interchangeably, though there is a recognized distinction in the meaning of the two words.'*

(Quoting from Samuel Williston, Law of Contracts 1-4, § 648 (3rd edition Jaeger 1961).

as a source of law.[59] Whether a specific practice is considered a trade usage depends on how regularly it is observed, how long it has existed, and how widespread it is.

Trade usages depend on the capacity of the merchant community to self-organise and select those usages which are beneficial to the community: '*when a usage has become uniform in an active commercial community that should warrant enough for supposing that it answers the needs of those who are dealing upon the faith of it.*'[60] There are instances when a usage develops that is not beneficial although this is rare. In a competitive market surviving usages can be assumed to benefit the parties.[61] A usage that stands in the way of economic efficiency would soon give way to another one. This is an acceptable presumption as it is better to tolerate a rare unreasonable usage than go through the effort and costs of trying to establish general rules to define precisely when a trade usage is reasonable.[62]

An example of a damaging trade usage is the practice of giving indemnity letters in exchange for a clean bill of lading. As speed is of the essence, the captain of the ship is asked to sign a clean bill of lading, even when he has not been given the opportunity to inspect the goods or if the goods do not conform. The captain is then given a letter of indemnity to exonerate the carrier from responsibility. This practice is widespread, yet it is not only fraudulent, but also counterproductive as it diminishes trust in the bill of lading and damages its value. Parties have argued in court that this is an enforceable trade usage. In a famous English case this was accepted by the trial court and by the court of appeal, but it was struck down by the House of Lords.[63] The House of Lords stated that trust is the foundation of trade and that if doubt arises about the trustworthiness of a clean bill of lading this is damaging for international trade.

The legal authority of the trade usage does not come from enforcement in the courts. There are two main views on the legal authority of trade usages.

59 See for instance the Uniform Commercial Code, which recognises trade usages as a source of law in all 50 states of the USA.

See Section 346 of the German Code of Commerce which obliges courts to take into consideration trade usages.

60 Judge Learned Hand in *Kunglig Jarnvagsstyrelsen v Dexter and Carpenter* 299 F. 991 (S.D.N.Y. 1924).

61 Jim C Chen, 'Code, Custom, and Contract: The Uniform Commercial Code as Law Merchant' (1992) 27 Texas International Journal 91, 123/124

This is especially so as reputation is vital in international trade. The enforcement of the lex mercatoria also depended on reputation. A sanction was for instance the exclusion from commercial fairs (see page 132 of professor Chen's article).

See also:

Kerry Lynn Mackintosh, 'Liberty, Trade, and the Uniform Commercial Code, When Should Default Rules Be Based on Business Practices?' (1996) 38 William & Mary Law Review 1465, 1478

62 Jim C Chen, 'Code, Custom, and Contract: The Uniform Commercial Code as Law Merchant' (1992) 27 Texas International Journal 91, 135

63 *Brown Jenkinson & Co v Percy Dalton* [1957] 2 Lloyd's List L. R.1 (C.A.).

The first is that as long as a usage is not recognised by a court it does not have legal authority and the second view is that a ruling by a court is merely declaratory and the ruling itself is not the source of the legal authority.[64] The first view causes a paradox: if a usage is only law after its recognition, then it should not pose any obligation upon the parties given that the trade usage did not exist before the ruling.[65] In that case, only trade usages that have been affirmed in judicial decisions are binding. This would lead to the court confirming that a specific usage is binding, yet not enforcing it in the current case, as the usage did not exist prior to the decision. It is therefore more reasonable to assume that a court recognises a trade usage, but that the legal authority does not come from this decision. That legitimacy comes from its usage by the merchant community. The authority of trade usages can thus come from domestic law (if trade usages are a source of law under domestic law), from the lex mercatoria (of which they are a source), and the business community (which creates and uses them).

The place of general principles of law in international commercial law generates more debate. General principles of law are sources of public international law, domestic law, and transnational commercial law. According to Lord Mustill their practical applicability in commercial law is limited because they are not specific enough.[66] Despite this criticism phrases like 'general principles of law', 'principles of commercial law' and similar are regularly found in choice of law clauses. Courts must then find a way to translate these general and sometimes vague principles into concrete rules. At other times courts and tribunals apply them without the parties having referred to them, either to interpret the law or to interpret the contract.

There are different theories on how general principles function as a source of international commercial law.[67] They could be a way of ordering the legal system or as guidance to understanding similar concepts in different laws.[68] In that case they would not be sources of law. They can also be seen as sources of law for gap filling purposes or to interpret the law.[69] This gap-filling method can be found in the CISG, which states that for matters covered by the convention, but not explicitly discussed in it, decisions should be based on the conventions' underlying general principles.[70] De Ly analyses that in the Netherlands and Belgium general principles are recognised as a source

64 Roy Goode, 'Usage and its Reception in Transnational Commercial Law' in Jacob S Ziegel and Shalow Lerner (editors), *New Developments in International Commercial and Consumer Law, proceedings of the 8th Bienal Conference of the International Academy of Commercial and Consumer Law* (Hart Publishing 1998) 12.

65 Ibid.

66 Michael Mustill, 'The New Lex Mercatoria: The First Twenty-Five Years' (1998) 4 Arbitration International 86,92.

67 Filip de Ly, *International Business Law and Lex Mercatoria (*T.M.C Asser Instituut 1992) 193.

68 Ibid.

69 Ibid, 194.

70 CISG Article 7 (2).

of law and are applied regularly. In France they are applied less frequently, but they are a formal source of law, and in Germany they are recognised as a method to interpret the law.[71]

General principles of law as defined by article 38 of the ICJ are sources of public international law. General principles are also a source of domestic law. They can thus derive their legal authority from domestic law or from international law. General principles of transnational commercial law pose a conundrum. If they are reduced to the general principles of law under article 38, they become so abstract as to lose their practical importance for international commerce. If on the other hand general principles of law are defined in a concrete way that is applicable to international commerce, they serve an important purpose in interpreting the law. If they are concrete rules, they will lose some of their universality because they are applied in state courts, which means that domestic law influences how these principles are interpreted and applied. Therefore, general principles of commercial law are on the juxtaposition of public international law, transnational commercial law, and domestic law and how they are defined and interpreted varies between jurisdictions.

4.5 Codified non- state rules as a source of law

International organisations, trade associations, and private groups create codified non-state rules. This can be with the goal of harmonising international commercial law and providing security and predictability to international transactions.

Apart from being codified, the crucial difference between uncodified non-state rules and codified non-state rules is that the legal position of the first is clearer. Trade usages and general principles of law are recognised in the domestic legal order as sources of law. They thus have a direct standing under the law. This is not the case for codified non-state rules. They are usually not recognised as a source of domestic law.[72] Their status as a source of law often comes from their association or assimilation with uncodified non-state rules. That is to the say the codified rule is seen as a reflection or expression of a general principle of law or a trade usage. They can also get their authority from the contract (if they are incorporated by reference or used as the applicable law) or from their position as legal doctrine/scholarship. This section explores the different types of codified non-state rules.

Upon adoption model laws become part of domestic law. The model law might be changed during the adoption. Model laws might be transferred almost one on one or they could merely serve as an inspiration for the drafters of the domestic law. The adopted model law is now part of the domestic

71 Filip de Ly, *International Business Law and Lex Mercatoria* (T.M.C Asser Instituut 1992), 194–199.

72 Although some jurisdictions do explicitly recognise certain codified non-state rules: Ukraine for instance recognises the UPICC and Incoterms as trade usages (Official Note of the High Commercial Court of Ukraine No.01-8/211, 07.04.2008).

law of the state. The original model law continues to exist in parallel to the state. The question is then what the legal authority of the model law is. Model laws are aimed at legislators. This makes the provisions less suitable as contractual rules, but this is not an intrinsic reason why private parties could not include a model law in their contract by reference. For instance, the parties could state that electronic commerce in the contract should be defined as per the relevant UNCITRAL Model Law.

Their legal authority beyond contractual rules is more difficult to ascertain. The purpose of model laws is to convince legislators to adopt their provisions. Their advocacy is aimed at the state and not at the contracting parties. As they are aimed at legislators, they are unlikely to be used as contractual rules. They are therefore unlikely to develop into trade practices and usages. If the model law has been adopted by many legislations this could increase the persuasive value of the provisions of the model law. The principles of the model law could become accepted international commercial law principles. This could ensure a development of some of the provisions of the model law into international commercial law doctrine or general principles of international commercial law.

Model contracts and model terms are aimed at the parties to the contract. Businesses use them as models or incorporate parts in their contract. They serve as contractual rules and derive their legal authority from the contract. Model contract terms could develop into trade usages if they are used frequently and consistently. They then take on a legal value beyond that of a contractual rule, as their application would not be dependent upon being included in the contract. They would be treated as implied terms of the contract.

The two most prominent sets of contract terms are the Incoterms and the UCP. The Incoterms are based upon pre-existing trade terms. Trade terms are interpreted differently in different ports and states.[73] The ICC chose the most prevalent meaning, and this can differ from local interpretations.[74]

The Incoterms are firstly contractual rules. They will apply when contracted into. Some consider them to be trade usages.[75] In 1968 Schmitthoff wrote that they are usages, which have to be contracted in to.[76] In 1980 Ramberg described the Incoterms as usages.[77] Case law is diffuse; there is some support for the claim that they are trade usages but also case law that

73 Hans van Houtte, *The Laws of International Trade* (Sweet & Maxwell 1995),149.

74 Ibid, 150.

75 Filip de Ly, *International Business Law and Lex Mercatoria* (T.M.C Asser Instituut 1992) 173.

76 Clive M Schmitthoff, 'The Unification or Harmonisation of Law by Means of Standard Contracts and General Conditions' (1986) 17 International & Comparative Law Quarterly 551,554.

77 Jan Ramberg, 'Incoterms 1980' in Norbert Horn and Clive M Schmitthoff (editors), *The Transnational Law of International Commercial Transactions* (Kluwer 1982) 151.

confirms their status as contractual rules.[78] The majority opinion is that the Incoterms are contractual rules.[79] The European Court of Justice affirmed that usages such as Incoterms have the status of a contractual term and should be applied as part of the contract in the same way as all relevant terms, including those that are used in '*international commercial usage.*'[80]

Not all Incoterms are equally established. An older more established term like FOB is more likely to be considered a trade usage than a newer term such as DDP. Incoterms are seen as trade usages when parties include a trade term such as FOB in their contract without any specific reference to the Incoterms and the court decides that the trade term should be interpreted in accordance with the Incoterms. The Incoterms are in that case the standard for interpreting trade terms and take on the role of trade usages. They can also be considered usages if the parties describe in their contract how the transfer of risk takes place without reference to a trade term, but the court interprets this transfer of risk clause in accordance with the corresponding Incoterm.

The UCP are contractual rules. They are voluntary in name but in practice they are usually not as getting a documentary credit with an established bank is almost impossible without using the UCP. The question is what this says about the legal authority of the UCP as a source of law. Dalhuisen believes the UCP to be customary law.[81] Already in 1968 Schmitthoff saw the UCP as being in a transitional stage from usage to custom.[82] There is thus support for considering them as more than contractual rules. On the other hand, it can be argued that the UCP cannot be seen as custom or trade usages because the provisions tend to be biased in favour of the bank.[83] Although merchants use them frequently they do this because they cannot get a documentary credit without including them and not because they feel any moral obligation about adhering to the UCP.[84] They are thus not custom as a sense of obligation is required for a usage to be custom. Could they be trade

78 Filip de Ly, *International Business Law and Lex Mercatoria* (T.M.C Asser Instituut 1992) 173.

79 Ibid, 174
And
Anne-Katherine Drettmann, 'Would English law on trade usages benefit from adopting a more formal approach such as seen in other jurisdictions as well as in international conventions?' (2009)
http://www.cisg.law.pace.edu/cisg/biblio/drettmann.html.

80 Electrosteel Europe SA v Edil Centro SpA (2011) Case C-87/10 ECLI:EU:C:2011:375.

81 Jan H Dalhuisen, *On Transnational and Comparative Commercial, Financial and Trade Law Volume I, - The New Lex Mercatoria and its Sources* (Hart Publishing 2001) 160.

82 Clive M Schmitthoff, 'The Unification or Harmonisation of Law by Means of Standard Contracts and General Conditions' (1986) 17 International & Comparative Law Quarterly 551,554.

83 Norbert Horn, 'The Use of Transnational Law in the Contract Law of International Trade and Finance' in Klaus Peter Berger (Editor), *The Practice of Transnational Law* (Kluwer Law International 2001) 79.

84 Ibid.

usages? They are used consistently and regularly, so based on observation it could be concluded that they are trade usages. They are applied more consistently than the Incoterms and there is thus a basis to consider them trade usages.[85] Yet, it might be asked whether merchants would adhere to them if they were not in the contract or whether they would choose to contract out of them if possible.

The UCP are considered contractual terms in most jurisdictions.[86] The first article of the UCP states that they are applicable when they are included in the contract and therefore they present themselves as contractual rules.[87] Although their usage is pervasive the unequal relationship between the bank and the merchant would prevent them from being considered customary law. It is also questionable whether they are trade usages. They could be considered as trade usages between banks which use them voluntarily and have considerable influence on the development of the UCP. Whether they should be considered trade usages between banks and third parties is more questionable. Businesses do not use the UCP spontaneously. For this reason, the UCP are rightly more contractual rules than trade usages, despite the high frequency of usage.

Guides and opinions are a diffuse category of non-state rules that serves to unite those rules that do not fall under any of the other categories. These include guidelines, commentary, legal opinions etc. The origins of these documents are international organisations, trade associations, study groups, think thanks, and other private initiatives. These documents do not serve as sources of law but can have persuasive value and contribute to the development of accepted international commercial practices and doctrine.

An example is the CISG Advisory Council. This is an independent group that publishes legal opinions on the interpretation of the CISG, based on case law and on the legislative history of the CISG.[88] These opinions have no direct legal standing but gain persuasive authority if applied by courts to interpret the CISG. They could therefore serve towards developing the principles underlying the CISG and the concrete rules of how the CISG should be interpreted.

85 Filip de Ly, *International Business Law and Lex Mercatoria (*T.M.C Asser Instituut 1992) 182.

86 Olugbenga Bamodu, 'Extra-national Legal Principles in the Global Village: a Conceptual Examination of Transnational Law', (2001) 4 International Arbitration Law Review 6, 14.

87 UCP 600 –Article 1: Application of UCP.

The Uniform Customs and Practice for Documentary Credits, 2007 Revision, ICC Publication no. 600 ("UCP") are rules that apply to any documentary credit ("credit") (including, to the extent to which they may be applicable, any standby letter of credit) when the text of the credit expressly indicates that it is subject these rules.

88 CISG Advisory Council: http://www.cisgac.com/

An example of a CISG best practice guide would be: John P McMahon, *Applying the CISG: Guides for Business Managers and Counsel*, (May 2010) http://www.cisg.law.pace.edu/cisg/guides.html.

International organisations do substantive work in this area. The ICC publishes handbooks, best practice guides, and other similar type instruments.[89] UNCITRAL also publishes these types of documents as well as for instance case law digests.[90] UNIDROIT publishes instruments in this category such as their legal guide to contract farming.[91] Trade associations produce legal opinions and best practice guides.[92]

Guides and opinions are aimed at legislators, legal professionals, and the business community. Some of these can be used during contractual negotiations as guidelines. Others could be used as contractual rules. They would therefore derive their authority from the contract.

Guides and opinions are used by courts to help interpret international and transnational commercial law. They can be considered as contributing to the formation of legal doctrine if they are cited frequently by courts, legislators, and policy makers. Their legal value would partly be determined by the institution (a document produced by an international organisation would have stronger persuasive value than that written by a private individual.) Furthermore, the origins of the instrument are important. For instance, the UNCITRAL case law digests are based on existing case law. This might be foreign case law or arbitral awards and thus not a source of law in the forum,

89 Examples are:
Policy and Business Practices: Developing Neutral Legal Standards for International Contracts
http://store.iccwbo.org/content/uploaded/pdf/Developing_Neutral_Legal_Standards_Int_Contracts.pdf
ICC Principles to Facilitate Commercial Negotiation
http://store.iccwbo.org/t/ICC-Principles-to-Facilitate-Commercial-Negotiation.

90 Examples are:
UNCITRAL Legal Guide on International Countertrade Transactions (1992)
http://www.uncitral.org/uncitral/en/uncitral_texts/sale_goods/1992Guide_countertrade.html
Promoting confidence in electronic commerce: legal issues on international use of electronic authentication and signature methods (2007)
http://www.uncitral.org/pdf/english/texts/electcom/08-55698_Ebook.pdf
UNCITRAL Digest of Case Law on the United Nations Convention on Contracts for the International Sale of Goods (2012)
http://www.uncitral.org/pdf/english/clout/CISG-digest-2012-e.pdf
UNCITRAL 2012 Digest of Case Law on the Model Law on International Commercial Arbitration
http://www.uncitral.org/uncitral/en/case_law/digests/mal2012.html.

91 Examples are:
Contract Farming Legal Guide
http://www.unidroit.org/instruments/contract-farming/legal-guide
Guide to International Master Franchise Arrangements (Second Edition 2007)
http://www.unidroit.org/guide-to-international-master-franchise-second-edition.

92 Examples are:
ISDA: opinions, and other documentation materials:
http://www2.isda.org/functional-areas/legal-and-documentation/
GAFTA: Guidelines for Appropriations, letters of credits, insurance terms
http://www.gafta.com/Contracts-2016.

but it would carry persuasive value, nonetheless. A best practice guide that reflects only the author's opinion would be less persuasive. If that best practice guide is based on long standing commercial practices, then it might be used as evidence of these practices and would have a stronger position. The dissimilar origins and authors make it difficult to pinpoint the legal authority of this category of codified non-state rules. The two main points of reference would be: their inclusion in the contract and their stance as legal doctrine/scholarship in the tradition of civil law.

4.6 Restatements of law

Restatements of law in international contract law aim to restate regional or global (commercial) contract law in the form of a set of principles and concrete rules. They are intended to be used by contracting parties as the applicable law but are also used for other purposes, such as to interpret international and transnational commercial law. The most successful example is the UNIDROIT Principles of International Commercial Contracts.[93] Regional examples are the Principles of European Contract Law and the Principles of Latin American Contract Law. This section explores these three restatements to understand their functioning and their place as a source of law.

The UPICC were designed to create a neutral contract law for international business transactions.[94] The first edition was published in 1994, the second edition in 1998, and the third in 2010.[95] The drafters made a conscious decision not to seek approval from the UNIDROIT council. They were drafted outside the constraints of the institution and no formal approval from states was necessary. The UNIDROIT Council did formally approve the second and following editions of the Principles thus bringing them under the umbrella of the institution. The UPICC contain both general contract law principles and specific rules. The commentary on the Principles, are considered an intrinsic part of the document.[96] They are a work of comparative study that mainly drew their inspiration from the UCC, the CISG, the

93 UNIDROIT developed two further sets of Principles: the ALI/UNIDROIT Principles of Transnational Civil Procedure (the ELI/UNIDROIT Principles of Transnational Civil Procedure are currently under development) and the Principles of Reinsurance Contract Law (PRICL)

Parts of this analysis of the UNIDROIT Principles appeared before in: Johanna Hoekstra, 'The Normative Influence of the UNIDROIT Principles of International Commercial Law on Courts' (2019) 23 The Vindobona Journal of International Commercial Law and Arbitration 54.

94 David Oser, *The Unidroit Principles of International Commercial Contracts: A Governing Law* (Martinus Nijhoff 2008) 2.

95 They were updated in 2016 with regards to long term contracts: http://www.unidroit.org/english/governments/councildocuments/2016session/cd-95-03-e.pdf.

96 Michael Joachim Bonell, 'The Law Governing International Commercial Contracts and the Actual Role of the UNIDROIT Principiles' (2018) 23 Uniform Law Review 15, 21.

Dutch Civil Code, the Civil Code of Québec, and the Restatement (Second) of the Law of Contracts and existing trade usages and general principles of commercial law.[97] UNIDROIT cooperated with UNCITRAL to ensure that the UPICC were compatible with the CISG.[98]

The UPICC are '*intended to enunciate rules which are common to (most of) the existing legal systems and at the same time to select the solutions which seem best adapted to the special requirements of international trade.*'[99] The Principles are based on existing law but also form an innovative approach to international commercial law.[100] They are not merely descriptive of the current state of law but they also suggest how the law should develop. Therefore, the Principles use the authority of the current law and build upon this to provide a more unified approach suitable for international commerce.

They can derive authority from being included in the contract, either by reference or as the applicable law. Their legal authority beyond the contract is less clear. They are the first instrument of its kind in international contract law although there is the concept of restatements of law in the US. Therefore, there is some understanding as to the legal nature of the instrument. Restatements of Law in the US are highly persuasive for courts in the application and interpretation of the law; they also regularly serve as inspiration for policy makers. They are so persuasive because they are based on existing case law. This is a crucial difference with the UPICC which are the product of a comparative legal study between a range of jurisdictions.

Just like model contract terms the Principles could develop to become trade usages or like a model law they could develop into general legal principles. The UPICC can develop into accepted international commercial law practices. They would form a point of reference for contracting partners, legal counsel, and adjudicators and can be used to interpret the contract or the law. They would thus form an international commercial law doctrine.

There is an extensive and on-going discussion about whether the UPICC are considered part of the lex mercatoria.[101] They could be used to describe the current state of certain parts of the lex mercatoria.[102] They would thus be a reflection of the lex mercatoria. Caution is advisable: '*It is not up to the Principles to advance themselves as general principles of law or as lex mercatoria [...] The* UNIDROIT *standards will only be part of the lex mercatoria if they*

97 Louis Marques, *International Uniform Commercial Law: Towards a Progressive Consciousness* (Ashgate, Aldershot 2005) 3.

98 Stefan Eberhard, *Les Sanctions de L'Inexécution du Contrat et les Principes Unidroit* (Cedidac UNIL Centre du Droit Lausanne 2005) 7.

99 Michael Joachim Bonell, 'The Unidroit Principles of International Commercial Contracts: towards a new lex mercatoria?' [1997] International Business Law Journal 145,146.

100 Ibid,147.

101 Jan Ramberg, *International Commercial Transactions* (ICC Kluwer Law International Norstedts Juridik AB, 1998) 21.

102 David Oser, *The Unidroit Principles of International Commercial Contracts: A Governing Law* (Martinus Nijhoff 2008) 47.

are recognised as such by the business community and its arbitrators.'[103] Suffice to say opinions differ, from cautiously optimistic to negative. The inherent quality of the UPICC is not necessarily disputed, but their nature is different from that of the lex mercatoria. If the lex mercatoria restricted to uncodified non-state rules, the UPICC could not be part of this.

Concluding, the UPICC do not have a direct standing as a source of law. They are contractual rules. They also have a place as international commercial law doctrine or at the very least they could develop into this. They could also gain legal authority from being considered trade usages or custom.[104] Bonell writes that it is not whether the Principles are applicable in theory which should determine their legitimacy, but whether they are applied in practice.[105] They would thus derive their legitimacy from their recognition and usage by the international business community, courts, and arbitral tribunals.

The Principles of European Contract Law (PECL) were developed by the Commission on European Contract Law (commonly referred to as the Lando Commission after its president Ole Lando) with the aim to enunciate the rules of contract law, which are common to European states. This commission was a private initiative and the work was done independently of the EU institutions although the European Commission showed some interest during the initial stages of the project.[106] The work started in 1982 and the PECL were published between 1995 and 2003.[107] The PECL, unlike the UNIDROIT Principles, are annotated with a list of comparative references. As with the UPICC the authors did not merely use the most commonplace solution, they innovated on existing solutions. The PECL are intended for international and domestic contracts and for consumer contracts as well as for commercial contracts. Whereas the UPICC are aimed at solely international commercial transactions the PECL are aimed at all contracts. The aim of the PECL is to create general principles and rules that could someday become part of the contract law of the member states.[108] They are therefore aimed at harmonising domestic contract law as well as creating transnational contract law.

103 Hans van Houtte, *The Laws of International Trade* (Sweet & Maxwell 1995) 184.

104 The relationship between the UNIDROIT Principles and the lex mercatoria is further explored in chapter 10.

105 Michael Joachim Bonell, 'The UNIDROIT Principles and Transnational Law' (2000) 5 Uniform Law Review, 199, 200.

106 Ole Lando, 'The Common Core of European Private Law and the Principles of European Contract Law' (1998) 21 Hastings International and Comparative Law Review 809, 819.

107 Part I, dealing with performance, non-performance and remedies, was published in 1995. A revised version of Part I alongside Part II was published in 1998. Part III deals with issues of assignment, assumption, statutes of limitation, procedural issues, capitalisation of interest and the effects of illegality and was published in 2003. Part III is published separately whereas Part I and II are integrated into one document.

108 David Oser, *The Unidroit Principles of International Commercial Contracts: A Governing Law* (Martinus Nijhoff 2008) 3.

The pre-amble of the PECL cites five functions. First of all, they can be used as the choice of law in a contract, second they can be used as an inspiration by courts, third they can be used as a basis for harmonisation of contract law, fourth they represent a modern formulation of the lex mercatoria, and fifth they are a foundation for European legislation.[109] The last function has become the most important. The practical applicability of the PECL has been limited for several reasons. The Lando Commission no longer exists which means that there is no structural framework to update the PECL, although a working group has published some revisions.[110] In contrast the UPICC, which were first published a year before the PECL, already had three updates. The lack of an institutional framework behind the PECL also means that they are not promoted in a structured and consistent manner and this contributes to less frequent usage. Another reason is that the PECL have become a basis for further projects in European legal harmonisation and attention has shifted away from them.[111]

What is the legal standing of the PECL? They could be used as contractual rules or the applicable law and derive their authority from the contract. Their value beyond that is subject to debate. The PECL were not prepared under the umbrella of an organisation, but that is in itself not a reason to disqualify the PECL as a source of law.[112] They can form part of a European contract law doctrine and help with the study of legal systems and be a '*language of communication among students and scholars from different countries.*'[113]

They could of course develop into trade usages or general principles of law in the same way as the UPICC could. In practice they are used less frequently than the UPICC and therefore their development into trade usages and general principles is less likely. However, the PECL are contributing to the development of general principles of European contract law. This does not happen only through their usage by the business community or their application by the courts but also through serving as a foundation stone for the creation of a European contract law.

The PECL became one of main foundations for the (Draft) Common Frame of Reference ((D) CFR). In the early 2000s the European Commission published several reports that included reflections on the PECL

109 Jan M Smits, 'Convergence of Private Law in Europe 'in Esin Örucü and David Nelken (Editors), *Comparative Law, A Handbook* (Hart Publishing 2007) 233.

110 Principes Contractuels Communs – Projet de Cadre Commun de Référence (Association Henri Capitant des Amis de la Culture Juridique Française & Société de Législation Comparé, 2008). These revisions were made by several members of the Study Group towards a European Civil Code, but this was done independently from this group.

111 Michael Joachim Bonell, 'The CISG, European Contract Law and the Development of a World Contract Law' (2008) 56 American Journal of Comparative Law 1, 11/12.

112 David Oser, *The Unidroit Principles of International Commercial Contracts: A Governing Law* (Martinus Nijhoff 2008) 122.

113 Jan M Smits, 'Convergence of Private Law in Europe' in Esin Örucü and David Nelken (Editors), *Comparative Law, A Handbook* (Hart Publishing 2007) 233.

and these formed the starting point of the DCFR.[114] The Research Group on EC Private Law (Acquis Group) researched and published the Principles of Existing EC Contract Law (Acquis Principles) as a preliminary to the DCFR.[115] The Study Group on a European Civil Code and the Acquis Group published the DCFR in 2009. Like the Lando Commission, these are private groups consisting of individuals who were not appointed by their governments. There is an overlap in membership between the three groups.

The DCFR was to serve as the basis for the Common Frame of Reference (CFR). The exact scope and the legal authority the CFR will have is unclear. The (D) CFR is also intended as a basis for an eventual European civil code. If a European Civil Code is not feasible, then it could serve as a basis for (optional) contract law instruments and other legislation. The DCFR encompasses several other areas of private law (such as tort law) in addition to contract law.

In turn the DCFR was used to develop the proposal for a Regulation of the European Parliament and the Council on a Common European Sales Law (CESL).[116] This proposal was published in October 2011. This instrument was intended to cover sale contracts. The CESL covered some areas, which are not included in the CISG (such as pre-contractual information duties, defects of consent, unfair contract terms, and electronic contracts). CESL was meant for consumer contracts and for business contracts if one of the contracting parties is a SME. It was to be an opt-in instrument. It had strong support from the European Parliament, but the backing from the European Council, the business community, consumer organisations, and national parliaments was weaker.[117] The ICC issued a statement expressing concern about the lack of harmony between the CISG and the CESL.[118] And with the ICC one can wonder why not more consideration was given to the CISG as the majority of EU states have ratified this.[119]

In 2014 the European Commission presented its Work Programme for 2015 and withdrew the proposal for the CESL.[120] The Commission stated it withdrew the proposal to transform this in a proposed instrument on ecom-

114 Communication to the European Parliament and the Council – A more coherent European contract law- An action plan (COM (2003) 68 of 12 February 2003
Communication from the Commission to the Council and the European Parliament on European contract law [COM (2001) 398 - Official Journal C 255 of 13.9.2001.

115 http://www.acquis-group.org/<

116 CESL: http://eur-lex.europa.eu/legal-content/en/ALL/?uri=CELEX:52011DC0636.

117 Viktor Elod Cserep, 'E Pluribus Unum - Out of Many, One Common European Sales Law'
(2017) 29 Pace International Law Review 199.

118 ICC Position on the EC Proposal for Common European Sales Law: http://www.iccwbo.org/Advocacy-Codes-and-Rules/Document-centre/2012/ICC-Position-on-the-EC-proposal-for-a-Common-European-Sales-Law/.

119 The United Kingdom, Malta, and Ireland have not ratified the CISG.

120 See: http://www.epln.law.ed.ac.uk/2015/01/07/proposal-for-a-common-european-sales-law-withdrawn/.

merce.[121] The negative reactions of Member States made the viability of the CESL questionable. In June 2015 the European Commission began a public consultation for the development of this new instrument, which cumulated into a proposal for two new directives on ecommerce in December 2015.[122] The PECL are thus serving to facilitate the Europeanisation of contract law. Their main legal and moral authority stems from their contribution to European contract law, in academic writings and in legislation, rather than from their usage by courts to interpret and apply the law.

There are several other private harmonisation initiatives in Europe such as the Trento Common Core Project that charts existing law in Member States to find a common core[123] and the Preliminary Draft for a European Code by the Academy of European Private Lawyers.[124] Currently there are no concrete plans to draw up a European contract law. The plans for this, along with the more ambitious plans for a European Civil Code, have been under discussion as far back as 1989 when the European Parliament initiated a study on this subject.[125] This idea resurfaced on several occasions, yet there are important questions about its feasibility.[126] One of the core areas of an eventual European Civil Code would most likely be contract law as most

121 http://www.europarl.europa.eu/EPRS/EPRS-Briefing-545732-Commissions-2015-work-programme-FINAL.pdf.

122 Public consultation on contract rules for online purchases of digital content and tangible goods

http://ec.europa.eu/justice/newsroom/contract/opinion/150609_en.htm

In December 2015 the Commission adopted two proposals for directives: one on the supply of digital content and one on the online sales of goods.

http://europa.eu/rapid/press-release_IP-15-6264_en.htm

Directive (EU) 2019/770 of the European Parliament and of the Council of 20 May 2019 on certain aspects concerning contracts for the supply of digital content and digital services has now been adopted. The directive for the online sale of goods was expanded to cover the sale of goods in general (so as not to create two distinct regimes):

Directive (EU) 2019/771 of the European Parliament and of the Council of 20 May 2019 on certain aspects concerning contracts for the sale of goods, amending Regulation (EU) 2017/2394 and Directive 2009/22/EC, and repealing Directive 1999/44/EC (Text with EEA relevance.).

123 http://www.common-core.org/.

124 http://www.eurcontrats.eu/site2/.

125 The Private Law Systems in the EU: Discrimination on Grounds of Nationality and the Need for a European Civil Code, Working Paper, Directorate General for Research, p3 http://www.europarl.europa.eu/workingpapers/juri/pdf/103_en.pdf.

126 The question whether the EU has the legal competence to unify contract law falls outside of the scope of this book. For a debate on this see for instance: Esther van Schagen, 'The Proposal for a Common European Sales Law: How its Drafting Process Might Affect the Optional Instrument's Added Value for Contract Parties and its Success' in A Keirse and M Loos (editors), *Alternative Ways to Ius Commune* (Intersentia 2012).

experts are in agreement that more sensitive areas such as family law should be left out, at least initially.[127]

Following the publication of the UPICC and the PECL several other regional initiatives were launched focusing on the development of a restatement of law. These include the Principles of Asian Contract Law (PACL) and the Principles of Latin American Contract Law (PLACL). These instruments are private initiatives, mainly involving scholars from the region. The PLACL were published in 2017. They are developed by a group of legal scholars from various countries in Latin America. The pre-amble of PLACL states the purposes of the PLACL. These are similar to the pre-ambles of the UPICC and the PECL:

Article 1. Scope of application

(1) These Principles set forth general rules applicable to domestic and international contracts, but not to consumer contracts.
(2) These Principles apply when:
   a. The parties subject themselves to them, in part or in full.
   b. The parties have agreed that their contract be governed by general principles of law, the lex mercatoria, or the like.

Article 2. Functions

(1) These Principles apply to interpret international uniform law instruments and domestic law governing the contract.
(2) They may also be used as a model for national or international legislators.[128]

It can be envisaged that the PLALC will take on similar roles as the PECL and UPICC. Their legal authority can be determined in the same way. They can get their authority from their inclusion in the contract, they can develop into trade usages and general principles of law, and they can serve as accepted

127 For a further discussion of this see:

Jan M Smits, 'European Private Law: A Plea for a Spontaneous Legal Order' in Deirdre M Curtin, Jan M Smits et al. (editors), *European Integration and Law: Four Contributions to Celebrate the 25th Anniversary of Maastricht University's Faculty of Law* (Antwerp-Oxford 2006)

Pierre Legrand, 'Against a European Civil Code' (1997) 60 Modern Law Review 44

Hugh Collins, *The European Civil Code: The Way Forward* (Cambridge University Press 2008)

Geraint Howells, European Contract Law Reform and European Consumer Law -- Two Related but Distinct Regimes (2011) 7 European Review of Contract Law 173, 176.

128 Rodrigo Momberg & Stefan Vogenauer, the Principles of Latin American Contract Law: Text, Translation, and Introduction (2018) 23 Uniform Law Review 144, 153/154

This article contains the full draft in Spanish and the translation in English of the PLACL.

regional commercial practice and doctrine if they are applied by the courts, and they can be used as a foundation for the development of both domestic and regional contract law. Like the PECL they have no institutional support, and this could impact their future development. This impacts how well they can be promoted and how they can be updated to ensure they remain current. This could affect how frequently they are used as the PECL demonstrate. As a new instrument the development of the PLACL beyond contractual rules has not yet taken shape and it remains to be seen how they will be applied in practice.

4.7 Conclusion: assessing the role of non-state rules in domestic law and in the contract

This chapter analysed the role of non-state rules as a source of law and their role within the contract. The chapter discussed how the place of non-state rules as a source of domestic law influences their role within the contract. In domestic law there is a clear distinction between the different types of non-state rules. A convention that is ratified and has entered into force becomes part of domestic law. The convention is not the source of legal authority but the domestic law in which it has been incorporated is that source. Trade usages and general principles of law are often considered sources of domestic law. The specific principles and trade usages would differ per jurisdiction, as would their specific role (for instance, whether they are implied terms of the contract or should be explicitly contracted into). Legal doctrine/scholarship can be recognised as a (subsidiary) source in domestic law or at least carry persuasive value. The domestic legal authority of these non-state rules thus comes from their direct standing as a recognised source of (domestic) law.

Codified non-state rules can have legal authority in domestic law if they are equated or assimilated with sources of domestic law. That is to say, if they are seen and applied as trade usages, general principles of law, or legal scholarship/doctrine. They can thus have indirect standing as a source of law in the national legal system through that assimilation.

There are two key measurements in understanding how non-state rules derive their authority from domestic law. The first is whether they have a direct standing as a source of domestic law and the second is whether they can be assimilated or linked with specific sources of law. If a codified non-state rule is used as trade usages or general principles of law if, the codified non-state rule derives its authority from its linkage with these sources of law.

The second issue this chapter focused on is how non-state rules derive their authority from being included in the contract. This is tied with the discussion above on the status of non-state rules in domestic law. Non-state rules can derive additional authority from their inclusion in the contract. They take on different roles and would have the authority of contractual terms, principles through which the contract should be interpreted, or even as governing substantive law, depending on the choices that the parties have made. That legal authority would be restricted to the specific contractual relationship and is dependent upon what is allowed by the domestic law or laws that have jurisdiction over the contract (which could include the lex fori, the lex arbitri, and the lex contractus). This chapter thus concludes that non-state rules, despite originating outside the state, often have a status in domestic law, either through explicit recognition as a source of law or through assimilation with a source of law. Their inclusion in the contract gives non-state rules further authority, but only for that specific contractual relationship.

Together with the previous chapters, this chapter has answered the question of what the nature of non-state rules is. After discussing the definition of non-state rules and their legal authority in chapter 2, examining the wider place of non-state rules in international commercial law in chapter 3, and analysing the shifting role of non-state rules as a source of law in domestic law and in the contract in this current chapter 4 the first part of the book has provided an understanding of how the legal authority of non-state rules can be understood. The quality of non-state rules as a source of law can be asserted in the same ways as a domestic source of law: origin, process through which they were created, reason why they were created, and substance. However, that does not sufficiently clarify their legal authority. For that we must look at what gives non-state rules their legitimacy. This can either be through domestic law (if they are considered a source of law) or through the transnational business community. That legal authority can be understood and measured through the support they have in the business community and through their application in courts and tribunals. It is especially the latter that is important because it is a way to measure and understand both the support that they have from within the business community as well as from legal professionals, courts, and tribunals. Given the importance of application the next two parts of this book focus on issues related to this application.

The next part focuses on when non-state rules can be applied as the governing law of the contract. It analyses this by examining both the agency of the parties and that of the courts to use non-state rules as the applicable law.

Part 2

Application of non-state rules as the governing law of the contract

5 Party autonomy in international commercial contracts

5.1 Introduction

The previous chapters examined the nature of non-state rules and came to the key conclusion that the legal authority of non-state rules can be measured through their application. Therefore, the second and third part of this book concentrate on the application of non-state rules. Part 2 (chapters 5, 6 and 7) examines the agency of the parties and the courts to choose non-state rules as the substantive law governing the contract. This current chapter five focuses on the interaction between private international law and non-state rules through an exploration of party autonomy. It discusses whether a choice for non-state rules would be acceptable and concludes that this is not allowed in most jurisdictions, although they can usually be included by reference in addition to an applicable state law. This is followed by chapter six which focuses on the extension of party autonomy to include non-state rules. Chapter 7 finally examines the role of non-state rules in international arbitration and concludes that overall, in arbitration there is considerably more leeway to use non-state rules. Courts will also enforce arbitral awards based on non-state rules because of the more extensive concept of party autonomy under arbitration laws. Together these chapters lead to an understanding, under which circumstances non-state rules can be applied as the substantive law governing the contract. This discussion ensures first of all clarity around the use of non-state rules as the governing law and how these are applied, and second contributes to the overall discussion in this book through furthering the understanding of the legal authority of non-state rules when these serve as the governing law.

This chapter starts by discussing what it means if non-state rules are applied as the governing law. It then examines the concept of party autonomy with regards to choice of law.[1] The chapter analyses the three main approaches to choice of law clauses in commercial contracts, which are:

- Choice of law is not permitted or severely restricted
- The need for a clear link between the contract and the chosen law.
- Choice of law is permitted even when such a link is absent.

1 This chapter does not discuss choice of jurisdiction as this is less pertinent in a discussion on the application of non-state rules.

The three examples used to examine these three different approaches are Brazil, the USA, and the EU.

5.2 Using non-state rules as the governing law

If non-state rules are applied as the governing law this means that the dispute between the parties is solved using only non-state rules to regulate all the issues. This happens when the parties made a choice of law for non-state rules or if in absence of a choice of law the court or tribunal decides to apply non-state rules as the applicable law.

The application of non-state rules as the substantive governing law delocalises the contract to the transnational sphere. This means that the court or tribunal should not apply non-state rules within the framework of a specific national legal system but as much as possible detach it from domestic law. The court/tribunal faces two significant hurdles in this process: deciding how non-state rules should be interpreted and how any gaps should be filled.

If a court applies a foreign law, it should apply and interpret this, as it would be applied/interpreted in its home jurisdiction. As a consequence, non-state rules should be interpreted as intended by the originators and promulgators (which could be an international organisation, the international business community, or a trade association). This means referring to official commentary, traveaux préparatoires, academic commentary etc. This causes difficulties because courts might not be aware of how the rules should be interpreted, contradictory interpretations exist, or there is no information available. 'Iuris Novit Curia' does not apply to the application of a foreign law (or non-state rules) and courts often interpret the law as they would interpret the lex fori as evidenced by experiences with the CISG.[2]

If the parties have made a choice for arbitration, the tribunal is faced with the same questions on how to interpret non-state rules. First, the arbitral tribunal could be composed of lawyers or other legal experts but that is not necessarily the case. Most arbitration laws/rules allow the parties to choose whomever they want as the arbitrator. This includes business experts and other professionals without a legal background. There is of course again the risk of bias in interpretation; this could be either because of the specific legal system the arbitrator is from, or because they use their own sense of justice to decide what 'the right approach' is to the dispute. The latter is not necessarily a bad thing as one of the reasons the parties might choose arbitration is because they prefer for 'common sense' to prevail over 'legal technicalities.' Arbitrators can and do interpret the law more loosely sometimes to ensure commercial efficiency even if from a legal perspective an interpretation in line with the principles underlying the rules is preferable.

2 John O. Honnold, Documentary History of the Uniform Law for International Sales: The studies, deliberations and decisions that led to the 1980 United Nations Conventions with Introductions and Explanations 1 (1989).

The second issue is how the gaps would be filled. Should the court turn towards the lex fori or towards the putative applicable law? If the parties have not indicated anything in their contract, then the court would apply its own private international law to decide which law to use to fill the gaps. Tribunals have more leeway in deciding which law to apply as they are not held by the same restrictions as courts, who need to follow their private international law. They might refer to *the lex arbitri*, putative applicable law, or another law of their choosing.

If the parties, make a choice for non-state rules as the governing law and do not mention any state law in the contract then ideally the court/tribunal should use the non-state rules to cover every single aspect of the dispute. This would cover the capacity of the parties, validity of the contract, formation and execution of the contract, and remedies among other issues.

This is not necessarily possible. The lex mercatoria, general principles of law, and trade usages are not complete, are not written down, and are flexible and subject to conflicting opinions on interpretation. The gaps would need to be filled by referring to a substantive law, other non-state rules (like the UPICC), or the courts/tribunal's owns sense of justice. The latter is problematic as it is unpredictable but could very well field acceptable dispute resolutions, especially in the case of arbitration where the procedure is less judicial.

The emergence of codified non-state rules provides a partial solution. The CISG is a convention and was not designed to function as a standalone instrument but was always to be embedded in a national law. The CISG covers formation of the contract, obligations of the buyer and seller, performance and non-performance, and remedies, and also contains general principles of interpretation. However, it does not deal with several key issues including validity of contract and capacity of the parties. Therefore, applying the CISG or similar conventions as the sole applicable law would be difficult.

Incoterms, the UCP, and other similar trade terms only cover part of the contract and whilst they play an important role and are often included in contracts, they would not be able to fulfil the role of governing law because of their limited scope.

The most promising option would thus be the restatements of law, the UNIDROIT Principles or one of the regional restatements, the PECL or the PLACL. These are mostly complete, come with extensive commentary, and form a coherent whole. The UNIDROIT Principles having been tested the most thoroughly in practice and having been updated already three times since their initial publication and are the most complete instrument. There are still several issues that are not covered of which capacity is the most important.[3] The UPICC do cover general contract law principles, formation of the contract including validity, agency, third party rights, assignment, performance, non-performance, limitations, long-term contracts, multi-party contracts, and

3 UNIDROIT Principles, chapter 3 validity, section 1: general provisions article 3.1.1.

remedies.[4] This means that they form a (almost) complete contract law instrument that can be applied and interpreted without reference to national law.

If the UPICC are applied in arbitration, then the procedure becomes almost completely detached from any jurisdiction. Whilst the UPICC cover most issues that can arise in a dispute, the UNILEX database shows that in most of the cases where the UPICC are applied as the governing law, this is in conjunction with an applicable domestic law, even if only as a fall-back option.[5] The database also contains examples of where it seems that the UPICC are applied as the sole governing law.[6] It is thus possible to solve a dispute using non-state rules without needing to refer to a domestic law.[7]

5.3 Choice of law in international commercial contracts

Party autonomy can facilitate economic transactions as it gives the parties to the contract a measure of control and therefore enhances predictability and certainty as to the consequences of the contractual relationship. This makes trading abroad more accessible and this can be positive for economic growth.

A long historical overview of party autonomy falls beyond the remit of this chapter so a couple of points will suffice.[8] One of the earliest references to the modern concept of party autonomy was in 16th century France, where the parliamentary lawyer, Charles Dumoulin was consulted by Mr and Mrs de Ganay who wished to know the law applicable to their matrimonial regime. The couple possessed properties in both Paris and in the Bourgogne, which had different laws at the time. In his response Dumoulin stated that marriage is a contract and that the matrimonial regime is found by looking at the intentions of the parties. The parties make a tacit choice for the applicable law to their marriage and this choice can be deducted by looking at the

4 UNIDROIT Principles of International Commercial Contracts 2016.

5 See for instance: ICC International Court of Arbitration 18795 where the tribunal applied the UPICC 'supplemented if necessary, by the law of country x' and International Arbitration Court of the Chamber of Commerce and Industry of the Russian Federation 233/2012 where the UPICC were applied supplemented by Russian law.

6 See for instance: Centro de Arbitraje de México (CAM) 30-11-2006 where the parties agreed for the UPICC to be applied and ICC International Court of Arbitration 12889 where the contract was silent on the applicable law and the tribunal proposed the UPICC which the parties accepted.

7 Although non-state rules would of course give way to mandatory laws and international public policy (in the same way as a foreign domestic law would.).

8 For a more thorough historical exposé see for instance:

Veronique Ranouil, *L'Autonomie de la Volonté : Naissance et Evolution d'un Concept* (Presses Universitaires de France 1980)

Matthias Lehmann, 'Liberating the Individual from Battles between States: Justifying Party Autonomy in Conflict of Laws' (2008) 41 Vanderbilt Journal of Transnational Law 381

Hessel E Yntema, 'Autonomy' in Choice of Law' (1952) 1 The American Journal of Comparative Law 341

Henri Battifol, *Les Conflits de Lois en Matière des Contrats* (Librairie du Recueil Sirey 1938).

first marital residence. Dumoulin thus advanced the theory that a contract can be submitted to another law than the law of the place where the contract was concluded, and that the intentions of the parties (explicit or implied) should be the point of departure to find the applicable law to the contract.[9] The Parisian parliament agreed with this hypothesis, and consequently the custom of Paris where the couple established themselves upon getting married was held to be the applicable law.

In the common law party autonomy was considered by Lord Mansfield in the 18th century: '*The general rule established ex comitate et jure gentium is, that the place where the contract is made, and not where the action is brought, is to be considered in expounding and enforcing the contract. But this rule admits of an exception where the parties (at the time of making the contract) had a view to a different kingdom.*'[10] This general rule is known as the vested rights theory: that a state should have a say over all that takes place on its territory. Therefore, the lex loci contractus should be the applicable law. The second point is that parties can select a different applicable law if that is their wish. In the US, in the case of *Wayman v Southard*, the Supreme Court expressed in 1825 that '*in every forum a contract is governed by the law with a view to which it was made.*'[11]

The tendency of the courts in the US, England, and France was to recognise party autonomy, although the concept was contested at times.[12] In the US Joseph Beale wrote: '*the applicable law is a matter of state sovereignty and [...] it is thus beyond reach of the parties.*'[13] Yet, in *Pritchard v Norton* the Supreme Court expressed that: '*the laws we are in search of... is that which the parties have, either expressly or presumptively, incorporated into their contract as constituting its obligation.*'[14] The gap between courts (which generally accepted choice of law clauses) and scholars (who were more doubtful of whether these should be allowed) led to the Restatement (First) of the Conflicts of Law (1934) being silent on the issue.[15] This can, at least partly, be ascribed to the influence of Joseph Beale on the Restatement (First) for

9 See for more on this case: Georges R Delaume, 'L'Autonomie de la Volonté en Droit International Privé' (1950) 39 Revue Critique de Droit International Privé 321.

10 *Robinson v. Bland* W. Bl. 234, 96 E.R. 129 (1760).

11 *Wayman v. Southard* 10 Wheat. (23 U.S.) 1 (1825)
'*in every forum a contract is governed by the law with a view to which it was made*'
And later confirming this: *Pritchard v Norton* 106 U.S. 1224 (1882).

12 Mathias Reimann, 'Savigny's Triumph? Choice of Law in Contracts Cases at the Close of the Twentieth Century' (1998–1999) 39 Virginia Journal of International Law 571, 575.

13 Joseph H Beale, *A Treatise on the Conflicts of Laws Volume 2: Choice of Law* (Baker, Voorhis & Co 1935) 1079/1080
See also Joseph H Beale, 'What Law Governs the Validity of a Contract?' (1910) 23 Harvard Law Review 260 for a further treatment of this issue
Joseph Beale was a proponent of the vested rights doctrine. He also noted that allowing party autonomy would decrease certainty for the parties because they could never be sure whether on grounds of public policy their choice would be refused.

14 *Pritchard v Norton* 106 U.S. 1224 (1882).

15 Mathias Reimann, 'Savigny's Triumph? Choice of Law in Contracts Cases at the Close of the Twentieth Century' (1998–1999) 39 Virginia Journal of International Law 571, 575.

which he was the Chief Reporter.[16] Taking into account the case law of the US Supreme Court it is evident that courts endorsed the principle of party autonomy.[17] On the issue of party autonomy there was thus a gap between theory and practice. Practice was more likely to subscribe to party autonomy than theory where there were severe differences of opinion.[18] In the end practice prevailed and when the Restatement (Second) of the Conflicts of Law was published in 1971 it recognised the parties' freedom to choose the applicable law.[19]

In the UK the concept of party autonomy developed following Lord Mansfield's initial considerations. This came to be known as the proper law of the contract doctrine.[20] There are three stages to this process whereby the court establishes first whether the parties have made an express choice of law, second the court looks at whether there is an implied choice of law, and only when no choice is made the court establishes the applicable law.[21] In 1937 Lord Atkin said: *'the proper law is the law which the parties intended to apply'*[22] In 1939 this was confirmed by Lord Wright under the caveat that the choice (express or implied) is made in good faith and should not be made to avoid public policy.[23]

In France the idea of party autonomy that started with Dumoulin developed relatively unchallenged. Although the Code Napoleon did not address the issue of party autonomy directly, courts continued to affirm the principle.[24] In 1910 the Cour de Cassation affirmed party autonomy.[25] In a dispute

16 Symeon C Symeonides, 'Party Autonomy in International Contracts and the Multiple Ways of Slicing the Apple' (2014) 39 Brooklyn Journal of International Law 1123, 1125 (who notes that others resisted Beale's view upon this issue)
Joseph H Beale, 'What Law Governs the Validity of a Contract?' (1910) 23 Harvard Law Review 260.

17 See for instance Mathias Reimann, 'Savigny's Triumph? Choice of Law in Contracts Cases at the Close of the Twentieth Century' (1998–1999) 39 Virginia Journal of International Law 571.

18 Hessel E Yntema, 'Autonomy' in Choice of Law' (1952) 1 The American Journal of Comparative Law 341.

19 Restatement (Second) of Conflict of Laws s 187 http://www.kentlaw.edu/perritt/conflicts/rest187.html.

20 Chris M V Clarkson and Jonathan Hill, *Jaffey on the Conflicts of Laws* (Second Edition, Oxford University Press 2002) 198
Lord Mansfield is also credited with beginning the process of absorbing the lex mercatoria into the common law through his qualification of trade customs as legal rules (see for this Filip de Ly, *International Business Law and Lex Mercatoria* (T.M.C Asser Instituut 1992) 17).

21 Chris M V Clarkson and Jonathan Hill, *Jaffey on the Conflicts of Laws* (Second Edition, Oxford University Press 2002) 198.

22 *R. v. International Trustee for the Protection of Bondholders Aktiengesellschaft* [1937] A.C. 500

23 *Vita Food Products, Inc. v. Unus* Shipping Co., Ltd. [1939] A.C. 277.

24 Private international law is not extensively codified in French law. Articles 3, 4 and 5 of the Civil Code give some general principles to the courts. Article 3 covers the applicable law to immovable property and the applicable law to French citizens with regards to personal status and covers applicability of mandatory laws. Article 4 states that even when the law is silence the judge must still decide on the issue whereas article 5 prohibits the judge to deduct general principles from individual cases.

25 *Arrêt American Trading Company*, Cour de Cassation, Chambre Civil, 5 Décembre 1910, Revue Droit International, 1911, 395.

regarding spoiled merchandise during a maritime transport one of the questions raised was that of the applicable law. The court stated that the applicable law to contracts between parties of different nationalities is the law of the place where the contract is concluded *unless the parties have chosen a different law*.[26] In 1959 the Cour de Cassation affirmed again that the applicable law is the one the parties choose.[27] Thus the dominant view in both Europe and the US favours party autonomy.[28]

Choice of law clauses are not accepted to the same degree in all jurisdictions. In Latin America theories such as the vested rights doctrine and territorialism were persuasive, especially through the influence of scholars who were involved in drafting private international law legislation.[29] Some Latin American states still have a limited recognition of party autonomy.[30]

Criticism levelled against party autonomy mainly concerns the protection of parties, the state, or society. There can be a perceived clash between party autonomy and fundamental values such as access to justice and protection of

26 *'Attendu, d'autre part, que la loi applicable aux contrats, soit en ce qui concerne leur formation, soit quant à leurs effets et conditions, est celle que les parties ont adoptée ; que si, entre personnes de nationalités différentes, la loi du lieu où le contrat est intervenu est en principe celle à laquelle il faut s'attacher, ce n'est donc qu'autant que les contractants n'ont pas manifesté une volonté contraire ; que non seulement cette manifestation peut être expresse, mais qu'elle peut s'induire des faits et circonstances de la cause, ainsi que des termes du contrat .'*

27 *'La loi applicable aux contrats est celle que les parties ont adoptée : à défaut de la déclaration expresse de leur part, il appartient aux juges du fond de rechercher d'après l'économie de la convention et les circonstances de la cause, quelle est la loi qui doit réagir les rapports des contractants.'*

Arrêt Fourrures Renel, Cour de Cassation, Chambre Civil, 6 Juillet 1959,

Note Henri Battifol, Revue Critique du Droit International Privé [1959] 708

28 Giesela Rühl, 'Party Autonomy in the Private International Law of Contracts: Transatlantic Convergence and Economic Efficiency' (2007) 3 Comparative Research in Law & Political Economy Research Paper, 4

http://digitalcommons.osgoode.yorku.ca/clpe/227

See also: Russell J Weintraub, 'Functional Developments in Choice of Law for Contracts' (1984) 187 Recueil des Cours Académie du Droit International 271

29 Maria Mercedes Albornoz, 'Choice of Law in International Contracts in Latin American Systems' (2010) 6 Journal of Private International Law 23, 49.

30 Argentina (although caselaw has widened the acceptance of party autonomy), Bolivia, Brazil, El Salvador, Honduras, Nicaragua, and Uruguay have restricted party autonomy to a degree

(Lauro Gama Jr, 'Prospects for the UNIDROIT Principles in Brazil' (2011) 16 Uniform Law Review 613

Lauro da Gama e Souza Jr. 'The UNIDROIT Principles of International Commercial Contracts and their Applicability in the MERCOSUR Countries' (2012) 36 Revue Juridique Thémis 375)

In other Latin American countries party autonomy is accepted without restrictions. For instance, Paraguay which has recently adopted The Hague Principles on Choice of Law (this will be discussed further on in the chapter) and Venezuela which has incorporated provisions from the *Inter-American Convention on the Law Applicable to International Contracts* into its 1998 Private International Law Act.

the weaker party.[31] The degree to which party autonomy should be extended is questioned. Symeonides writes that in his analysis of American choice-of-law cases, which he has conducted for over 30 years, he has come across many cases where one of the parties uses choice of law to the detriment of the other party.[32] An example of how the rights of the parties can be negatively affected are cases where one of the parties was not part of the original contract, such as when a bill of lading (containing a choice of law clause) is sold on to a third party that is now bound by a choice of law that he had no say in and may not protect his rights sufficiently.[33] In developing states there is concern that unrestricted party autonomy can give multinational companies further influence to the detriment of smaller local businesses.[34] Multinationals can impose a choice of law and jurisdiction clause on weaker parties and as such exclude the developing state where the contract is performed from the judicial process. As it is more expensive to present a case in a foreign forum and to deal with an unfamiliar law (additional legal costs, translation costs etc.) this can be detrimental for smaller local businesses as it limits their access to justice.

Muir Watt discusses that only private interests are promoted when a case is put before a forum that has no connection to the case and is governed by a law, which is not connected to either the contract or the forum. This forum would be less concerned with protecting societal interest than a forum, which has a substantive connection to the case.[35] It limits the control the state has over activities taking place on its territory, including protecting local companies, employment, and wider societal issues such as environmental protection. Thus, extensive party autonomy can negatively affect the interests of society, which is why states curb the effects through (international) public policy and mandatory laws.

Party autonomy is directly linked to freedom of contract: as the parties shape the contract to their intentions they choose the applicable law to fit these intentions.[36] Party autonomy comes from the freedom of the parties to

31 Cecilia Fresnedo de Aguirre, 'Party Autonomy - A Blank Cheque?' (2012) 17 Uniform Law Review 655, 658.

32 Symeon C Symeonides, 'The Hague Principles on Choice of Law for International Contracts: Some Preliminary Comments' (2013) 61 American Journal of Comparative Law 873, 878

These cases do not just include B2B contracts, but also B2C contracts.

33 Horatia Muir Watt, 'Party Autonomy in international contracts: from the making of a myth to the requirements of global governance' (2010) 6 European Review of Contract Law 250, 275.

34 Ingeborg Schwenzer, and Pascal Hachem, 'The CISG- Successes and Pitfalls' (2009) 57 The American Journal of Comparative Law 457, 464.

35 Horatia Muir Watt, 'Party Autonomy in international contracts: from the making of a myth to the requirements of global governance' (2010) 6 European Review of Contract Law 250, 275.

36 Matthias Lehmann, 'Liberating the Individual from Battles between States: Justifying Party Autonomy in Conflict of Laws' (2008) 41 Vanderbilt Journal of Transnational Law 381, 415.

contract, which also gives the parties the freedom to localise their contract where they wish.[37] As such party autonomy is directly connected to that cornerstone of contract law: freedom of contract, where the parties are best situated to understand which law (and forum) will form the best legal framework for their contractual relationship.

5.4 Restricted party autonomy

Brazil is an example of a country with a globalised economy where choice of law clauses are regularly not enforced.[38] Private international law in Brazil can be categorised as (more) rigid (than European or American conflicts of law)[39] and it restricts the autonomy of the parties in court litigation.[40]

The 1942 Introduction to the Civil Code (which regulates the application and interpretation of the law) contains the relevant private international law articles.[41] Article 9 discusses the applicable law. The main rule is that the applicable law is the lex loci contractus or when the contract is concluded by correspondence, the law of the residence of the offeror. The exception is when the obligation is to be executed in Brazil, as then Brazilian law is the applicable law.[42] Brazilian private international law differs from European and US private international law as the latter two use various points of connection to determine the applicable law to the contract (in the absence of the choice of the parties), whereas Brazilian law primarily relies on the lex loci contractus. The law is silent on what happens when the parties include a choice of law clause in their contract. The previous Introduction, which dates from 1916 stated that the lex loci contractus was the applicable law *unless the parties made a different choice*.[43] It should be noted that despite

37 Henri Battifol, *Les Conflits de Lois en Matière des Contrats* (Librairie du Recueil Sirey 1938).

38 Dana Stringer, 'Choice of Law and Choice of Forum in Brazilian International Commercial Contracts: Party Autonomy, International Jurisdiction and the Emerging Third Way' (2005–2006) 44 Columbia Journal of Transnational Law 959.

39 Carmen Tiburcio, 'Private International Law in Brazil: A Brief Overview' (2013) 1 Panorama of Brazilian Law 11, 37.

40 Brazil is a signatory of the *New York Convention of 1958 on Recognition and Enforcement of Arbitral Awards. The Brazilian Arbitration Act* also allows free choice-of-law (Article 2, §1 and §2). The comments on party autonomy in Brazil should therefore be read strictly in the context of court litigation.

41 *Lei de Introdução às Normas do Direito Brasileiro/ decreto-lei* (n. 4657/42).

42 The original text in Portuguese reads:

Art. 9o Para qualificar e reger as obrigações, aplicar-se-á a lei do país em que se constituirem.

§ 1o Destinando-se a obrigação a ser executada no Brasil e dependendo de forma essencial, será esta observada, admitidas as peculiaridades da lei estrangeira quanto aos requisitos extrínsecos do ato.

§ 2o A obrigação resultante do contrato reputa-se constituido no lugar em que residir o proponente.

43 Nadia de Araujo. Fabiola I Guedes de C. Saldanha, 'Recent Developments and Current Trends on Brazilian Private International Law Concerning International Contracts' (2013) 1 Panorama of Brazilian Law 73, 77.

this liberal choice of words there were also many exceptions when Brazilian law would be applicable regardless of the law chosen by the parties.[44] Yet it does mean that the general principle of party autonomy with regards to choice of law was recognised in Brazilian law prior to 1942.

The change in the new Introduction created uncertainty as to the autonomy of the parties. Some experts argue that the absence of this principle from the Introduction means that choice of law is no longer recognised because it was omitted from the legislation whilst others state that party autonomy is still possible if the concept is recognised under the lex loci contractus, and yet others have argued that the omission in the law does not mean that choice of law clauses are not allowed because it is not expressly disallowed either.[45] These commentators point to the continuation of the law and that the principles underlying the law stay the same unless these are expressly changed and that since choice of law was recognised in the 1916 Introduction it still stands as the 1942 law does not indicate that this has changed.[46] The latter seems to be the minority opinion.[47] Courts generally react with a restrictive interpretation and often do not uphold choice of law clauses.[48] There is no real consensus as there are also cases where the choice of the parties was upheld.[49] Courts seem to favour the application of Brazilian law and maximise the use of the public policy exception in their application of private international law.[50] An important and pragmatic reason for falling back on Brazilian law is an overburdened judicial system that does not allow the courts much time for individual cases and of course applying the lex fori saves the court time.[51]

The new Brazilian Civil Procedural Code allows for choice of forum clauses in international contracts but does not discuss choice of law clauses.[52] Brazil has signed the Inter-American Convention on the Law Applicable to International Contracts, which permits the parties to choose the applicable law, but it has not ratified the convention. The law was updated in the early

44 Ibid.

45 Ibid, 78.

46 Carmen Tiburcio, 'Private International Law in Brazil: A Brief Overview' (2013) 1 Panorama of Brazilian Law 11, 23.

47 Ibid.

48 Dana Stringer, 'Choice of Law and Choice of Forum in Brazilian International Commercial Contracts: Party Autonomy, International Jurisdiction and the Emerging Third Way' (2005–2006) 44 Columbia Journal of Transnational Law 959, 973.

49 Nadia de Araujo and Fabiola I Guedes de C. Saldanha, 'Recent Developments and Current Trends on Brazilian Private International Law Concerning International Contracts' (2013) 1 Panorama of Brazilian Law 73, 80.

50 Dana Stringer, 'Choice of Law and Choice of Forum in Brazilian International Commercial Contracts: Party Autonomy, International Jurisdiction and the Emerging Third Way' (2005–2006) 44 Columbia Journal of Transnational Law 959,

51 Maria Mercedes Albornoz, 'Choice of Law in International Contracts in Latin American Systems' (2010) 6 Journal of Private International Law 23, 48.

52 For the full text see: http://www.planalto.gov.br/ccivil_03/_Ato2015-2018/2015/Lei/L13105.htm

2000s yet the articles on private international law were not changed.[53] This indicates that enlarging choice of law is currently not a priority.

Among Brazilian scholars there seems to be a consensus that private international law should be updated to expressly allow for choice of law in litigation.[54] Restrictions on party autonomy have a negative effect on the economy as it raises contracting costs substantially.[55] In the area of sale of goods contracts uncertainty is diminished with the 2014 entry into force of the CISG in Brazil as this raises predictability on the substance of the law although of course that does not enhance the agency of the parties to choose the applicable law.[56] Given the restrictions placed on party autonomy in general it is not surprising that in Brazilian private international law a choice of law for non-state rules would not be acceptable outside of arbitration.[57]

5.5 A substantive connection between the applicable law and the contract

Other jurisdictions allow for choice of law clauses but impose certain restrictions on these. Most states in the US for instance restrict the choice to a law, which has a substantive connection with the contract. Private international law in the US is regulated at state level and not at federal level.[58] It should be taken into account, that conflicts of law legislation cover interstate contracts as well as international contracts. The main focus within legislation and debate

53 Lauro da Gama e Souza Jr, 'the UNIDROIT Principles of International Commercial Contracts and their Applicability in the MERCOSUR Countries' (2012) 36 Revue Juridique Thémis 375, 416.

54 Ibid, 418.

55 Dana Stringer, 'Choice of Law and Choice of Forum in Brazilian International Commercial Contracts: Party Autonomy, International Jurisdiction and the Emerging Third Way' (2005–2006) 44 Columbia Journal of Transnational Law 959, 983.

56 See for more on this: Iacyr de Aguilar Viera, 'The CISG and Party Autonomy in Brazilian International Contract Law' (2013) 1 Panorama of Brazilian Law 173.

57 Lauro Game Jr, 'Prospects for the UNIDROIT Principles in Brazil' (2011) 16 Uniform Law Review 613, 641

The author also discusses that in arbitration this would be different as a choice for non-state rules would be acceptable per the *Brazilian Arbitration Act*

(Article 2: At the parties' discretion arbitration may be in law or equity. §1 – The parties may freely choose the rules of law applicable in the arbitration, as long as their choice does not violate good morals and public policy.

§2 – The parties may also stipulate that the arbitration shall be conducted under general principles of law, customs, usages and the rules of international trade.).

58 Through the Commerce Clause (Article 1, Section 8. Clause 3 of the US Constitution) Congress has power to '*regulate commerce with foreign Nations, and among the several states, and with the Indian Tribes.*' Congress does not attempt to regulate every aspect of international commerce. Federal courts sometimes interpret the Clause restrictively although at other times their interpretation is more far-reaching. This is often depending on the current constitution of the Supreme Court. Although this seldom has effect on private international law aspects it should still be kept in mind that federal law plays a key part in international commerce (for instance, trough the ratification of conventions.)

is on interstate conflicts of law more than on international disputes.[59]As space precludes discussing each individual state's private international law this section focuses on two pieces of legislation: The Restatement (Second) of the Conflicts of Law and the Uniform Commercial Code.

The Restatement (Second) of the Conflicts of Law was published in 1971 by ALI. Restatements are codifications of general legal principles that are deducted from case law. They try to establish the common denominators in case law to understand how courts approach and interpret the law. They aim to provide a true description of the current state of the law, but they also contain prescriptive elements as they indicate what direction the law should take. Restatements are not binding on the courts, but they are considered highly authoritative. According to the ALI they are more than a treatise and less than a code.[60] Twenty-three states have adopted legislation that has the same approach as the Restatement (Second) of the Conflicts of Law.[61] Therefore, the Restatement is an important document for understanding how party autonomy is approached in the US. In the Restatement (Second)

59 Mathias Reimann, 'Parochialism in American Conflicts Law' (2001) 49 American Journal of Comparative Law 369, 388.

60 As first stated by Benjamin Cardozo *The Growth of Law* (Yale University Press 1924) p 9.

61 States that follow the Restatement (Second) on choice of law: Alaska, Arizona, Colorado, Connecticut, Delaware, Idaho, Illinois, Iowa, Kentucky, Maine, Michigan, Mississippi, Missouri, Montana, Nebraska, New Hampshire, Ohio, South Dakota, Texas, Utah, Vermont, Washington, West Virginia.

12 other states follow a traditional approach (Alabama, Florida, Georgia, Kansas, Maryland, New Mexico, Oklahoma, Rhode island, Sour Carolina, Tennessee, Virginia, and Wyoming), 4 states follow the significant contacts approach (Arkansas, Indiana, Nevada, North Carolina), 2 states follow the better law approach (Michigan and Wisconsin), and the remaining states follow the combined modern approach (California, District of Colombia, Hawaii, Louisiana, Massachusetts, New Jersey, New York, North Dakota, Oregon, and Pennsylvania.)

See for this: Symeon C Symeonides, 'Choice of Law in the American Courts in 2015: Twenty-Ninth Annual Survey' (2016) 64 American Journal of Comparative Law,

http://papers.ssrn.com/sol3/papers.cfm?abstract_id=2709668

Note that the above is valid for choice of law in contracts and not necessarily in other legal matters like tort.

Another approach does not necessarily mean that party autonomy is treated differently. The law of New York for instance endorses party autonomy if there is a substantial relationship with the chosen law (unless the contract is worth more than $250,000 as in that case there is no need for a substantial relationship). Therefore, the approach is similar to that of the Restatement.

See *New York Law of General Obligations section 5-1401.*

Although states follow certain approaches to conflicts of law it is not so that in practice they always clearly adhere to that method:

Symeonides notes that conflicts of law cases often seem isolated from one another and that it is not always easy to find the methodological underlying principles in individual cases.

Symeon C Symeonides, 'The Choice-of-Law Revolution Fifty Years after Currie: An End and a Beginning' (2015) 2 University of Illinois Law Review 1847

Symeon C Symeonides, 'Choice of Law in the American Courts in 2019: Thirty-Third Annual Survey' (2020) 68 American Journal of Comparative Law,

https://papers.ssrn.com/sol3/papers.cfm?abstract_id=3511163.

the approach to party autonomy in contracts (both international and inter-state) can be found in §187:

(1) The law of the state chosen by the parties to govern their contractual rights and duties will be applied if the particular issue is one which the parties could have resolved by an explicit provision in their agreement directed to that issue.

(2) The law of the state chosen by the parties to govern their contractual rights and duties will be applied, even if the particular issue is one which the parties could not have resolved by an explicit provision in their agreement directed to that issue, unless either

   a. The chosen state has no substantial relationship to the parties or the transaction and there is no other reasonable basis for the parties' choice, or
   b. Application of the law of the chosen state would be contrary to a fundamental policy of a state which has a materially greater interest than the chosen state in the determination of the particular issue and which, under the rule of § 188, would be the state of the applicable law in the absence of an effective choice of law by the parties.

A choice of law is thus accepted if there is a substantial relationship between the law and the contract. This seems to pose stringent restrictions on choice of law, but the official commentary discusses that relationship should be interpreted in a broad manner and with respect for the will of the parties: *'Contracts are entered into for serious purposes and rarely, if ever, will the parties choose a law without good reason for doing so.'*[62] Thus, courts should give serious consideration to the chosen law even when the connection is not immediately obvious.

A substantial relationship can be any reasonable basis underlying the choice. This includes:

- Experience with this type of case
- Underdeveloped law in other states that have a more substantial relation with the contract
- More comprehensive law in a particular state
- Lex loci contractus
- Place of performance
- Place of domicile of one of the parties
- Place of incorporation of one of the parties
- Principal place of business of one of the parties

This indicates willingness towards accepting choice of law clauses even when the connection with the contract is not straightforward.

62 http://www.kentlaw.edu/perritt/conflicts/rest187.html.

The leading cases point to a choice being honoured even when the relation between the contract and the choice of law is not immediately obvious. In *Radioactive, J.V v. Manson* it was held that the law of New York had sufficient connections with the contract despite neither party being based there and the contract not being concluded or executed there: '*New York federal and state courts have significant experience with music industry contracts, and the parties wanted to avail themselves of that experience by selecting a New York forum and New York law.*'[63] Therefore, the expertise of the law of New York in the music industry was deemed to be a substantial enough relationship.

In *Allstate Insurance Co. v. Hague*, the Supreme Court stated that '*for a state's substantive law to be selected in a constitutionally permissible manner, that state must have a significant contact or significant aggregation of contacts, creating state interests, such that the choice of its law is neither arbitrary nor fundamentally unfair.*'[64] The substantial relationship does restrict the options of the parties '*to reduce [...] insecurity*'[65] and could prevent the choice for a neutral law. Practice seems to suggest that a choice for a neutral law could be respected under certain circumstances if the parties can make clear what the relationship is, yet they cannot be certain their choice will be honoured.

Further limits are placed by '*the fundamental policy of a state which has a materially greater interest than the chosen state and which would be the state of the applicable law in the absence of choice of law by the parties.*'[66] Under the Restatement (Second) there are hence two questions for the court to consider when confronted with a choice of law clause: first of all, whether there is a substantial relationship with the chosen law, and second whether there is a fundamental policy of the otherwise applicable law that bears a closer relationship to the contract. Professor Symeonides conducts an annual survey into American choice of law cases. His conclusion, based on this long-standing work, is that in most cases when a choice of law clause is not honoured the reason is the public policy exception and not the absence of a substantial

63 *Radioactive, J.V, v Manson*, 153 F. Supp. 2d 462 (S.D.N.Y 2001).

64 *Allstate Insurance Co. v. Hague*, 449 U.S. 302,312–13 (1981)

Some American states' choice of law legislations also contain provisions where a substantial relationship to the chosen law is not required. The need for this substantial relationship is therefore not absolute.

65 Charles R Calleros, 'Towards Harmonization and Certainty in Choice of Law Rules for International Contracts: Should the U.S. Adopt the Equivalent of Rome I?' (2010) 28 Wisconsin International Law Journal 639, 666.

66 *§ 187. Law of the State Chosen by the Parties.*

relationship.[67] The main reasons for this are most likely a mix between the wide interpretation of the substantial relationship criterion and that lawyers already premeditate this criterion when advising clients on choice of law.[68] Third, in many cases parties would most likely wish to select a law that is connected to the case anyway as often this is the most practical choice.

Could party autonomy under the Restatement (Second) be extended to include non-state rules? The aforementioned article §187 states: *(1) The law of the state chosen by the parties to govern their contractual rights and duties will be applied if the particular issue is one which the parties could have resolved by an explicit provision in their agreement directed to that issue.* The wording law of the state is used throughout the article. State can refer to a foreign state or to a US state, but would not refer to rules that are emitted by an entity, which is not a state.

Comment C on subsection 1 reads: *'In the alternative, they may incorporate into the contract by reference extrinsic material which may, among other things, be the provisions of some foreign law.'* The Reporter's Notes to the Restatement provide some clarity on what this extrinsic material could be: *'may also stipulate for the application of trade association rules or well-known*

67 See for instance Symeon C. Symeonides, 'Choice of Law in the American Courts in 1996: Tenth Annual Survey' (1997) 45 American Journal of Comparative Law 447 where he reported that out of 100 cases the choice of law was not enforced in only six of these. In all six cases this was for public policy reasons.

For more recent examples see:

Symeon C. Symeonides, 'Choice of Law in the American Courts in 2013: Twenty-Seventh Annual Survey' (2014) 62 American Journal of Comparative Law 223 analysed several cases where the choice of law clause was not upheld by the court. Only in one of the cases discussed did the absence of a substantial relationship play a part in the decision. In the other cases the reason was the fundamental policy exception.

Symeon C. Symeonides, 'Choice of Law in the American Courts in 2014: Twenty-Eight Annual Survey' (2015) 63 American Journal of Comparative Law 299

Again, in the cases discussed the reasons for not enforcing a choice of law clause is fundamental public policy.

As an example, one of the cases discussed in the survey is *Exxon Mobil Corp. v. Drennen 2014 WL 4782974 (Tex. 2014).* This concerned a choice of law clause in an employment contract for New York law. The Texas Supreme Court reinforced the choice and noted that even if New York did not have a substantial relationship to the contract there was a reasonable basis for the choice because: *(1) New York had a well-developed body of law regarding employee stock and incentive programs and securities-related transactions; and (2) the choice of New York law assured a uniform treatment of Exxon's employee incentive programs in all states.*

68 An example of where choice of law was not accepted:

Curtis 1000, Inc. v. Suess 24 F.3d 941 (7th Cir. 1994), where in an employment contract a choice for Delaware law was not upheld by the Illinois Court because of the absence of a sufficient connection with the state of Delaware (the only connection was that the company was incorporated in Delaware)

(However other courts have enforced choice of law clauses whereby the incorporation of a company in a given state was sufficient evidence of a substantial relationship.)

commercial customs.'[69] This thus allows reference to non-state rules, which can be incorporated as contractual rules for any non-mandatory provisions.

In absence of a choice of law clause §188 states that '*the applicable law is the local law of the state which, with respect to that issue, has the most significant relationship to the transaction and the parties…*'[70] As the text clearly refers to state law it would be difficult to see how this could lead to the application of non-state rules. This becomes more evident when one reviews the points of contact to take into account to establish the most significant relationship. These points of contacts are: the place of contracting, the place of negotiation, the place of performance, the location of the subject matter of the contract, and the domicile, residence, nationality, place of incorporation, and place of business of the parties.[71] These all refer to a geographical place and thus all point to the law of a territorial entity. The same is true for special type contracts where the points of contact that determine the most significant relationship are all geographical.[72]

Work has now started on the Restatement (Third) on the Conflicts of Law.[73] The Restatement (Second) has little specific content on international conflicts of law situations, which can be explained by the insularity of American conflicts of law theories in the 60s and 70s as well as by a lack of international cases at the time.[74] It is likely that the new Restatement will consider international contracts in more depth because of the increase in international cases and trade. This could include further considerations of non-state rules as a choice of law.

69 Reporter's Notes Subsection 1, article 187.

70 §188 Law governing in absence of effective choice by the parties http://www.kentlaw.edu/perritt/conflicts/rest188.html

71 §188 Law governing in absence of effective choice by the parties http://www.kentlaw.edu/perritt/conflicts/rest188.html.

72 § 189-90 Land contracts-law of site.
http://www.kentlaw.edu/perritt/conflicts/rest189.html
§ 191 Contracts to sell interests in chattels-the place of delivery.
http://www.kentlaw.edu/perritt/conflicts/rest191.html
§ 192 Life insurance contracts-the domicile of the insured.
http://msgre2.people.wm.edu/2ndRestatement.html
§ 193Contracts of fire, surety, or casualty insurance-the principal location of the insured. http://www.kentlaw.edu/perritt/conflicts/rest193.html
§ 194Contracts of surety ship-the law governing the principal obligation. http://www.kentlaw.edu/perritt/conflicts/rest194.html
§ 195Contracts for the repayment of money-the place of repayment. http://www.kentlaw.edu/perritt/conflicts/rest195.html
§ 196 Contracts for the rendition of services-the place where the major portion of the services are to be rendered. http://msgre2.people.wm.edu/2ndRestatement.html
§ 197Contracts for transportation-place of departure or dispatch. http://www.kentlaw.edu/perritt/conflicts/rest197.html.

73 For the current status see: https://www.ali.org/projects/show/conflict-laws/.

74 Symeon C Symeonides, 'The Choice-of-Law Revolution Fifty Years after Currie: An End and a Beginning' (2015) 2 University of Illinois Law Review 1847, 1919.

NCCUSL and ALI first published the Uniform Commercial Code in 1952. The UCC is a model law that can be adopted by state legislators.[75] A permanent editorial board regularly proposes updates and publishes official comments on application and interpretation. The UCC consists mainly of variable default rules that are only applied if the contract is silent on the issue. The UCC makes explicit that it is a continuation of the lex mercatoria.[76] The UCC does not address itself specifically to merchants and most provisions are applicable to all, including consumers.[77] All US states have adopted the UCC.[78] States can make changes to the UCC. Mostly these changes are minor and concern, for example, the numbering of the articles, but in other cases they are more extensive. For instance, Louisiana has not adopted the second chapter of the UCC (concerning sale of goods) and uses separate legislation to cover these issues. The interpretation of the code also varies which means that, despite uniformity on paper, the UCC has not unified commercial law completely.[79]

Before the reforms in 2001 article §1-105 of the UCC discussed choice of law. This article states that when a transaction bears a reasonable relation to this state (the particular state in which the UCC is enacted) as well as to another state or nation the parties can choose either law to govern their transaction. It therefore reflects the substantial relationship criterion of the Restatement (Second). What a reasonable relationship is, does not become clear from the article.[80] The official Comments give guidelines and state that the reasonable relationship needs to comply with the criteria that were laid down by the Supreme Court in *Seeman v. Philadelphia Warehouse* and that the law chosen must be that *'of a jurisdiction where a significant enough portion of*

75 Professor Chen notes that the UCC is a Holy Roman Empire: it is not uniform, nor commercial, nor a code (Jim C Chen, 'Code, Custom, and Contract: The Uniform Commercial Code as Law Merchant' (1992) 27 Texas International Journal 91, 93)

It is not uniform as changes are made by the states when adopting the UCC, it is not strictly commercial as it not just applicable to merchants and it is also not a comprehensive code as is understood in the civil law tradition.

76 Official comments to §1-301:

it is in large part a reformulation and restatement of the law merchant and of the understanding of a business community which transcends state and even national boundaries

For more information on this see:

Bruce L Benson, 'The Spontaneous Evolution of Commercial Law' (1989) 55 Southern Economic Journal 644.

77 Jim C Chen, 'Code, Custom, and Contract: The Uniform Commercial Code as Law Merchant' (1992) 27 Texas International Journal 91, 106.

78 The District of Colombia, Puerto Rico, Guam, and the US Virgin Islands have also enacted the UCC.

79 Robert J Nordstrom and Dale B Ramerman, 'The Uniform Commercial Code and the Choice of Law' (1969) 4 Duke Law Journal 623, 624

80 Note UCC article 4A regarding fund transfers allows banks to choose an applicable law without a reasonable relation criterion. Article 8 gives the same leeway in the area of investment securities and article U.C.C. § 5-116(a) to letters of credits. Therefore, for certain types of contracts there is no need for a substantive relationship between the contract and the applicable law.

the making or performance of the contract is to occur or occurs.[81] Thus, a choice of law would be valid as long as there is a connection to either the conclusion or execution of the contract, the transaction is valid at the place of performance, and the choice is made in good faith. Different rules apply to special contracts (like bank deposits, investment securities, and rights of creditors.)[82]

§1-105 was replaced in the updated version of the UCC in 2001 with §1-301.[83] The Rome Convention significantly influenced the drafters.[84] This new article distinguished between an international contract and an interstate contract. In an international contract the law of any foreign nation could be chosen regardless of whether there was a relationship with the contract. In a domestic contract only the law of a US state can be chosen but the law did not need to be connected with the contract. Therefore, in a contract between a buyer from Arizona and a seller from France the parties could choose the unrelated Italian law. In a contract between a buyer from Arizona and a seller from Nevada the parties could not choose the unrelated Italian law, but they could choose the unrelated law of Montana. Most states adopted the 2001 version of the UCC, however the text of the article §1-301 proved less than popular. States that adopted the new version of the UCC retained the text of the original §1-105. Examples of how this looks are for instance the codes of Delaware[85] and Virginia.[86] In the end only the US Virgin Islands adopted the new text. In 2008 the editorial board subsequently withdrew it.

81 See: UCC § 1-105, Comment 1.

Subsection (1) states affirmatively the right of the parties to a multi-state transaction or a transaction involving foreign trade to choose their own law. That right is subject to the firm rules stated in the six subsections listed in subsection (2) and is limited to jurisdictions to which the transaction bears a 'reasonable relation.'

Seeman v. Philadelphia Warehouse Company., 274 U.S. 403, 47 S. Ct. 626, 71 L. Ed. 1123 (1927)

82 UCC § 1-105 (2)

83 Uniform Commercial Code (as amended March 8, 2008)

§ 1-301 Territorial Applicability; Parties' Power to Choose Applicable Law.

(c) Except as otherwise provided in this section:

(1) an agreement by parties to a domestic transaction that any or all of their rights and obligations are to be determined by the law of this State or of another State is effective, whether or not the transaction bears a relation to the State designated; and

(2) an agreement by parties to an international transaction that any or all of their rights and obligations are to be determined by the law of this State or of another State or country is effective, whether or not the transaction bears a relation to the State or country designated.

http://www.law.cornell.edu/ucc/1/1-301

84 U.C.C. § 1-301 Reporter's Note b (Proposed Draft, Nov. 2000)

85 § 1-301 Territorial applicability; parties' power to choose applicable law.

(a) Except as otherwise provided in this section, when a transaction bears a reasonable relation to this State and also to another state or nation the parties may agree that the law either of this State or of such other state or nation shall govern their rights and duties.

http://delcode.delaware.gov/title6/c001/sc03/index.shtml

This text is thus the same text as article § 1-105 in the previous version of the UCC.

86 Code of Virginia §8.1A-301. Territorial applicability; parties' power to choose applicable law

https://leg1.state.va.us/cgi-bin/legp504.exe?000+cod+8.1A-301.

Two major objections were made to article §1-301.The first was that extending choice of law in this way encourages forum shopping and this allows the parties to evade a law which is more closely connected to the contract but considered inconvenient by the parties.[87] SME might not be able to properly research what it entails if the applicable law is completely unrelated to the transaction. This could decrease security in business transactions. The second objection came from a different angle and asserted that the new article actually restricts choice of law as it distinguishes between B2C and B2B contracts, which the old article §1-105 does not do.[88]

There were also questions regarding the constitutionality of the amendment. The Full Faith and Credit Clause (Article IV, Section 1 of the Constitution) covers interstate duties with respect to public acts and judicial proceedings.[89] It was questioned whether the proposed amendment was constitutional in light of this clause and the *Allstate Insurance Co. v. Hague* decision. Applying the law of a state, which has no interest (even remotely) in the conflict infringes on the rights of a state that does have an interest in the outcome of the conflict and that consequently applying this unrelated law would violate the Full Faith and Credit Clause.[90] Others argued that the fundamental policy provisions in the law are enough to satisfy the demands of the Clause.[91] Case law confirms that the law of a state that has a stake in the dispute should be taken into account although it is not clear to what extent this should be done.[92] As several US states have conflicts of law legislation that does not require a substantial relationship between the contract and the applicable

87 Giesela Rühl, 'Party Autonomy in the Private International Law of Contracts: Transatlantic Convergence and Economic Efficiency' (2007) 3 Comparative Research in Law & Political Economy Research Paper 21
http://digitalcommons.osgoode.yorku.ca/clpe/227.

88 See section e of article § 1-301 for the provisions on consumer contracts: http://www.law.cornell.edu/ucc/1/1-301

A reasonable relationship to the chosen law is still required for consumer contracts and this law may not deprive the consumer of the protection of the law of its principal residence or that of the law where he receives the goods in sales of goods contract.

89 The text of the clause reads:

Full faith and credit shall be given in each state to the public acts, records, and judicial proceedings of every other state. And the Congress may by general laws prescribe the manner in which such acts, records, and proceedings shall be proved, and the effect thereof.

90 Richard K Greenstein, 'Is the Proposed UCC Choice of Law Provision Unconstitutional?' (2000) *73 Temple Law Review* 1159.

91 Ibid, 1179.

92 *Alaska Packers V. Industrial Accident Commission*, 294 U.S. 532 (1935)

This case considered an employment contract between an employer from California and an employee with a choice of law clause for Alaskan law. The employee was injured whilst working in Alaska. The Court reasoned that the Full Faith and Credit Clause permitted the court in California to apply its own law because

Prima facie every state is entitled to enforce in its own courts its own statutes, lawfully enacted. One who challenges that right, because of the force given to a conflicting statute of another state by the full faith and credit clause, assumes the burden of showing, upon some rational basis, that of the conflicting interests involved those of the foreign state are superior to those of the forum.

law it might be presumed that the proposed Article §1-301 would not have been contrary to the Full Faith and Credit Clause.[93] There are currently no plans to re-introduce a new updated version of the old Article §1-105 so for now this issue is shelved.

The discussion in the previous section concerned the choice for a state law. Under the current law parties enjoy freedom of choice provided that a reasonable relationship can be established to the chosen law. The wording of the UCC makes it explicit that the chosen law should be a state law: '*...when a transaction bears a reasonable relation to this state and also to another state or nation the parties may agree that the law either of this state or of such other state or nation shall govern their rights and duties.*' This wording does not sanction a choice of law for non-state rules.

When the 2001 text of §1-301 was drafted the question of non-state rules was addressed in the official comments:

> This Section does not address the ability of parties to designate non-legal codes such as trade codes as the set of rules governing their transaction. The power of parties to make such a designation as part of their agreement is found in the principles of Section 1-302. That Section, allowing parties' broad freedom of contract to structure their relations, is adequate for this purpose. This is also the case with respect to the ability of the parties to designate recognized bodies of rules or principles applicable to commercial transactions that are promulgated by intergovernmental organizations such as UNCITRAL or Unidroit. See, e.g., Unidroit Principles of International Commercial Contracts.[94]

This allows the parties to include non-state rules in the contract for any non-mandatory provisions. As discussed, the text of this article was not adopted, and the official comments are thus not applicable. The official comments above refer to Section §1-302. This section reads:

(a) Except as otherwise provided in subsection (b) or elsewhere in [the Uniform Commercial Code], the effect of provisions of [the Uniform Commercial Code] may be varied by agreement.
(b) The obligations of good faith, diligence, reasonableness, and care prescribed by [the Uniform Commercial Code] may not be disclaimed by agreement. The parties, by agreement, may determine the standards by which the performance of those obligations is to be measured if those standards are not manifestly unreasonable. Whenever [the Uniform Commercial Code] requires an action to be taken within a reasonable time, a time that is not manifestly unreasonable may be fixed by agreement.
(c) The presence in certain provisions of [the Uniform Commercial Code] of the phrase "unless otherwise agreed", or words of similar import,

93 See for instance the conflict of law legislation in Oregon and Louisiana.
94 UCC 1957, 1-302, Comment 2 (2001 Revision).

does not imply that the effect of other provisions may not be varied by agreement under this section.

Contrary to the 2001 text of §1-301 the text of §1-302 is widely adopted by state legislations. Parties could use their rights to vary from the UCC and incorporate non-state rules when this does not run contrary to the obligations described in sub-article b. As the parties themselves can choose the standards by which these obligations are measured (provided these are reasonable) this gives the parties considerable leeway to include non-state rules by reference The parties would still need to choose a governing state law and this would not displace any mandatory provisions of the applicable law. The official comments discuss the possibility to use non-state rules:

> An agreement that varies the effect of provisions of the Uniform Commercial Code may do so by stating the rules that will govern in lieu of the provisions varied. Alternatively, the parties may vary the effect of such provisions by stating that their relationship will be governed by recognized bodies of rules or principles applicable to commercial transactions. Such bodies of rules or principles may include, for example, those that are promulgated by intergovernmental authorities such as UNCITRAL or UNIDROIT (see, e.g., UNIDROIT Principles of International Commercial Contracts), or non-legal codes such as trade codes.[95]

As a large part of the UCC consists of variable rules this would give non-state rules a significant role in regulating the contract

Article §4-103 on bank deposits and collections confirms the possibility to vary from the default rules.[96] Article §4-103 (b) even goes so far as to state that in certain cases specific non-state rules could be applied without the consent of all those involved in the contract.[97] Clearinghouses insert rules in contracts for cheques and credit cards that affect millions of people without meaningful agreement from the parties.[98] Professor Symeonides questions the justification given in the official comments that such transactions involve a great number of people which makes it quasi impossible to get consent from all the parties, as it gives *'private for-profit entities'* a great deal of power to impose rules upon

95 See for the full official comments on this article: http://nebraskalegislature.gov/laws/ucc.php?code=1-302.

96 Article 4-103 regarding bank deposits and collections states: (a) The effect of the provisions of this Article may be varied by agreement, but the parties to the agreement cannot disclaim a bank's responsibility for its lack of good faith or failure to exercise ordinary care or limit the measure of damages for the lack or failure. However, the parties may determine by agreement the standards by which the bank's responsibility is to be measured if those standards are not manifestly unreasonable.
http://www.law.cornell.edu/ucc/4/article4.htm

97 UCC §4-103 (b) Federal Reserve regulations and operating circulars, clearing-house rules, and the like have the effect of agreements under subsection (a), whether or not specifically assented to by all parties interested in items handled.

98 David V Snyder, 'Private Lawmaking' (2003) 64 Ohio State Journal 371, 397.

people who a) had no say in whether these should be included in the contract and b) had no democratic say in the rule making process.[99] These are often consumers or SME that do not have any realistic alternative beyond accepting these rules, as all companies with similar services impose them.

If no choice of law clause is included in the contract then the UCC states that *b) In the absence of an agreement effective under subsection (a), and except as provided in subsection (c), the Uniform Commercial Code applies to transactions bearing an appropriate relation to this state.* Sub section C lists a number of articles on the applicable law in special type contracts. The comments state furthermore that if the case has a reasonable relation to a state which has enacted the UCC as well as to other jurisdictions '*the question what relationship is appropriate is left to judicial decision.*' In multistate transactions it could be suitable to apply the UCC based on its comprehensiveness, uniformity, and its understanding of business which transcends state and national boundaries even when it does not represent the most significant relationship to the contract.[100]

As the UCC is not a conflict of law legislation it can only indicate when it is applicable and not which other laws might be applicable. Therefore, the UCC does not indicate a situation in which non-state rules could govern the contract in absence of a choice of law clause.

Some US States have enacted legislation that allows for a choice of law without the need for a substantial or reasonable relationship. These are Oregon[101] and Louisiana.[102] Several other states such as Texas,[103] California,[104] New York,[105] Delaware,[106] and Illinois[107] have enacted legislation that allows

99 Symeon C Symeonides, 'Contracts subject to Non-State Norms' (2006) 54 American Journal of Comparative Law 209, 220.

100 Official comments §1-301. Territorial Applicability; Parties' Power to Choose Applicable Law (as amended 8 March 2008) http://www.law.indiana.edu/instruction/dhlong/5534/doc/ucc_amend_1-301.pdf.

101 Oregon: § 81.120 Choice of law made by parties http://www.oregonlaws.org/ors/2007/81.120.

102 Louisiana 2009 Louisiana Civil Code: CC 3540 - Party autonomy http://law.justia.com/codes/louisiana/2009/cc/cc3540.html.

103 Texas: Business and Commerce Code Title 9. Applicability of law to Commercial Transactions Chapter 271. Rights of the Parties to Choose Law Applicable to certain transactions.
http://www.statutes.legis.state.tx.us/Docs/BC/htm/BC.271.htm
Valid for any transactions with a value of at least $1 million.

104 New York General Obligation Law § 5-1401: NY Code - Section 5-1401: Choice of law http://codes.lp.findlaw.com/nycode/GOB/5/14/5-1401#sthash.b6TuVwoN.dpuf
Transactions over $ 250,000.

105 California Civil Code Section 1646.5
http://law.onecle.com/california/civil/1646.5.html;
Transactions over $ 250,000.

106 Delaware Code Annual title 6, § 2708
http://delcode.delaware.gov/title6/c027/sc01/index.shtml;
Transactions over $ 100,000.

107 Civil Procedure (735 ILCS 105/) Choice of Law and Forum Act.
http://www.ilga.gov/legislation/ilcs/ilcs5.asp?ActID=2018&ChapterID=56
Transactions over $ 250,000.

a choice of law clause for that state without the presence of a reasonable relationship provided that the transaction in the contract is worth more than a certain amount of dollars.[108]

To summarise, under the UCC and the Restatement (Second) of the Conflicts of Law it is not possible to choose non-state rules as the law of the contract. It is possible to incorporate these into the contract, in addition to a choice for a state law. Under the variation by agreements rules of the UCC and the incorporation by reference rules of the Restatement the contracting parties have considerable leeway to use non-state rules, but not as the applicable law.

5.6 Choice of law without borders

The third approach to party autonomy requires no substantive connection between the contract and the governing law. In the EU, choice of law in contracts is regulated by the Rome I Regulation on the Law Applicable to Contractual Obligations.[109] Rome I entered into force in 2008. It was preceded by the Convention on the Law Applicable to Contractual Obligations (known as the Rome Convention), which entered into force in 1991. The Rome Convention was signed by the then Member States of the European Community. On accession of new Member States adhesion treaties to the Rome Convention were concluded. Partly due to the cumbersome nature of this process the decision was made to convert the Convention into a Regulation.

The UK was not automatically a party to Rome I, but it opted in.[110] Denmark decided not to opt into the Rome I Regulation and the Rome

108 Note that California, Delaware, Illinois and New York allow the parties to choose their own law as the applicable law in these cases whereas Texas allows the parties to choose any law and not just the law of Texas.

109 Regulation (EC) No 593/2008 of the European Parliament and of the Council of 17 June 2008 on the law applicable to contractual obligations (Rome I)
http://eur-lex.europa.eu/legal-content/EN/TXT/?uri=celex%3A32008R0593.

110 The Protocol on the Position of the United Kingdom and Ireland on Policies in Respect of Border Controls, Asylum and Immigration, Judicial Cooperation in Civil Matters and on Police Cooperation
http://eur-lex.europa.eu/LexUriServ/LexUriServ.do?uri=OJ:C:2004:310:0353:0355:EN:PDF

Protocol no. 4 (1997) (United Kingdom and Ireland annexed to the Treaty on European Union (TEU) and to the Treaty establishing the European Community (TEC) art. 1-4)

Commission Decision of 22 December 2008 on the request from the United Kingdom to accept Regulation (EC) No 593/2008 of the European Parliament and the Council on the law applicable to contractual obligations (Rome I)
http://eur-lex.europa.eu/LexUriServ/LexUriServ.do?uri=OJ:L:2009:010:0022:0022:en:PDF

Following the UK exiting the EU the UK is no longer part of the Rome I Regulation and no decisions have yet been made on how UK private international law will develop after December 2020.

Convention is therefore still applicable in Denmark. All other EU member states and their overseas territories automatically became parties to the Regulation. Rome I is applicable to all contracts concluded on or after 17 December 2009.

The Rome I Regulation favours party autonomy:

(11) The parties' freedom to choose the applicable law should be one of the cornerstones of the system of conflict-of-law rules in matters of contractual obligations.

Rome I does not cover all aspects of the contract and excludes several important areas from its scope such as legal capacity, obligations arising out of family relations, obligations arising out of matrimonial property regimes, obligations arising out of negotiable instruments, obligations arising out of arbitration, obligations arising out of company law, power of agency, obligations arising out of trusts, pre-contractual obligations, obligations arising out of specific insurance contracts, and evidence and procedure.

Article 3 is the primary article that concerns choice of law:

A contract shall be governed by the law chosen by the parties. The choice shall be made expressly or clearly demonstrated by the terms of the contract or the circumstances of the case. By their choice the parties can select the law applicable to the whole or to part only of the contract. The chosen law does not need to have a substantive relationship to the contract.

As can be seen from this paragraph dépeçage is allowed. This enhances the freedom of the parties further. The second section of Article 3 allows parties to change the applicable law if this does not affect the formal validity of the contract or the rights of third parties.

The third and fourth paragraph place some limits on the effects of the chosen law. Paragraph 3 states that mandatory provisions of the putative applicable law cannot be derogated from.[111] Paragraph 4 states that mandatory provisions of community law cannot be derogated from if the putative applicable law is that of a Member State.[112] Article 9 specifies that mandatory laws of the forum shall be applied and that mandatory laws of the country where the contract is executed may be applied. Finally, article 21 states that the public policy concerns of the forum can override the applicable law.[113]

111 3. Where all other elements relevant to the situation at the time of the choice are located in a country other than the country whose law has been chosen, the choice of the parties shall not prejudice the application of provisions of the law of that other country which cannot be derogated from by agreement.

112 4. Where all other elements relevant to the situation at the time of the choice are located in one or more Member States, the parties' choice of applicable law other than that of a Member State shall not prejudice the application of provisions of Community law, where appropriate as implemented in the Member State of the forum, which cannot be derogated from by agreement.

113 22 The application of a provision of the law of any country specified by this Regulation may be refused only if such application is manifestly incompatible with the public policy (ordre public) of the forum.

These constraints do not limit the choice of the parties but can limit the effects of that choice.

The Regulation imposes special conditions on choice of law in consumer and employment contracts. In those cases, the choice cannot be made to deprive the consumer or employee from any mandatory provisions of the otherwise applicable law.[114] There are also special provisions for insurance and carriage of passenger's contracts whereby only a limited number of laws constitute an acceptable choice.[115] Therefore, Rome I limits the freedom of choice in specific cases for protectionist reasons, but in commercial contracts the choice of law is not limited by such constraints.

The above concerns the choice for a state law. Would it be possible for parties to choose non-state rules as the applicable law to the contract? Article 3 does not mention the word state at all. However, if one combines this with Article 1 of the preceding Rome Convention: *'The rules of this Convention shall apply to contractual obligations in any situation involving a choice between the laws of different countries,'* it seems as if a choice of law for non-state rules is not allowed. This was confirmed in court.[116] This has not been without controversy. This *'strange positivistic feature, a throwback to an earlier age, is at odds with current commercial and judicial practice.'*[117]

In the *Bank Shamil of Bahrain v. Beximco* the choice of law clause stated that the contract was subject to the Sharia and would be governed in accordance with English law. Both the trial court and the Court of Appeal ruled that English law was the applicable law. The Court of Appeal stated that under the Rome Convention only a choice for the law of a country is permissible.[118]

114 See article 6 consumer contracts and article 8 individual employment contracts.

115 See article 7 Insurance Contracts and Article 5(2) for the carriage of passengers.

116 An example would be *Halpern v Halpern* [2007] EWCA Civ 291

This case concerned inheritance issues whereby the parties had agreed on Jewish law as the applicable law.

Lord Justice Waller of the Court of Appeal stated:

'the starting point for the Rome Convention was a point accepted by all countries party to that convention, that laws could not exist in a vacuum; by 'laws' were meant laws enforceable in the courts of countries whether parties to the Convention or other states'

And (quoting Dicey, Morris & Collins, the Conflicts of Law, 14th Edition (Sweet & Maxwell 2006)

'Article 1(1) of the Rome Convention makes it clear that the reference to the parties' choice of the law to govern a contract is a reference to the law of a country. It does not sanction the choice or application of a non-national system of law, such as the lex mercatoria or general principles of law'

For the full text see: http://www.nadr.co.uk/articles/published/ArbitLRe/Halpern%20v%20Halpern%202007.pdf.

117 Friedrich K Juenger, 'The Inter-American Convention on the Law Applicable to International Contracts Some Highlights and Comparisons' (1994) 42 American Journal of Comparative Law 381,384.

118 *Shamil Bank of Bahrain EC v Beximco and others* [2004] EWCA Civ 19, English Court of Appeal; See for more on this case for instance:

Jason C T Chuah, 'Impact of Islamic Law on Commercial Sale Contracts – A Private International Law Dimension in Europe' (2010) 4 European Journal of Commercial Contract Law 191.

When the Rome I regulation was drafted the proposed Article 3 (2) read: *'Parties shall be allowed to choose as the applicable law the principles and rules recognised internationally or in the community.'*[119] According to the accompanying explanatory memorandum, this wording meant to authorise a choice for the UPICC, PECL, or a possible future Community instrument. It excluded the lex mercatoria, which is not precise enough and private codifications that are not adequately recognised by the international community.[120] The latter refers to standard terms and conditions elaborated by trade associations. It is interesting that the authors made a distinction between the lex mercatoria and codified non-state rules and did not assimilate the two. This proposal would have given parties considerable freedom to choose non-state rules as the applicable law. The final version of the Rome I Regulation did not include this proposed text, as it was not supported by the Council and European Parliament. So, would parties have any possibility to use non-state rules in the final version of Rome I?

The first paragraph of Article 3 does not give any context to the word law. Based on this paragraph it could be argued that a choice for non-state rules is acceptable. However, if one reads the entire Regulation the grounds for this position are not firm. The Preamble at different points refers to the law of a country. Nowhere does the Preamble specifically state that the choice is limited to the law of a country, but by regularly using this wording it is apparent that this is what is meant with the word law. This becomes even more obvious further on in article 3. Paragraph 3 reads:

Where all other elements relevant to the situation at the time of the choice are located in a country other ***than the country whose law has been chosen****, the choice of the parties shall not prejudice the application of provisions of the law of that other country which cannot be derogated from by agreement.*

This implies that what is meant in the first paragraph by law is the law of a country. Consequently, this would exclude a choice for non-state rules as the law of the contract.

The Preamble states *this Regulation does not preclude parties from incorporating by reference into their contract a non-state body of law or an international convention*. Parties can thus incorporate non-state rules, but they cannot choose these as the applicable law. An exception is made for an eventual future EU contract law instrument.[121] The now defunct CESL would

119 Proposal for a Regulation of the European Parliament and the Council on the law applicable to contractual obligations (Rome I) COM (2005) 650 final), http://eur-lex.europa.eu/LexUriServ/LexUriServ.do?uri=COM:2005:0650:FIN:EN:PDF.

120 Comments on the European Commission's Proposal for a Regulation of the European Parliament and the Council on the law applicable to contractual obligations (Rome I) - Max Planck Institute for Comparative and International Private Law (2007) 226, 230 http://scholarship.law.duke.edu/cgi/viewcontent.cgi?article=2612&context=faculty_scholarship.

121 *(14) Should the Community adopt, in an appropriate legal instrument, rules of substantive contract law, including standard terms and conditions, such instrument may provide that the parties may choose to apply those rules.*

have been such an instrument. It is not clear what the exact scope of this statement in the Preamble is. It is not an article in the Regulation. It is not clear from the text what is meant by a non-state body of law. This should be interpreted wider than the text of the proposed article 3 which allowed a choice for non-state rules but excluded for instance the lex mercatoria.[122] At the same time the exact legislative authority of this statement is not explicit. Is it so that the non-state rules would be simple contractual rules when applied by reference or would they be considered an applicable law (just not the sole applicable law)?[123] It is also not evident whether the incorporated non-state rules should be interpreted in light of the applicable state law. The exact weight that should be accorded to non-state rules incorporated by reference is not clarified and is left to the interpretation of the courts of the EU Member States. In a 2005 Italian case the court stated that a reference to *'the laws and regulations of the international chamber of commerce, **Paris**, France' as the applicable law was not valid.*[124]It was too vague and Italian private international law does not permit a choice for non-state rules. Although the Rome I Regulation makes it clear that if included in the contract non-state rules should be applied by reference it does not specify what the court should do if the contract states that non-state rules are the governing law. A reference to non-state rules as the governing law could lead to these being applied to the extent that they do not conflict with the mandatory rules of the applicable state law, they could also be applied in a more restrictive way to interpret the contract, they could be used as implied terms of the contract, or the choice could even be ignored.

Under the Rome I Regulation, the general rule when the parties have not made a choice is that the applicable law is that of the country where the party that performs the characteristic performance has his habitual residence (article 4.2). The characteristic performance is usually the non-pecuniary performance. Article 4.1 lists special type contracts. In the case of a sales contract the law of the country where the seller has his habitual residence is the applicable law. Article 4.3 furthermore states that if another country has a closer connection to the contract, then that law shall be the applicable law. Article 4.4 states that if the applicable law cannot be found under paragraphs 1 and 2 then this shall be law of the country with which the contract has the closest connection. It becomes clear from reading article 4 as well as article 5 (the law applicable to contracts of carriage), article 6 (consumer contracts), article 7 (insurance contracts), and article 8 (individual employment contracts) that the otherwise applicable law under Rome

122 Jason C T Chuah, 'Impact of Islamic Law on Commercial Sale Contracts – A Private International Law Dimension in Europe' (2010) 4 European Journal of Commercial Contract Law 191, 195.

123 Olugbenga Bamodu, 'The Rome I Regulation and the Relevance of Non-State Law' in Peter Stone and Youseph Farah (Editors), *Research Handbook on EU Private International Law* (2015 Edward Elgar Publishing) 221/222.

124 Tribunale Padova - Sez. Este, 11 January 2005. Available at: http://www.unilex.info/principles/case/1004.

I always refers to the law of a country. In absence of a choice of law clause the Rome I Regulation can thus only lead to the application of the law of a country. It is interesting to note that Article 3 does not refer as explicitly to the law of a country and that there is thus a clear distinction between the two Articles. This seems to leave some small scope to claim that the omission of the word 'country' from Article 3 was intended to convey a larger concept of the word law, even if a more holistic reading of the Regulation seems to counter that claim and disallows for non-state rules as the applicable law.

5.7 Conclusion: choice of law and non-state rules

Party autonomy and freedom of contract are intrinsically linked. Parties can shape the law in the same way as they shape their contract.[125] Especially in B2B contracts there is considerable freedom for the parties to choose the forum and the applicable law.

The majority of jurisdictions support party autonomy.[126] Restrictions are sometimes placed upon what laws can be chosen. These restrictions can include the need to prove a substantial relationship between the choice of law and the contract. The restrictions can also go further, especially in speciality contracts and limit the choice further. This chapter discussed the examples of Brazil, the USA, and the EU to show three different approaches to party autonomy. Whereas party autonomy is restricted in Brazil, both the US and the EU allow the parties to choose the applicable law. Behr points out that the major difference is that under Rome I the parties can go to court knowing their choice will be respected whereas in the US this is more ambiguous, even if in practice in the vast majority of cases choice of law is respected.[127] American and European private international laws are converging and therefore the differences between their approaches should not be overstated.[128] Choice of law is usually restricted to the law of a country or a regional jurisdiction and does not allow for a choice for non-state rules.

125 Matthias Lehmann, 'Liberating the Individual from Battles between States: Justifying Party Autonomy in Conflict of Laws' (2008) 41 Vanderbilt Journal of Transnational Law 381.

126 For other countries see for instance Yongping Xiao & Weidi Long, 'Contractual Party Autonomy in Chinese Private International Law' (2009) 11 Yearbook of Private International Law 193.

127 Volker Bëhr, 'Rome I Regulation, A Mostly Unified Private International Law of Contractual Relationships within most of the European Union' (2010) 29 Journal of Law and Commerce 233, 242.

128 Mathias Reimann, 'Savigny's Triumph? Choice of Law in Contracts Cases at the Close of the Twentieth Century' (1998–1999) 39 Virginia Journal of International Law 571, 573
See also:
Ole Lando, 'New American Choice-of-Law Principles and the European Conflicts of Law of Contracts' (1982) 30 American Journal of Comparative Law 19
Giesela Rühl, 'Party Autonomy in the Private International Law of Contracts: Transatlantic Convergence and Economic Efficiency' (2007) 3 Comparative Research in Law & Political Economy Research Paper 4
http://digitalcommons.osgoode.yorku.ca/clpe/227.

Conflicts of law legislations lead to the application of a state law in the absence of a choice of law clause. General rules in absence of a choice of law by the parties mainly use geographical criteria to determine the applicable law: residence of the seller, place of execution of the contract, or the place where the contract was made. By using geographical connection points this would never lead to the application of non-state rules which cannot be traced back to a physical territory.

It is often possible to incorporate non-state rules by reference, that is to say in addition to an applicable state law. In practice this means that non-state rules play a key role in the contract although legislation does not clarify whether incorporating by reference means that they are contractual rules or an additional applicable law. This difference would especially affect how they are interpreted. If they are contractual rules, they should be interpreted in light of the contract and the applicable law. If they are an additional applicable law, they should be interpreted autonomously in light of the principles underlying the instrument.

Commercial contract law is often composed of mainly variable rules that the parties can derogate from. These default rules only come into play when the parties have not incorporated any specific provisions in their contract on those same issues. Conventional law can also allow for this. For instance, the CISG in article 6 specifies that parties can derogate from or vary the provisions of the convention.

This leads to two conclusions. The first is that a choice of law clause that refers solely to non-state rules as the governing law of the contract would be problematic in most jurisdictions. It would usually lead to the court applying its conflicts of law legislation to find the applicable state law. It is possible to incorporate non-state rules for any non-mandatory provisions provided that there is an applicable state law. The second conclusion is that through their inclusion by reference non-state rules can play a key role in determining the rights and obligations of the parties. If the lex fori allows for non-state rules to be chosen as the applicable law to the contract, then the legitimacy for the application of non-state rules is provided by lex fori, however if they are applied as contractual rules then that legitimacy mainly comes from the applicable law (which is not necessarily the lex fori.)

The next chapter goes further into depth on the issues regarding a choice of law for non-state rules and examines jurisdictions that extend the concept of party autonomy to include non-state rules and analyses some of the objections against allowing non-state rules as the applicable law to the contract.

6 Non-state rules and private international law

6.1 Introductory remarks

The previous chapter examined how far the autonomy of the parties to choose the applicable law to the contract extends. The key question the chapter answered was whether a choice for non-state rules as the applicable law, is allowed in litigation. In many jurisdictions this is not possible as choice of law almost exclusively refers to a choice for a state law. This current chapter analyses the relationship between private international law and non-state rules to understand more fully the limited applicability of non-state rules as the governing law of the contract, what the reasons behind these limitations are, and whether there are any exceptions to this general rule.

The chapter first examines how international conventions on choice of law deal with non-state rules. The chapter then analyses several jurisdictions where a choice of law for non-state rules is possible. This can either be expressly by direct reference to non-state rules in the law, implicitly through a definition of law that can be interpreted more widely than just state law, or if so interpreted by the courts if the law is ambiguous or silent on the issue. The final part of the chapter analyses the reasons why party autonomy in choice of law usually does not extend to non-state rules and whether these reasons are convincing.

6.2 International legislation

There are only few private international conventions focusing on choice of law in international contracts. Choice of law therefore remains primarily an area of domestic law or EU law. There is no general choice of law in (commercial) contracts convention. There are some examples of private international law conventions that discuss choice of law, albeit these are more limited in scope (either regionally or contract type).

The Inter-American Convention on the Law Applicable to International Contracts (the Mexico City Convention) was drafted by the Organisation of American States (OAS) to create a uniform choice of law regime in the

Americas.[1] Article 7 discusses the applicable law: *'The contract shall be governed by the law chosen by the parties.'* There is no need for a substantive relationship between the contract and the choice of law. The article does not specifically say that this law must be a state law. The Spanish version uses the word derecho, which is a wider concept than ley. In arbitration rules and laws the word derecho is often used instead of ley to indicate a broader approach to choice of law. The English language variants of these legislations often use 'rules of law' and 'law' to distinguish between a broader and a more restricted concept of law. However, the OAS Convention uses the word law in its English version. Article 17 of the OAS Convention defines the word law: *'For the purposes of this Convention, "law" shall be understood to mean the current law in a State, excluding rules concerning conflict of laws.'* This would indicate that non-state rules are excluded. However, the main purpose of this Article seems to be the exclusion of private international law which limits the effect of renvoi as renvoi can have unintended consequences for the parties to the contract.

Article 9 determines the applicable law in the absence of a choice of law: *'If the parties have not selected the applicable law, or if their selection proves ineffective, the contract shall be governed by the law of the State with which it has the closest ties.'* This refers to the law of a state and excludes non-state rules. Article 9 continues with: *'shall also take into account the general principles of international commercial law recognized by international organizations.'* Some non-state rules would thus be applied regardless of whether the parties have included them in the contract. This might include the UPICC as these were recognised and endorsed by UNIDROIT.

Article 10 reads: *'In addition to the provisions in the foregoing articles, the guidelines, customs, and principles of international commercial law as well as commercial usage and practices generally accepted shall apply in order to discharge the requirements of justice and equity in the particular case.'* This gives a prominent place to non-state rules as an equitable tool, both in the absence of a choice of law or when a choice of law is made. This article was debated amongst scholars and no consensus was reached whether under the convention the parties could choose non-state rules as the governing law.[2]

1 Signed by Bolivia, Brazil, Venezuela, Mexico, and Uruguay, but only ratified by Mexico, and Venezuela: http://www.oas.org/juridico/english/sigs/b-56.html

Note that whereas current Brazilian internal law has a restrictive view on party autonomy this convention would have significantly extended the scope of party autonomy in Brazil.

2 For instance, Professor Michaels believes that the article intended to refer to state law only (See Ralf Michaels, 'Non-State Law in the Hague Principles of Choice of Law in International Contracts' (2014) 7 http://papers.ssrn.com/sol3/papers.cfm?abstract_id=2386186) whereas Professor Juenger is convinced that the article can be interpreted to allow for non-state rules as a choice of law (Friedrich K Juenger, 'The Inter-American Convention on the Law Applicable to International Contracts Some Highlights and Comparisons' (1994) 42 American Journal of Comparative Law 381)

Professor Fresnedo de Aguirre is in agreement that non-state rules can be chosen 'within certain limits' (Cecilia Fresnedo de Aguirre, 'Party Autonomy - A Blank Cheque?' (2012) 17 Uniform Law Review 655, 666).

This OAS Convention was only ratified by Venezuela and Mexico so the exact extent of party autonomy under this instrument has not been tested extensively in practice.[3] It can be seen as indicative that Supreme Court decisions in both Mexico and Venezuela have demonstrated a permissive attitude for non-state rules as a choice of law.[4]

The Hague Convention of 1955 (Convention on the Law Applicable to the International Sale of Goods) applies to conflicts of law in the international sale of goods.[5] It entered into force in 1964 and currently has eight members.[6] The convention allows parties to choose the applicable law. Article 2 only mentions the option to choose the domestic law of a country.[7] This article leaves no room to choose non-state rules. There are no additional articles that allude to the possibility to choose non-state rules or incorporate these in the contract. It can be concluded that under this Convention a choice of law for non-state rules is not permissible.

Article 3 determines that the law applicable to the contract in the absence of a choice made by the parties is the law of the state where the seller has his place of business, except in some specific cases when it is the law of the country where the buyer has his place of business.[8] This territorial determinant excludes any possible application of non-state rules.

3 In April 2017 Venezuela announced their departure from the OAS. It is unclear at the time of writing how this will affect the position of the conventions and treaties signed under the OAS.

The Private International Law Act of Venezuela has incorporated the Mexico City Convention and therefore even if the convention is denounced the rules are likely to stay the same.

4 Claudia Madrid Martínez, 'Notas Sobre La Lex Mercatoria: entre el Silencio del Legislador Europeo y el Silencio de los Estados Americanos' in J. Moreno Rodríguez and D. Fernández Arroyo (editors) *Derecho internacional privado y Derecho de la Integración. Libro Homenaje a Roberto Díaz Labrano* (CEDEP 2003) 333.

5 This includes most goods with the exception of sales of securities, sales of ships and of registered boats or aircraft, or to sales upon judicial order or by way of execution http://www.hcch.net/index_en.php?act=conventions.text&cid=31.

6 These are Denmark, Finland, France, Italy, Norway, Sweden, Switzerland, and Niger. http://www.hcch.net/index_en.php?act=conventions.status&cid=31.

7 Article 2

A sale shall be governed by the domestic law of the country designated by the Contracting Parties. Such designation must be contained in an express clause, or unambiguously result from the provisions of the contract.

8 Article 3

In default of a law declared applicable by the parties under the conditions provided in the preceding Article, a sale shall be governed by the domestic law of the country in which the vendor has his habitual residence at the time when he receives the order. If the order is received by an establishment of the vendor, the sale shall be governed by the domestic law of the country in which the establishment is situated.

Nevertheless, a sale shall be governed by the domestic law of the country in which the purchaser has his habitual residence, or in which he has the establishment that has given the order, if the order has been received in such country, whether by the vendor or by his representative, agent or commercial traveller.

In case of a sale at an exchange or at a public auction, the sale shall be governed by the domestic law of the country in which the exchange is situated or the auction takes place.

The Hague Convention on the Law Applicable to Contracts for the International Sale of Goods of 1986 was drafted to replace the 1955 Convention. This document covers choice of law in article 7. The wording used in the article is *'a contract of sale is governed by the law chosen by the parties.'* Article 8 concerns the applicable law in absence of a choice of law clause and refers expressly to the law of a state.[9] This indicates that a wider interpretation of the word law could be used when applying article 7. Yet, if one looks at article 15 the word law is defined further: *'In the Convention "law" means the law in force in a State other than its choice of law rules.'* This is the same as under the OAS Convention and therefore it is unclear whether choice of law is restricted to a state law. This convention has not entered into force and given its completion date it is not likely that it ever will so no further work has been done on the interpretation.

The protocols of the Cape Town Convention allow the parties to choose the applicable law (Article VIII of the Aircraft Protocol, Article VI of the Railway Protocol, Article VIII of Space Protocol, and Article VI of the MAC Protocol.) These are drafted in the same way with point 2 of the article stating that the parties can agree on the law, which is to govern their contractual rights. Point 3 of the Articles clarifies this by qualifying this choice as the law of a State.

The Hague Principles on Choice of Law in International Commercial Contracts (The Hague Principles) were elaborated by the HCCH. The Hague Conference decided on this undertaking because there is currently a great deal of ambiguity regarding choice of law clauses and there is no comprehensive international legislation. Instead of elaborating a convention the HCCH decided to draft a model law. Research indicated that the probability that a convention would be ratified by a large number of countries was small (because of the difficulties of agreeing on rules regarding concepts such as mandatory laws) and that therefore the costs would outweigh the benefits.[10] A model law is cheaper to draft and more versatile and flexible in usage. The Principles can be used by courts or arbitral tribunals as guidance or they can be adopted by states.

Choice of law is discussed in the second article:

1. A contract is governed by the law chosen by the parties.
2. The parties may choose-
   a) The law applicable to the whole contract or to only part of it; and
   b) Different laws for different parts of the contract.

9 To the extent that the law applicable to a contract of sale has not been chosen by the parties in accordance with Article 7, the contract is governed by the law of the State where the seller has his place of business at the time of conclusion of the contract.
http://www.hcch.net/index_en.php?act=conventions.text&cid=61.

10 Symeon C Symeonides, 'The Hague Principles on Choice of Law for International Contracts: Some Preliminary Comments' (2013) 61 American Journal of Comparative Law 873.

3. The choice may be made or modified at any time. A choice or modification made after the contract has been concluded shall not prejudice its formal validity on the rights of third parties.
4. No connection is required between the law chosen and the parties or their transaction.

The term law is not specified further. The official commentary stipulates that with law is meant the law of a state.[11] The official notes also discuss that The Hague Principles are not applicable in contracts between businesses belonging to separate territorial units of one nation state (unless domestic law says otherwise). The notes do not specify whether the parties can choose the law of such a territorial unit, provided that they themselves are from different countries.

So far this is familiar territory, but Article 3 pushes the concept of party autonomy further and explicitly allows the parties to choose non-state rules as the applicable law:

> The law chosen by the parties may be the rules of law that are generally accepted on an international, supranational or regional level as a neutral and balanced set of rules, unless the law of the forum provides otherwise.

The article itself does not define what exactly rules of law are although it gives some criteria to help establish which rules constitute an acceptable choice. These guidelines seem to disallow rules elaborated by trade associations and other professional bodies, as these are not neutral. This is supported by the official commentary, which states that neutral should be understood as a neutral, impartial body that represents diverse legal, political, and economic perspectives. A set of rules made by an impartial, neutral body also excludes the lex mercatoria, general principles of law, or other such formula. The Principles are silent on trade usages and their application is left to the governing law.[12] The Principles leave it to the forum whether a choice for non-state rules is possible. The last point is a drawback as this brings an element of uncertainty to the instrument. Nor was it necessary as The Hague Principles are a model law and states could adapt the provisions regardless.

The official notes define rules of law as rules, which do not emanate from state sources, thus equating these with non-state rules. The official notes elaborate the criteria mentioned above and give some examples of acceptable choices.[13] International treaties and conventions are an acceptable choice as are non-binding instruments formulated by established international bodies and independent groups of experts. The instruments mentioned by name are the UNIDROIT Principles, the PECL, and the CISG. Finally, the notes also mention that as the number of non-state rules is growing this list should

11 Commentary 2.5.
12 Commentary 3.13.
13 Commentary 3.4-3.13.

not be considered exhaustive. These conditions are imprecise: what is a set of rules and why can only sets of rules be chosen? What is generally accepted and neutral?[14]

The official commentary gives no solution on gap filling if the applicable non-state rules are not complete but reminds the parties that they should take this into account when deciding on choice of law. As The Hague Principles do not cover the applicable law in the absence of a choice of law clause this issue is not dealt with further. This could be problematical, as non-state rules do not form a complete legal system. Therefore, if the parties choose a non-state law, but no other applicable law, it would be up to the forum to decide on how the gaps should be filled. As different private international laws could lead to different applicable laws this heightens uncertainty. It would have been better if the Principles could have included an article indicating how any gaps should be filled. This would have provided security for the parties, as the approach to gap filling would then be uniform.

In the original working draft no limits were placed on which non-state rules could be chosen.[15] This proved too controversial because of the different views of states on this matter so the Working Group added the conditions set forth in article 3.[16] Michaels argues that if this choice is made possible, then there should be no conditions so that the parties can be certain their choice would be accepted.[17] This would also be more in line with transnational legislation, as these normally do not define non-state rules. However, Symeonides argues that placing these conditions was the right approach: adding the requirements excludes the potential application of trade association rules, which can favour one of the parties too strongly.[18] At the same time, the parties are also protected through mandatory laws and international public policy against the application of biased rules. Of course, too much reliance on public policy and mandatory laws reduces the effects of the applicable law and this raises unpredictability for the contracting parties. Excluding the lex mercatoria is questionable. Whilst indeed this is not a well-defined body of law and its application is unpredictable, it is also the law that is most closely associated with the autonomy of the merchant community and which was developed by that community. If the Hague Principles truly place autonomy

14 Ralf Michaels, 'Non-State Law in The Hague Principles of Choice of Law in International Contracts' (2014)7
http://papers.ssrn.com/sol3/papers.cfm?abstract_id=2386136.

15 Ibid.

16 Genevieve Saumier, 'The Hague Principles and Choice of Non-State Rules of Law to Govern an International Commercial Contract' (2014) Brooke Journal of International Law 1,28

17 Ralf Michaels, 'Non-State Law in The Hague Principles of Choice of Law in International Contracts' (2014) 7
http://papers.ssrn.com/sol3/papers.cfm?abstract_id=2386186.

18 Symeon C Symeonides, 'The Hague Principles on Choice of Law for International Contracts: Some Preliminary Comments' (2013) 61 American Journal of Comparative Law 873, 893.
Cecilia Fresnedo de Aguirre, 'Party Autonomy - A Blank Cheque?' (2012) 17 Uniform Law Review 655, 667.

at the centre, then a choice for the lex mercatoria should be allowed. If the contracting parties deliberately choose the unpredictability and flexibility of the lex mercatoria then this choice is just as valid as a choice for the PECL for instance.

Although the Hague Principles represent a large step forward in extending party autonomy to non-state rules it should be kept in mind that an eventual effect from the Principles will not be felt for some time. This effect will depend on whether states adopt them, or courts and arbitral tribunals use them. So far Paraguay has adopted the Principles into their new private international law legislation.[19] Given that overhauls of private international law are few and far between there is unlikely to be a surge of adoptions of the Hague Principles.

6.3 Examples of extending party autonomy

The discipline of private international law was fully developed at the same time as the nation state and the two concepts are intrinsically linked.[20] The role of the state has changed through globalisation but private international law is still founded on the 19th century concepts of the nation state, a time when the paradigm of state sovereignty was paramount.[21] The connecting point for finding the applicable law is the state. The key principle is that as private commercial transactions are not covered by public international law, they are by necessity covered by a state law, and all that private international law should solve is which state covers the transaction.[22] Therefore, traditionally the discipline leaves little room for a choice of law for non-state rules. Applicable law is geographically and territorially confined.

The absence of the possibility to choose non-state rules can be explained on the basis that there is a presumption that the contract laws of (liberal) states are interchangeable because they are based on the same societal needs, and that as non-state rules are not based on those needs they are not interchangeable with state laws.[23] Muir Watt argues that this argument is not altogether logical because non-state rules could be qualitatively better than a given state law, and if mandatory laws and public policy form a safeguard

19 Paraguay Promulgates the Law based on the Draft Hague Principles on Choice of Law in International Commercial Contracts http://www.hcch.net/index_en.php?act=events.details&year=2015&varevent=392.

20 Ralf Michaels, 'Globalizing Savigny? The State in Savigny's Private International Law and the Challenge of Europeanization and Globalization' (2005) Duke Law School Legal Studies Research Paper Series, Research Paper N.74, 7

Kenneth C. Randall & John E. Norris, 'A New Paradigm for International Business Transactions' (1993) 71 Washington University Law Review 599, 607.

21 Ibid, 28.

22 Friedrich K Juenger, 'The Lex Mercatoria and Private International Law' (2000) 5 Uniform Law Review 171, 173.

23 Horatia Muir Watt, 'Party Autonomy' in international contracts: from the making of a myth to the requirements of global governance' (2010) 6 European Review of Contract Law 250, 261.

then it really does not matter whether non-state rules are based on those same societal needs. It is also dangerous to assume that the sole fact that the chosen law is a state law means that it provides for the same societal needs as the lex fori.[24]

Would it be easier for states where no substantive relationship is required to accept a choice of law clause for non-state rules than for countries where this is required? This would not necessarily be the case. If party autonomy is restricted to laws with a substantive relationship to the contract then the points of connection could include trade associations and international commercial custom.[25] When a choice for the law of New York is accepted on the basis that this law has significant experience with the music industry it is equally viable that a choice of law for the UNIDROIT Principles could be justified based on their expertise in international commerce.[26]

In the US there are two examples of state law that have a wider definition of the world law and potentially allow for a choice of law for non-state rules. These are Oregon and Louisiana. Neither of these requires a substantive connection between the chosen law and the contract.

The 2001 Oregon Choice of law codification uses the word 'law' instead of 'state law.'[27] This implies that it would be possible to choose a law, which is not attached to a state. However, if we lock further into the codification the definition of the word law is given in §81.100 '*any rule of general legal applicability adopted by a state, whether that rule is domestic or foreign and whether derived from international law, a constitution, statute, other publicly adopted measure or published judicial precedent.*'[28] This implies that the chosen law must be that of a state.

§81.100 defines a state as follows: '*"State" means the United States, any state of the United States, any territory, possession or other jurisdiction of the United States, any Indian tribe, other Native American group or Native Hawaiian group that is recognized by federal law or formally acknowledged by a state of the United States, and any foreign country, including any territorial subdivision or other entity with its own system of laws.*[29]' If one follows certain theories the merchant community could be seen as an independent entity with its own system of law (the lex mercatoria). This was discussed in chapter two. Therefore, would it be possible to argue that a choice of law for the lex mercatoria would be valid under Oregon law based on this definition? The

24 Ibid, 264/265.

25 Morris J Levin, 'Party Autonomy: Choice-of-Law Clauses in Commercial Contracts' (1957–1958) 46 Georgetown Law Journal 260.

26 *Radioactive, J.V, v Manson*, 153 F. Supp. 2d 462 (S.D.N. Y 2001).

27 Oregon: § 81.120 Choice of law made by parties: *Except as specifically provided (...) the contractual rights and duties of the parties are governed by the law or the laws that the parties have chosen*
http://www.oregonlaws.org/ors/2007/81.120.

28 § 81.100. Definitions for ORS 81.100 to 81.135 38 WLR 397 (2002)
http://www.oregonlaws.org/ors/2007/81.100.

29 § 81.100. Definitions for ORS 81.100 to 81.135 38 WLR 397 (2002)
http://www.oregonlaws.org/ors/2007/81.100.

prospect is interesting even if it is extremely doubtful whether the merchant community is a real coherent entity with its own clearly defined set of laws. As discussed in chapter two there is too much uncertainty over the content of the lex mercatoria, its legal boundaries, and it is difficult to regard merchants as a distinct community. It would thus be difficult to argue that under this article a choice of law for the lex mercatoria is viable, especially given that it is clear that with entity, it is likely to mean a geographical reference.

The key to a choice of law for non-state rules can be found in the official comments to Section 7, which state that the parties may select model rules or principles such as the UPICC as a choice of law.[30] Party autonomy in Oregon can thus be extended to include a choice for non-state rules. It seems that this is restricted to codified non-state rules given the way the comments are formulated and the example of the UPICC. It is unclear from the comments whether uncodified non-state rules would constitute an acceptable choice.

The Oregon code specifies that if parties have not made a choice of law then the court must find the most appropriate law for the contract. The court must first identify which states have a relevant relationship with the transaction, then identify whether there are any underlying public policies of the laws that are relevant, and third evaluate the relative strength and pertinence of these policies.[31] As the first step is to identify the states that have a relevant connection with this transaction it is evident that this excludes non-state rules.

The second example is that of Louisiana.[32] In the preliminary title of the civil code published in 1807 Louisiana codified its private international law

30 See: Annex III, Comments § 7(3) Report on Conflicts Law Applicable to Contracts – LC 2255 https://willamette.edu/wucl/centers/olc/reports/reports/adopted.html

'In exercising this autonomy, parties may select model rules or principles. For example, parties to an international contract may choose to have it governed by the Unidroit Principles of International

Commercial Contracts.'

For further information, see these articles:

James A R Nafziger, 'Oregon's conflicts law applicable to contracts' (2002) 38 Willamette Law Review 397 Symeon S Symeonides, 'Oregon's choice of law codification for contract conflicts: an exegesis' (2007) 44 Willamette Law Review 205.

31 § 81.130 General rule

http://www.oregonlaws.org/ors/2007/81.130.

32 For a more in-depth discussion of private international law in Louisiana see the works by professor Symeonides. A small selection:

Symeon C Symeonides, 'The Conflicts Book of the Louisiana Civil Code: Civilian, American, or Original?' (2008) 83 Tulane Law Review 1041;

Symeon C Symeonides, 'Les Grands Problèmes de Droit international Privé et la Nouvelle Codification de Louisiane' (1992) 81 Revue Critique de Droit International Privé 223;

Symeon C Symeonides, 'Louisiana Conflicts Law: Two 'Surprises' (1994) 54 Louisiana Law Review 497;

See also:

Russell J Weintraub, 'Courts Flailing in the Waters of the Louisiana Conflicts Code: Not Waving but Drowning' (2000) 60 Louisiana Law Review 4;

Carol S Bruch, 'Codifications of Conflicts Law: The Louisiana Draft' (1987) 35 American Journal of Comparative Law 255.

but the provisions were limited and therefore mainly relied on case law.[33] In 1992 a specific conflicts of law codification was introduced. Regarding choice of law, this codification states: '*All other issues of conventional obligations are governed by the law expressly chosen or clearly relied upon by the parties, except to the extent that the law contravenes the public policy of the state whose law would otherwise be applicable.*'[34] This article does not say 'state law' or 'law of a state,' but only uses the word law. This leaves some discretion to the adjudicator to decide what law is. Professor Symeonides, who was the Rapporteur for the codification, has stated that a choice for non-state rules would be acceptable.[35] Unlike the Oregon codification the Louisianan Civil Code does not contain any definition of the word law.

If one contrasts Article 3540 with Article 3537 that contains the general rule in absence of a choice of law clause there is a clear distinction. Article 3547 states that '*except as otherwise provided in this Title, an issue of conventional obligations is governed by the law of the state whose policies would be most seriously impaired if its law were not applied to that issue.*[36] This article manifestly refers to the law of a state whereas the choice of law article only uses the word law. This indicates a deliberate decision to omit the word state from article 3540 and would therefore lead to a tentative conclusion that a choice of law for non-state rules is acceptable.

There are several categories of jurisdictions that allow for a choice of non-state rules. The first one is where the possibility to choose non-state rules is codified in law. This is for instance the case with Oregon (as discussed) and Paraguay (which has recently adopted the Hague Principles on Choice of Law.) The second category does not allow for this explicitly but implies the possibility by defining law in a broader way. Louisiana is an example of this. This is also the case in some other jurisdictions. For instance, Talpis advances that in Québec a choice of law for non-state rules would be acceptable per Article 3111 of the Québécois civil code.[37] The reasons are that the concept of autonomy in the Québécois civil code is far-reaching and in the first paragraph the article does not use 'law of a state' but 'law'[38]

33 Symeon C Symeonides, 'Louisiana Conflicts Law: Two 'Surprises' (1994) 54 Louisiana Law Review 497.

34 Louisiana Civil Code article 3540: http://www.legis.state.la.us/lss/lss.asp?doc=110561.

35 Symeon C Symeonides, 'Contracts subject to Non-State Norms' (2006) 54 American Journal of Comparative Law 209, 222.

36 Art. 3537 General rule
http://legis.la.gov/Legis/Law.aspx?p=y&d=110557.

37 Jeffrey Talpis, 'Retour Vers le Futur : Application en Droit Québécois des Principes d'Unidroit au Lieu d'une Loi Nationale' (2002) 36 Revue Juridique Thémis 609;

Article 3111 Code Civil du Québec. L'acte juridique, qu'il présente ou non un élément d'extranéité, est régi par la loi désignée expressément dans l'acte ou dont la désignation résulte d'une façon certaine des dispositions de cet acte. Néanmoins, s'il ne présente aucun élément d'extranéité, il demeure soumis aux dispositions impératives de la loi de l'État qui s'appliquerait en l'absence de désignation. On peut désigner expressément la loi applicable à la totalité ou à une partie seulement d'un acte juridique.

38 Ibid, 619–620.

The third category is those jurisdictions where case law indicates acceptance of a choice of law for non-state rules. An example is Venezuela where the Supreme Court accepted a choice of law for the lex mercatoria.[39] Venezuela and Mexico have ratified the OAS convention that could potentially allow a choice of law for non-state rules. Venezuela has incorporated the text of article 9 and 10 of the OAS Convention in its private international law regulation and this gives non-state rules a key role in international contracts.[40] These articles require the court to take into account principles of international commercial law as accepted by international organisations, trade usages, and customs.

The Supreme Court of Colombia has stated that parties can choose non-state rules as the law of the contract provided these do not run counter to public policy and mandatory legal provisions.[41] This gives a significant place to non-state rules, but in the context of an applicable state law. It is not clear from this case, which exact conditions the choice of law clause must meet and whether all non-state rules would be an acceptable choice.

In 2005 the Bundesgericht in Switzerland stated that opinions are divided on whether the parties can choose non-state rules as the law of the contract and this choice could be affirmed with regards to sets of general principles prepared independently and with an equilibrium and comprehensiveness comparable to domestic law such as the UNIDROIT Principles.[42] In this case the parties included the FIFA rules in their choice of law clause and the Court stated that rules such as these prepared by private organisations could not be considered as the applicable law. A caveat should be placed here; the choice of law clause included a reference to Swiss law as well as to the FIFA Rules. It is unclear whether the decision of the Bundesgericht should be

39 Maria Mercedes Albornoz, 'Choice of Law in International Contracts in Latin American Systems' (2010) 6 Journal of Private International Law 23, 37;

citing the case: *Banco Union v Banque Worms* [1989] Corte Suprema de Justicia, 144 Gaceta Forense 507.

40 Artículo 30 y 31 de la Ley de Derecho Internacional Privado venezolana.

41 *Rafael Alberto Martínez Luna y María Mercedes Bernal Cancino vs. Granbanco S.A*, Corte Suprema de Justicia, 21.02.2012

It concerned a civil claim against a bank by two Colombian citizens with regards to a loan agreement. The plaintiffs claimed that as a result of the financial crisis in Colombia the contract became more onerous than when they contracted and that this created an imbalance in the contract. The lower courts ruled that there was not enough evidence to prove this. This was confirmed by the Supreme Court. The Supreme Court recognised that there is a general principle of revision of the contract under Colombian law, but that this case did not meet the criteria. The Court furthermore stated that this principle is part of the lex mercatoria. The court cited the UNIDROIT Principles articles 6.2.1.and 6.2.3 as evidence of this. In the reasoning the court then stated that parties can choose non-state rules:

'Indispensable aclarar que las partes pueden regular el contrato mercantil internacional por sus reglas, en cuyo caso, aplican de preferencia a la ley nacional no imperativa,'.

42 X AG v Y, Bundesgericht (2005) BGE 132 II 285 S 285

Available at: http://www.unilex.info/principles/case/1124.

interpreted in a way that would allow non-state rules to be the sole governing law.

In two Brazilian cases the Court applied the UNIDROIT Principles in absence of a choice of law clause. In both cases the court eschewed the traditional connecting point to establish the applicable law (the lex loci contractus) but stated that as there were multiple connecting points a more flexible approach was needed to decide the applicable law.[43] The Court then applied the CISG and the UNIDROIT Principles as an expression of the new lex mercatoria. This choice indicates that if private international law takes a more holistic approach that goes beyond territory to include other connecting factors to determine the applicable law then this could lead to the application of non-state rules.

Finally, private international law can refer to non-state rules outside of the context of the governing law. It can allow for parties to incorporate them by reference or for courts to use them to interpret the applicable law. The examples of the Rome I Regulation, the Restatement (Second) on the Conflicts of Laws, and the UCC were already discussed in the previous chapter. Other examples include Panama where the law states that the UNIDROIT Principles could be used as a subsidiary rule in addition to the applicable law or to interpret the law in international commercial contracts.[44] These private international laws thus accord an importance place to non-state rules but only in conjunction with an applicable state law.

6.4 Party autonomy without limits

This section examines the objections raised against extending party autonomy to include non-state rules. The main objections are lack of protection for the weaker party, lack of predictability for the parties, difficulties in establishing the content of non-state rules, and lack of completeness.

Non-state rules might not give the contracting parties the same rights as a state law. This would especially be problematic if the contracting parties have unequal bargaining power and therefore the choice is imposed upon them. An example is the UCP 600 whereby the bank is usually the stronger party and can impose their usage on the party that seeks a documentary credit.

Yet, it is not necessarily so, that the rights of the parties would inherently be better protected by choosing a state law. The same concerns that non-state rules raise can come into play when parties choose a state law. It is not always possible to know in advance with sufficient certainty whether a

43 Noridane Foods S.A. v. Anexo Comercial Importação e Distribuição Ltda. (2017) Court of Appeal of Rio Grande do Sul 70072362940
Abstract available at: http://www.unilex.info/principles/case/2035
Voges Metalurgia Ltda. v. Inversiones Metalmecanicas I.C.A. – IMETAL I.C.A. (2017) Court of Appeal State of Rio Grande do Sul 4-25.2016.8.21.7004192500
Abstract available at: http://www.unilex.info/principles/case/2042.

44 Ley N° 7 - Código de Derecho Internacional Privado de la República de Panamá, Articulo 86 & 87.

state law protects the rights of the parties. The approach to contract law differs between states whereby a more liberal approach that prioritises freedom of contract would not have the same protectionism in place as other states where the rights of the parties are balanced against each other through more state intervention. International public policy and mandatory laws do protect the parties against an imbalance of rights in non-state rules in the same way as they can against an imbalance of rights in a foreign state law. The fact that non-state rules fold before mandatory provisions already provides some guarantee of protection to the parties if there is a severe misbalance in rights. Thus, the choice of forum can be just as crucial or even more crucial in protecting the rights of the parties

Symeonides is sceptical about allowing parties to choose non-state rules as the law of contract: *'Nevertheless, history cannot – and the merchant community will not – protect the individual contractor, much less the consumer, of the 21st century, the contemporary state can and will.'*[45] He discusses that there is a lot of attention (and praise) for those non-state rules which have been designed by respected institutions like UNIDROIT and UNCITRAL, but that it should not be forgotten that many instruments are not like those 'paragons' of transnational commercial law and are utilitarian instruments drafted by organisations that have a direct (financial) stake in the outcome of disputes, these would for instance be the rules promulgated by banking clearing houses and trade associations.[46]

There is a tendency for these instruments to be biased towards the service provider or the seller, who is a member of the association as the instrument serves to protect the business interests of the group.[47] The quality of, for instance, the UPICC is not in question, but that the recognition of the UPICC as a choice of law sets precedent for more questionable instruments that are not of a similar quality.[48] Scholars might concentrate on those instruments that are drafted by respected institutions and this leads to a general assumption that the quality of non-state rules is high.[49] It should be noted that standard contract terms set up by trade associations have a long history and can count on strong support from the business community who resort to these far more frequently to regulate the contract than that they resort to for instance the UPICC.

Snyder identifies three types of private law making.[50] The first type is private law making by institutions such as ALI. The instruments drafted by these organisations need to be adopted by a legislature or applied by the court. These would for instance include international conventions. They do

45 Symeon C Symeonides, 'Contracts subject to Non-State Norms' (2006) 54 American Journal of Comparative Law 209,210.
46 Ibid, 220.
47 Ibid
48 David Oser, *The Unidroit Principles of International Commercial Contracts: a Governing Law* (Martinus Nijhoff 2008) 24.
49 Ibid.
50 David V Snyder, 'Private Lawmaking' (2003) 64 Ohio State Journal 371,371.

not become law unless they have been ratified by the state. The second type, are rules made by trade associations. These usually only affect a limited number of parties: only direct participants in the specific trade and they have little bearing on outsiders.[51] The third category is that of rules which affect other parties beyond the direct participants in a specific trade.

These include rules for users of financial products such as cheques, credit cards, and letters of credits. For example, the UCC gives clearing houses power to impose their rules on all who use a cheque regardless of whether these users consent to this.[52] These are non-state rules that people cannot avoid unless they stop using cheques. The UCP 600 are drafted by a private organisation (ICC) and imposed by other private organisations (banks). The UCP are imposed not just on the parties to the documentary credit, but also involve third parties such as the carrier of the goods who issues the bill of lading.[53] It is virtually impossible for parties to avoid them unless they do not take out a letter of credit, which would hamper their business in other ways. Officially the UCP are variable, yet in practice the disproportionate difference in bargaining power between a bank and most traders would make this impossible. Therefore, for all intents and purposes the UCP impose themselves as law upon the contracting parties despite being non-state rules.

Trade associations form a closed community. The landscape of trade associations is diverse with many functioning as a resource for information and they take a more or less focused approach to lobbying policy makers to ensure their interests are taken into account. Others function as an almost completely independent private institution. They have their own dispute mechanisms and regulations. This is especially common in the commodity trade.[54] If traders want access to the resources of the association they will need to join. In some cases, it might be very difficult or even impossible to trade outside the confines of the organisation.[55] Members agree to stick to the rules and bring any disputes to the association. Of course, the organisation has no power of enforcement of decisions and in theory members might decide to ignore the decision of the association in case of conflict. These decisions often take the form of an arbitral award and can be enforced in the same way as any other arbitral award. In practice members usually adhere to

51 There are more examples of private institutions that have an entry system for members and operate under their own rules. For instance, stock exchanges (Gillian K Hadfield, Privatizing Commercial Law: Lessons from the Middle and Digital Ages, (2000) Working Paper No.195, 17).

52 (b) Federal Reserve regulations and operating circulars, clearing-house rules, and the like have the effect of agreements under subsection (a), whether or not specifically assented to by all parties interested in items handled.

53 David V Snyder, 'Private Lawmaking' (2003) 64 Ohio State Journal 371, 391.

54 Lisa Bernstein, 'Opting out of the Legal System: Extra-legal Contractual Relations in the Diamond Industry' (1992) 21 Journal for International Legal Studies 115
Lisa Bernstein, 'the Law Merchant in a Merchant Court: Rethinking the Code's Search for Immanent Business Norms' (1996) 144 University of Pennsylvania Law Review 1776.

55 Lisa Bernstein, 'Opting out of the Legal System: Extra-legal Contractual Relations in the Diamond Industry' (1992) 21 Journal for International Legal Studies 115.

the rules and decisions. Reputations mechanisms play a key role in this.[56] A merchant adheres to the rules of the association because if he does not then the other traders will avoid doing business with him and the merchant might end up expulsed from the association and the benefits it provides (such as access to other traders (or even the entire trade), access to information and other resources.) Whilst in individual cases members might perceive some injustice overall the system is beneficial because it supports and advances the trade.

Some non-state rules are drafted to protect the interests of only one of the parties. This becomes especially problematic when these rules impose themselves upon parties that have no knowledge of these rules or have no choice but to consent to their application, as there is no practical alternative available. This could be to the detriment of the rights of the weaker parties, depending on rules chosen.

The second argument against allowing a choice for non-state rules is that the unfamiliarity of the court with their application could lead to unexpected results. The choice of a foreign law does not necessarily represent a safer choice for the parties. Lando refers to a study made by Max Rheinstein who analysed 40 cases in which American courts applied a foreign law. Rheinstein found that out of the 40 cases in 32 instances the law was not applied correctly, and in four of the remaining cases it was doubtful whether the application of the foreign law was correct.[57] Even if the parties know the foreign law well the result could be different than expected because of how the rules are interpreted and applied. Overall, courts have a preference to apply the lex fori, instead of a foreign law, even if this foreign law is designated through conflicts of law.[58]

> While the degree of freedom available to the parties would not increase significantly by permitting to choose a non-state law, the degree of uncertainty would increase. This is only in part due to the difficulty of ascertaining the exact content of the lex mercatoria. Even assuming that the parties chose a codified restatement of the lex mercatoria, such as the UNIDROIT Principles or the PECL, there would be considerable uncertainty in respect for example of gaps and legal standards that need concretisation by the judge. These restatements have to be interpreted autonomously and in the light of principles of international trade: but how can any gaps be integrated, or legal standards interpreted in the cases where there are no underlying principles and no generally

56 Gillian K Hadfield, Privatizing Commercial Law: Lessons from the Middle and Digital Ages, (2000) Working Paper No.195, 12.

57 Ole Lando, 'Principles of European Contract Law and UNIDROIT Principles: Moving from Harmonisation to Unification' (2003) 8 Uniform Law Review 123.

58 Friedrich K Juenger, the Lex Mercatoria and Private International Law (2000) 5 Uniform Law Review 171, 176.

acknowledged principles in international trade that permit autonomous interpretation?[59]

Moss raises two important issues: first, the content of non-state rules can be difficult to ascertain and second, even if the first problem is circumvented by choosing codified non-state rules there are no clear general principles for an autonomous interpretation of these rules. This raises the important point of interpretation. There is no real (body of) (international) (case) law on how non-state rules should be interpreted. This leads to different interpretations and therefore to more uncertainty for the contracting parties. Yet, this problem of interpretation is not exclusive to non-state rules as was seen from Rheinstein's study and is also relevant in the application of foreign law, where such principles of interpretation exist but might not be known to the judge who is applying this law. Non-state rules are applied less often (especially in court litigation) and there is thus limited case law available to guide their interpretation. This would especially be problematic for unwritten non-state rules whose content is the most ambiguous. On others, such as the UNIDROIT Principles there is a wide amount of material available regarding interpretation, which could ensure consistency.

The other issue that Moss mentions is that non-state rules are not complete. Domestic law is needed to fill in the gaps. An example is an ICC case, which was to be decided by applying the lex mercatoria as expressed by the UPICC.[60] At the time the UPICC did not cover the issue of illegality so the tribunal resorted to French law for this issue.[61] Thus although non-state rules were applied ultimately recourse to a state law was necessary to supplement the non-state rules. This decreases predictability for the parties as they might not know in advance which state law will be applied. This could be the putative applicable law, the lex fori, or even another law that the court/tribunal judges to be the most appropriate. The interaction between state law

59 Giudetta Cordero Moss, *Norwegian National Report to the XVII Congress of the International Academy of Comparative Law Contracts without a Proper Law in Private International Law and Non-State Law* (2006) *as* quoted in Lena Gannagé, 'Le Contrat Sans Loi en Droit International Privé' (2007) 11 Electronic Journal of Comparative Law 1,16.

60 ICC Award No. 11018 (2002).

61 *'The lex mercatoria is not yet very elaborated on nullity as a consequence of illegality. For instance, the UNIDROIT Principles of International Commercial Contracts or the Principles of European Contract Law do not deal with invalidity arising from illegality. However, many principles of the lex mercatoria related to nullity in general are relevant in the present case. Moreover, to the extent necessary, French law that is very elaborate on the issue of nullity will be taken into consideration as an additional source of law.'*

http://www.unilex.info/case.cfm?pid=2&do=case&id=1420&step=FullText

The 2010 version of the UNIDROIT Principles does cover this issue

See for instance: Michael Joachim Bonell, 'The New Provisions on Illegality in the UNIDROIT Principles 2010' (2011) 16 Uniform Law Review 517

Giles Guniberti, 'Le Nouvel Article 3.3.1 Des Principes Unidroit 2010 Sur le Contrat Violant une Règle Impérative: un Regard Critique du Point de Vue du Droit International Privé' (2013)18 Uniform Law Review 490.

and non-state rules can lead to unexpected results. Parties can consider this issue in advance and decide to use non-state rules for parts of the contracts whereas they will have other parts governed by a state law or other non-state rules (dépeçage). This choice could prove difficult, as one of the reasons why the parties might choose non-state rules in the first place is that they could not agree on a state law. As non-state rules are less complete than most state laws this issue is germane to a choice for non-state rules.

The main objections against non-state rules as the governing law thus are: balance of the rights of the parties (which includes protection of weaker parties), the undemocratic element of non-state rules (no public sanction), the difficulties in establishing the content, the interpretation of non-state rules, and their lack of completeness.

Are these arguments enough to disallow a choice for non-state rules? First of all, many objections against extending party autonomy to non-state rules are not inherent to just these, but also occur when a foreign law is chosen. A foreign state law might not provide the protection or the freedom that the lex fori does. Mandatory rules and public policy can protect the rights of the parties although this does interfere with the autonomy of the parties and can lead to unpredictability as to the application of the law. The more safeguards there are in place to protect the parties, the less it protects the freedom of the parties to choose the applicable law. It is in between these that a balance must be found.

The lack of public/state sanction of non-state rules is less relevant as the forum has not publicly approved a foreign state law either and would usually apply this at the request of the parties. Of course, the foreign state law has public approval in another state. However, does that public approval meet the standards of the forum? What of a law passed in an undemocratic state by an authoritarian regime? Is that public approval more acceptable than the private approval of non-state rules? Especially if those rules are drafted by a neutral organisation composed of members from a wide array of countries or by merchants in that specific trade? This standpoint becomes even more difficult to maintain if one takes into account that some non-state rules such as international conventions might precisely have this public approval in other states like the example of the CISG shows (non-state rules in the UK, publicly approved law in France).

If non-state rules are the product of the international merchant community, then these reflect the societal needs of that community, and these needs could be just as valid as the societal needs of a nation. Non-state rules can be more flexible than state laws. They are quicker to draft, and they can be amended with the same ease. This means that these instruments are faster to respond to concerns of the market and might better represent the view of the international business community than some state laws do. There is competition between different non-state rules and those that are chosen regularly have popular backing and therefore a type of public support. If merchants are not happy with certain non-state rules, they will simply not use them. If specific non-state rules are used frequently that must mean that the participants are content with their functioning.[62]

This does not address those situations where there is a power disparity between the parties. In that case the weaker party cannot object to the choice of law and cannot set up an alternative system. There will also be a lack of incentive for the private entity to respond to the objections and adapt the rules, as there is no competition on the market. The state could provide a legal structure in which non-state rules operate. In the previous sections it could be seen that The Hague Principles on the Conflicts of Law, the Oregon state legislation, and the original proposal for the Rome I legislation all include conditions on what type of non-state rules are allowed as a choice of law. Codified non-state rules provide clarity and coherence. However a restriction on choice also decreases security for the parties, as they cannot be sure whether their choice will be honoured, unless the legislation is explicit enough to take away any doubts.[63]

Non-state rules are less complete than state laws and therefore recurrence to a state law for gap filling purposes will often be necessary. The original proposal to the Rome I Regulation included that if parties choose non-state rules any matters not settled by these would be governed by *'general principles underlying them, or failing such principles, in accordance with the law applicable in the absence of a choice under this Regulations.'*[64] There is the issue of how these general principles would be discovered and interpreted, yet the inclusion of such a gap filling rule in private international law would help to deal with the problem of incompleteness. The court could use several mechanisms to full these gaps; it could use its private international law to find the putative applicable law, use the lex fori, or apply general principles of law. In all cases this would lead to a degree of unpredictability for the parties. This cannot be avoided, as non-state rules are incomplete. Even the UPICC, which is without a doubt the most complete instrument cannot provide for every single eventuality (although their completeness by now is such that they are almost self-contained.)

6.5 Conclusion: party autonomy and non-state rules

There are some serious objections against allowing a choice of law for non-state rules. Most of these objections are not exclusive to non-state rules and also apply to a choice for a (foreign) state law. The most substantial objections are that non-state rules are often incomplete and that they may raise

62 David V Snyder, 'Private Lawmaking' (2003) 64 Ohio State Journal 371,425.

63 Ralf Michaels, 'Non-State Law in The Hague Principles of Choice of Law in International Contracts' (2014) http://papers.ssrn.com/sol3/papers.cfm?abstract_id=2386186.

64 Proposal for a Regulation of the European Parliament and the Council on the law applicable to contractual obligations (Rome I) COM (2005) 650 final Article 3 http://eur-lex.europa.eu/legal-content/EN/TXT/PDF/?uri=CELEX:52005PC0650&from=EN.

problems of interpretation: these issues lead to uncertainty as to how the law will be applied. In most cases either the lex fori or the otherwise applicable law would be used to resolve such problems, but that in itself may lead to uncertainty as to how the law and non-state rules interact, and how they are interpreted by the court.

There are two important reasons for allowing the parties to choose non-state rules as the applicable law: first, the risks associated with choosing non-state rules are not intrinsically different from the risks associated with choosing a state law. Second, if parties are given the autonomy to choose the applicable law because it is believed that they know what is the best law for their particular situation and should therefore have the freedom to make that decision, then equally they should be given the agency to determine whether they want to choose non-state rules as the applicable law. Enhancing the freedom of the parties will enhance the expression of the will of the parties in the contract.

It is unclear how often the parties now include a choice of law for non-state rules in the contract. Even if this information were available it would not give a complete understanding of the wishes of the parties as most jurisdictions do not allow for a choice of law for non-state rules outside of arbitration and therefore the parties would refrain from choosing these in the first place. Additionally, any database can only measure how often non-state rules come up in courts. It would not measure how frequently they are chosen by the parties, as most contracts are executed without any litigious conflicts or are solved through a private dispute resolution mechanism which is usually confidential. Therefore, it is difficult to gauge how necessary an extension of party autonomy to include non-state rules is.

Allowing non-state rules as the applicable law in litigation would enhance their legal authority because not only would their status be on par with a foreign applicable law, it would also contribute to their development. A major drawback of restricting the choice of the parties to state law is that under those circumstances courts can only play a modest role in developing the understanding and interpretation of non-state rules.[65] As arbitral awards are usually not published or are heavily redacted, they cannot assume the same role in developing non-state rules as court decisions can. If non-state rules are applied regularly by courts and an authoritative body of interpretation is developed this would lead to a fuller understanding of non-state rules and this would ensure a more predictable application which would enhance certainty for the contracting parties and further legal harmonisation.

65 Genevieve Saumier, 'The Hague Principles and Choice of Non-State Rules of Law to Govern an International Commercial Contract' (2014) Brooke Journal of International Law 1,21.

7 Non-state rules and arbitration

7.1 Introduction

This chapter examines the application of non-state rules in international commercial arbitration. Chapters 5 and 6 discussed the use of non-state rules as the sole applicable law to the contract and concluded that this is not allowed in most jurisdictions, although there are some exceptions. By contrast in arbitration it is usually possible to choose non-state rules as the sole applicable law. This chapter focuses especially on the link between arbitration and litigation, that is to say when an award based on non-state rules gets challenged in the courts. Understanding the role of non-state rules in arbitration contributes to a better understanding of the legal authority of non-state rules because the arguments advanced by the parties, by attorneys, and by arbitrators on (the application of) non-state rules can shed light on how these are supported and perceived. This contributes to understanding in which capacity non-state rules are used as the applicable law in arbitration, either at the initiative of the parties or in the absence of a choice of law clause.

Arbitration plays a significant role in international commercial dispute resolution and many contracts, especially high value contracts, contain an arbitration clause. Therefore, arbitration is important for the development of transnational commercial law, including non-state rules. At the same time, arbitration does not have a formal system of precedent and awards are mostly confidential so it does not contribute to the creation of transnational law in the same way as court decisions can. Therefore, it is especially through the challenge of an arbitral award that we can learn how the contracting parties, the tribunal, and the court interact with non-state rules given that these court decisions are mostly publicly available.

This chapter analyses first whether the parties can make a choice of law for non-state rules in arbitration. It should be kept in mind that courts are attached to a national, international, or European judicial order whereas the arbitrator is not attached to a specific legal order and therefore, the decisions the arbitrator makes do not affect domestic, international, or European law.[1] It means that even if the application of non-state rules is permissible in one of these orders it is not necessarily so in the others. The second part of the chapter examines situations when arbitral awards based on non-state rules are reviewed in courts. As arbitral proceedings and awards are confidential it is difficult to get a complete picture of how non-state rules are applied in arbitration and by focusing on the enforcement/challenge of arbitral awards in the context of court proceedings it is possible to formulate a better understanding on when and how non-state rules are applied in arbitration.

7.2 National legislation on arbitration and non-state rules

Arbitrators can render decisions in law or as amiable compositeur. In the latter case, the arbitrator is not bound to apply any law.[2] The arbitrator decides based on what he considers to be just, equitable, and fair. If an arbitrator is acting as amiable compositeur he can apply non-state rules, but the legal authority of these would not be important. The arbitrator is not bound to apply any rules of law so the status of the rules he applies is irrelevant. The arbitrator can only act as amiable compositeur with the consent of the parties.[3] Acting as amiable compositeur is not the same as applying non-state rules such as the lex mercatoria as in those cases the arbitrator is applying a law and should follow this law regardless of his personal opinions on the substance.[4] So if an arbitrator is acting as amiable compositeur and wants to apply the UNIDROIT Principles this is possible and if he does not agree with a specific rule he can either change the rule or not apply it. The arbitrator is not bound to follow the UPICC. If the arbitrator is rendering a decision in law and has been instructed to apply the UPICC then he should apply the Principles as they are, regardless of whether he personally agrees with the content.

1 Guillaume Busseuil, 'L'Avenir des Principes Unidroit Relatifs aux Contrats de Commerce International et des Principes Européens du Droit du Contrat: du Droit Mou ou Droit Dur ?' [2004] Centre de Droit Civil des Affaires et du Contentieux Economique 16.

2 When acting as amiable compositeur the arbitrator might apply a law but he a) is not compelled to do so and b) when he does, he can apply and interpret the law with more flexibility. It is also possible for courts to render decisions as amiable compositeur if the legislation allows this. For instance, in France the judge can act as amiable compositeur if the parties request this (article 12.4 of the Civil Procedural Code (Le litige né, les parties peuvent aussi, dans les mêmes matières et sous la même condition, conférer au juge mission de statuer comme amiable compositeur, [...]).

3 This is the case in many national arbitration laws such as English Arbitration Act (Section 46.1 (b), the Swiss Private International Law Act (article 187.2), and the French Code of Civil Procedure (article 1497) as well as international arbitration rules such as those of the ICC (article 21.3).

4 Lord Justice Mustill, 'Contemporary Problems in International Commercial Arbitration: A Response' (1989) 17 International Business Lawyer 161,162
'Amiable composition and lex mercatoria have nothing in common at all, except that each has a name in a foreign language.

As the exact content of uncodified non-state rules in general and the lex mercatoria in particular can be hard to establish there is a risk of the arbitral tribunal following their sense of what is fair and just when rendering a decision based on the lex mercatoria and therefore more or less acting as amiable compositeur without authorisation from the parties.

The question whether the arbitrator can apply non-state rules if he is rendering a decision in law is more pertinent to understanding the legal authority of non-state rules. Although there are differences between countries the overall tendency is to allow for non-state rules as the applicable law in arbitration. According to the civil procedure code of The Netherlands the arbitrator can apply any rule of law that he deems appropriate.[5] The Dutch Supreme Court confirmed an arbitral award based on non-state rules and did not question the choice of law made by the parties.[6] The parties in this case had chosen as the applicable law *'the general legal rules and principles regarding international contractual obligations enjoying a wide international consensus, including the UNIDROIT Principles.'*

French arbitration law allows the tribunal to decide the case according to the rules of law chosen by the parties or those it deems appropriate in absence of a choice of law clause.[7] The text uses the words *règles de droit* and not *lois* and this suggests that non-state rules are an acceptable choice of law. The Italian civil procedure code states that the arbitrator shall render the decision according to the rules of law (*norme di diretto*) and not laws (*legge*).[8] These legislations allow the parties to choose non-state rules but also allow the arbitrator to apply non-state rules in the absence of a choice of law clause.

In the USA the Federal Arbitration Act (FAA) does not discuss the applicable law to the contract. Section 2 of the FAA discusses reasons to invalidate an award and does not mention anything with regards to the applicable law

5 Article 1504

1. The arbitral tribunal decides according to the rules of law.
2. If the parties have made a choice of law the arbitral tribunal decides according to the rules of law chosen by the parties. If the parties have not made a choice of law the arbitral tribunal decides the applicable rules of law.
3. The arbitral tribunal can act as amiable compositeur if instructed so by the parties.
4. In all cases the arbitral tribunal must take into consideration the applicable trade usages.

6 *Bae Systems Plc v. Ministry of Defence and Support For Armed Forces of the Islamic Republic Of Iran*, Hoge Raad 22 May 2015, ECLI:NL:HR:2015:1272.

7 Code de Procédure Civile: Article 1511:
Le tribunal arbitral tranche le litige conformément aux règles de droit que les parties ont choisies ou, à défaut, conformément à celles qu'il estime appropriées. Il tient compte, dans tous les cas, des usages du commerce.

8 Codice di Procedura Civile, Libro IV Dei Procedimenti Speciali, Titolo VIII: Dell'Arbitrato Art. 822.
Gli arbitri decidono secondo le norme di diritto, salvo che le parti abbiano disposto con qualsiasi espressione che gli arbitri pronunciano secondo equità.

as a reason to invalidate an award.[9] Section 10 discusses enforcement, but does not mention the applicable law as a reason to refuse enforcement.[10]

The FAA does not include a general public policy defence, but federal courts have held that violation of public policy can make an award unenforceable.[11] The US Supreme Court has not pronounced itself on whether the application of non-state rules is considered a violation of public policy.[12] The estimation is that, given the high threshold for declaring an arbitral award unenforceable, it can be assumed that the simple application of non-state rules would not be sufficient grounds to invalidate an award.[13]

In *Mitsubishi v Soler Chrysler-Plymouth* the Supreme Court stated that federal policy is in favour of arbitration; especially in the field of international commerce.[14] The Court confirmed that the arbitral tribunal does not owe any allegiance to the law of a particular state and is free to apply a law of its choosing.[15] The favourable attitude towards arbitration coupled with the acknowledgment that arbitration does not belong to the domestic legal order strongly supports the thesis that the simple application of non-state rules is not enough to violate public policy and that therefore parties can choose non-state rules as the applicable law.

In England the court of appeal declared in 1983 in *Bank Mellat v Helleiniki Techniki SA* that '*our jurisprudence does not recognise the concept of arbitral procedures floating in the transnational firmament unconnected with any municipal system of law.*'[16] This view evolved over the years. In *DST v Rakoil* the enforcement of an award, rendered in Switzerland, based on the lex mercatoria was sought and granted despite the arbitrator not acting as amiable

9 9 U.S. Code § 2 - Validity, irrevocability, and enforcement of agreements to arbitrate; A written provision [....] to settle by arbitration [...] shall be valid, irrevocable, and enforceable, save upon such grounds as exist at law or in equity for the revocation of any contract.

10 9 U.S. Code § 10 - Same; vacation; grounds; rehearing.

11 Symeon C Symeonides, 'Contracts subject to Non-State Norms' (2006) 54 American Journal of Comparative Law 209,214.

12 Ibid.

13 Ibid;

See also:

Kenneth M Curtin, 'Contractual Expansion & Limitation of Judicial Review' (2000) 15 Dispute Resolution Journal 56, 59.

14 *Mitsubishi v. Soler Chrysler-Plymouth*, 473 U.S. 614 (1985)

'The strong presumption in favor of freely negotiated contractual choice-of-forum provisions is reinforced here by the federal policy in favor of arbitral dispute resolution, a policy that applies with special force in the field of international commerce.'

15 *Mitsubishi v. Soler Chrysler-Plymouth*, 473 U.S. 614 (1985).

16 *Bank Mellat v. Helleiniki Techniki* [1983] 3 WLR 783 (CA)

This was also affirmed in *Amin Rasheed Shipping Corporation v Kuwait Insurance Company* [1983] 2 All. E.R. 884:

'Contracts are incapable of existing in a legal vacuum. They are mere pieces of paper devoid of all legal effect unless they were made by reference to some system of private law which defines the obligations assumed by the parties to the contract by their use of particular forms of words and prescribes the remedies enforceable in a court of justice for failure to perform any of those obligations.'

compositeur.[17] This concerned an oil exploration agreement between an enterprise in the UAE and a German Company. The contract contained a choice of forum clause for ICC arbitration, but no choice of law clause. The arbitrators decided on internationally accepted principles of law as the applicable law. The tribunal awarded damages to DST. DST brought proceedings for enforcement in England where Rakoil had assets. Rakoil appealed on the basis that English public policy prevented the enforcement of an award made on the application of *'unspecified, possibly ill-defined, internationally accepted principles of law.'* The appeal was rejected.

> DONALDSON M.R I agree… that parties can validly provide for some other system of law to be applied to an arbitration tribunal. Thus, it may be … that the parties could validly agree that a part, or then whole, of their legal relationships should be decided by the arbitral tribunal on the basis of a foreign system of law, or perhaps on the basis of principles of international law… I see no reason why an arbitral tribunal in England should not, in a proper case, where the parties have so agreed, apply foreign or international law.

The court thus recognised that an award based on principles of international law does not violate public policy. The influence of this case on the acceptability of non-state rules as a choice of law is debatable as it was argued that the court was not concerned with the issue of the applicable law, but only with enforcement of an award made in a country where the lex arbitri allows for non-state rules as the applicable law.[18] The ruling therefore remains ambiguous on the exact status of non-state rules.

This has changed with the adoption of the English Arbitration Act of 1996. This still uses the wording law and not rules of law.[19] Despite this the Act allows a choice for non-state rules according to section 46 (1) (b): *'the arbitral tribunal shall decide the dispute…if the parties so agree, in accordance with such other considerations as are agreed by them determined by the tribunal.'* What these other considerations are is not discussed further, but the article is wide enough to include non-state rules. In the well-known case of *Channel Tunnel Group Ltd v Balfour Beatty Construction Ltd* the applica-

17 *Deutsche Schachtbau – und Tiefbohrgesellschaft mbH v Ras Al Khaimah National Oil Co* [1987] 3 WLR 1023 (CA) known as *DST v. Rakoil*
(This case eventually went to the House of Lords, but this particular issue was not considered further.).

18 Michael Joachim Bonell, *An International Restatement of Contract Law: the UNIDROIT Principles of International Commercial Contracts* (2nd edition. Transnational Publishers 1997), 149.

19 English Arbitration Act 1996, Article 46
(1) The arbitral tribunal shall decide the dispute—
(a) in accordance with the law chosen by the parties as applicable to the substance of the dispute, or
(b)if the parties so agree, in accordance with such other considerations as are agreed by them or determined by the tribunal.

ble law was the principles common to French law and English law and this choice was accepted by the courts in England without question.[20]

'*In England, an express choice by the parties of lex mercatoria will be given effect, but will not be viewed under the new Arbitration Act as choice of an applicable law and it would appear that any implied choice by the parties of lex mercatoria as the applicable law, either alone or in addition to a designated municipal law, cannot be given effect.*'[21] The parties can thus choose non-state rules as the applicable law but the exact legal status of that choice is not clear.

The law does not seem to view non-state rules as law or equivalent to law, but allows for their application, nonetheless. When an arbitrator is applying non-state rules, he is not applying a law, but neither is he acting as amiable compositeur. Section 46(3) excludes the application of non-state rules without an express choice made by the parties.[22] The case law of *DST v Rakoil* suggests that the application of non-state rules by the arbitrator in absence of a choice of law clause will be valid if that arbitration took place under a lex arbitri that allows for this choice.[23]

7.3 Party autonomy and arbitration

The agency of the parties to choose non-state rules as the applicable law is thus larger in arbitration than in court litigation in most countries. In Brazil party autonomy is limited in litigation, but in arbitration the parties can choose the applicable law and they also have the right to choose non-state rules as the applicable law.[24]

The arbitral tribunal also has more rights to apply non-state rules in the absence of a choice of law clause. Under different arbitration laws and rules the Tribunal can apply non-state rules in the absence of a choice of law clause, even without making reference to a state law.

The reasons why a tribunal might choose non-state rules could include (a) double choice of law so these cancel each other out (b) complete silence which indicates the parties could not agree on a choice of law, (c) the parties

20 *Channel Tunnel Group Ltd and Another v Balfour Beatty Construction Ltd and Others*, [1993] AC 334 CA.

21 Stewart S Shackleton, 'The Applicable Law in International Arbitration under the New English Arbitration Act 1996' (1997) 13 Arbitration International 375, 379.

22 English Arbitration Act 1996 article 46 (3)

If or to the extent that there is no such choice or agreement, the tribunal shall apply the law determined by the conflict of laws rules, which it considers applicable.

23 And as the UK is a party to the New York Convention enforcement and recognition of a foreign arbitral award would fall under the scope of the convention.

24 Lauro Gama Jr, 'Prospects for the UNIDROIT Principles in Brazil' (2011) 16 Uniform Law Review 613, 640.

have not made a choice of law but refer to non-state rules in their contract,[25] (d) it is substantively the most appropriate choice according to the tribunal or (e) the circumstances are such that it is clear the parties want as little interference from state law as possible. When the parties do not include a choice of law clause, they could be more satisfied if the arbitrator applies non-state rules because these are perceived as more neutral. Especially in contracts between a state entity and a company the perceived neutrality of non-state rules can be very important. The state would not agree to any other state law but its own and the company could believe this law to be biased towards the state. Non-state rules would then be a neutral option that is preferred by both parties.

The most important reason why states allow greater freedom in arbitration is that as the arbitrator is detached from the domestic legal order his decisions do not influence the development of domestic law and as the forum is private it has no consequences for the legal system if the tribunal applies the law incorrectly. Consequently, it cannot be said that if non-state rules can be applied in arbitration this is because the law endorses the application of non-state rules as a choice of law. It rather flows from a positive attitude of the state towards arbitration as a dispute resolution mechanism that should be given freedom in form and substance. The parties should be free to shape the arbitration as they wish, including the substantive law. There is a certain symmetry in the fact that non-state rules can be applied when using a non-state dispute resolution body.

If non-state rules are applied within international arbitration the sphere in which the dispute is resolved is (almost) truly transnational. It is not completely detached from the legal order because the lex arbitri and the lex fori where the award is enforced play a role. Yet, for all intents and purpose an international arbitration decided according to non-state rules does exist in a transnational sphere because of the minimal connections with any domestic legal system.

Arbitral awards can shed led light on the acceptance of non-state rules by the business community. If non-state rules are chosen or applied with some frequency, this indicates a degree of support among the business community. Arbitral awards can in this way contribute to the formation of custom and usages, which in turn can be applied by courts. These awards can be used by courts to find the substance of uncodified non-state rules or as evidence of the acceptance of a non-state rule as a trade usage.

As arbitral proceedings and awards are confidential it is difficult to gauge how often the parties choose non-state rules. The ICC publishes a yearly statistic reports on arbitral awards rendered under their Tribunal. In 2018 only 2% of the contracts subject to an ICC Award contained a choice of law

25 See for instance ICC Case No 8501(1999) where the Tribunal decided to apply the CISG and the UPICC in absence of a choice of law clause on the basis that the parties had referenced the INCOTERMS and the UCP 500 in other contractual clauses (collected in Jean-Jacques Arnaldez, Yves Desrains and Dominique Hascher, Collection of ICC Arbitral Awards 1996–2000 (Wolters Kluwer 2009)).

clause for non-state rules.[26] UNILEX has 196 arbitral proceedings on their database where the UNIDROIT Principles were used in some capacity (not necessarily as choice of law and regardless of whether the usage was at the parties' initiative or that of the tribunal.)[27] Over a period of over 20 years these numbers are small but given the confidentiality of arbitral proceedings we do not know in how many more cases they were used.

7.4 Arbitration rules and non-state rules

The arbitration rules of the ICC refer in article 21.1 to 'rules of law' and in article 21.2 the applicability of relevant trade usages is specifically mentioned.[28] This is similarly worded to the civil law jurisdictions discussed in section 7.2. The UNCITRAL Arbitration Rules use the wording *rules of law*, but specify that this is restricted to the choice made by the parties.[29] When the arbitral tribunal decides the applicable law, the UNCITRAL Rules use the word law: '*the arbitration tribunal shall apply the rules of law designated by the parties as applicable to the substance of the dispute. Failing such designation by the parties, the arbitral tribunal shall apply the law which it determines to be appropriate.*'[30] Therefore, if the applicable law is determined by the arbitral tribunal, it can only choose a law and not rules of law.

Comparing the earlier versions of the ICC and UNCITRAL Rules demonstrates a progressive development towards a wider acceptance of possible choices of law. The Arbitration Rules of the ICC in an earlier version read '*the parties shall be free to determine the law to be applied by the arbitrator to the merits of the dispute. In the absence of any indication by the parties as to the applicable law, the arbitrator shall apply the law designated as the proper law by*

26 ICC, ICC Dispute Resolution 2018 Statistics (2019) ICC Publication No.898E, 13 Available online: www.iccwbo.org/dr-stat2018
(Compared to 87% for a state law of which the most popular is English law with 16% and the law of a US state with 12% (New York in half those cases), followed by France and Switzerland with both 9%).

27 http://www.unilex.info/principles/cases/arbitral_award
(Numbers dating from March 2020).

28 Article 21
1. The parties shall be free to agree upon the rules of law to be applied by the arbitral tribunal to the merits of the dispute. In the absence of any such agreement, the arbitral tribunal shall apply the rules of law, which it determines to be appropriate.
2 The arbitral tribunal shall take account of the provisions of the contract, if any, between the parties and of any relevant trade usages.
3 The arbitral tribunal shall assume the powers of an amiable compositeur or decide ex aequo et bono only if the parties have agreed to give it such powers.
http://www.iccwbo.org/products-and-services/arbitration-and-adr/arbitration/icc-rules-of-arbitration/.

29 The UNCITRAL Arbitration Rules (as revised in 2010) Article 35.1
http://www.uncitral.org/pdf/english/texts/arbitration/arb-rules-revised/arb-rules-revised-2010-e.pdf.

30 Ibid.

the rule of conflict which he deems appropriate.[31] It does not use the wording 'rules of law' or a similar formula. The 1976 version of the UNCITRAL arbitration rules stated that *'the tribunal shall apply the law designated by the parties as applicable to the substance of the dispute. Failing such designation by the parties, the arbitral tribunal shall apply the law determined by the conflict of laws rules which it considers applicable'.*[32] This again uses the term law instead of rules of law. In both cases the current versions of the rules thus mark a change to a more inclusive concept of the applicable law.

The Rules of Procedure of the Inter-American Arbitration Commission use the term law throughout and specifically state that if the parties have not made a choice the arbitrator should apply the conflicts of law legislation that they deem applicable.[33] As conflicts of law legislation can usually only lead to the application of a state law this would preclude non-state rules.

The ICSID Convention (Washington Convention) allows for the parties to choose non-state rules as the applicable law to the contract. It also allows for sources of international law to be the applicable law in the absence of a choice made by the parties.[34] Meant by this are the sources of international law as recognised under article 38 of the ICJ. Therefore, without the consent of the parties the tribunal is not free to apply non-state rules apart from those recognised under article 38 (which could be argued are not non-state rules in transnational commercial law as discussed in chapter 3.)

Overall, if we look at both domestic law and transnational instruments it can be concluded that a choice for non-state rules is almost always permissible in arbitration. The application of non-state rules in the absence of a choice of law clause is accepted in many jurisdictions and transnational instruments, but not in all. Therefore, the tribunal might need to apply a state law in the absence of a choice of law clause. The tribunal would in most cases be free to use non-state rules in addition to the applicable state law to either interpret the law or the contract.

31 International Chamber of Commerce, Rules of Conciliation and Arbitration - (Old) Conciliation and amended Arbitration Rules in force as from January 1, 1988 until December 31, 1997
http://www.jus.uio.no/lm/icc.conciliation.arbitration.rules.1988/doc.html.

32 UNCITRAL Arbitration Rules (1976 version)
http://www.uncitral.org/pdf/english/texts/arbitration/arb-rules/arb-rules.pdf.

33 Rules of Procedure of the inter-American Arbitration Commission (1988) as amended in 2002 Article 35

1. The arbitral tribunal shall apply the law designated by the parties as applicable to the substance of the dispute. Failing such designation by the parties, the arbitral tribunal shall apply the law determined by the conflict of laws rules that it considers applicable.

[...]

3. In all cases, the arbitral tribunal shall decide in accordance with the terms of the contract and shall take into account the usages of the trade applicable to the transaction.
https://www.law.cornell.edu/cfr/text/22/part-194/appendix-A.

34 article 42(1).

7.5 Arbitration, non-state rules and, court litigation

Arbitral awards come up in state courts when they are challenged or when they are enforced. Arbitral awards can be challenged on several grounds. The UNCITRAL Model Law on International Commercial Arbitration permits to challenge an award on the following grounds: if one the parties was incapacitated, if no proper notice was given, if the dispute does not fall under the scope of arbitration, if the composition of the tribunal or the procedure did not meet the criteria set out by the parties (unless these criteria were unlawful as determined by the law applicable to the arbitration procedure), if the court finds that the matter of the dispute is not arbitrable, or if the award is in conflict with public policy.[35] The application of non-state rules could be challenged if this did not meet the procedural process criteria or if their usage conflicts with public policy.

The New York Convention uses similar grounds as the UNCITRAL Model Law on when an award can be refused enforcement.[36] An award based on non-state rules could be refused enforcement under the New York Convention on grounds of public policy or non-respect of procedure. The arbitral award in *The Ministry of Defence and Support for the Armed Forces of the Islamic Republic of Iran v Cubic Defense Systems, Inc* was disputed in court by Cubic Defense systems.[37] They contested enforcement on the grounds that the arbitral tribunal had exceeded the terms of submission by issuing a ruling based upon legal theories not contemplated/asserted by the parties. The court decided that: *'The Tribunal's reference to and application of the* UNIDROIT *Principles and principles such as good faith and fair dealing do not violate Article V(1) (C) [of the 1958 New York Convention on the Recognition and Enforcement of Foreign Arbitral Awards.]'*[38]

Arbitral Awards cannot usually be challenged for wrongful application of the law although there are some exceptions. The English Arbitration Act of 1996 in its sections 68 and 69 gives the grounds for challenging the award: this can be done for serious irregularities (section 68) and points of law (section 69). The grounds mentioned in section 68 are: failure by the tribunal to comply with their general duties, the tribunal exceeding its powers, not conducting

35 The UNCITRAL Model Law on International Commercial Arbitration of 1985 (with amendments as adopted in 2006) Article 34
http://www.uncitral.org/pdf/english/texts/arbitration/ml-arb/07-86998_Ebook.pdf
The UNCITRAL Model Law on International Commercial Arbitration has been adopted by 72 states:
http://www.uncitral.org/uncitral/en/uncitral_texts/arbitration/1985Model_arbitration_status.html.

36 The New York Convention of the Recognition and Enforcement of Foreign Arbitral Awards (1958) Article V, http://www.uncitral.org/pdf/english/texts/arbitration/NY-conv/XXII_1_e.pdf.

37 *The Ministry of Defence and Support for the Armed Forces of the Islamic Republic of Iran v Cubic Defense Systems, Inc*, United States District Court, S.D. California, 7 December 1998.

38 Ibid.

the procedure as agreed by the parties, not dealing with all the issues, uncertainty with regards to effect of the award, fraud, irregularity in proceedings, or contrariety to public policy. Section 69 allows for an award to be challenged on points of law which can only be done if the rights of one of the parties are substantially affected, if the question is one the arbitration tribunal was asked to answer, and that either it is clear that the tribunal was wrong or that the question is one of such general public importance that a court decision would be prudent.[39] For an appeal under section 69 only questions of English law can be challenged: '*given the restriction on Court intervention where a law other than English law is applied, arbitrators may yet enjoy some freedom from sanction for the application of forms of law unrecognised in England, including lex mercatoria or general principles of law.*'[40] Therefore, the application of non-state rules could not be challenged under article 69.

The challenge or enforcement of an arbitral award becomes relevant for the legal authority of non-state rules when the Tribunal's choice of law is challenged. This is why challenges to arbitral awards where the parties made a choice of law for non-state rules are not as relevant to understand the legal authority of non-state rules.[41] If parties choose non-state rules as the applicable law, they usually would not challenge an award on this particular issue. They might disagree with the interpretation of the non-state rules by the tribunal, but not with the use of non-state rules itself. Therefore, if an arbitrator applies non-state rules at the request of the parties it would be difficult to challenge that the criteria of procedure have not been respected on this particular issue.

If the arbitrator applies non-state rules without being mandated to do so through the arbitration agreement and/or the contract at the basis of the dispute, this could be grounds to challenge an award on the premise of non-respect of procedure. The pivotal question concerns the validity of the use of non-state rules as law or rules of law.

There are several classic cases that deal with this issue. In *Fougerolles* the arbitral tribunal applied general principles of law in absence of a choice of law clause in the contract.[42] This case concerned an agency agreement under which Fougerolles was engaged as an intermediary to negotiate a contract for its principal. The respondents terminated the agency contract before the claimant was able to conclude the negotiations. Fougerolles sued the bank for unlawful termination. The arbitral tribunal based their award on

39 English Arbitration Act of 1996, articles 67, 68 and 69.

40 Stewart S Shackleton, 'The Applicable Law in International Arbitration under the New English Arbitration Act 1996' (1997) 13 Arbitration International 375,389.

41 Examples of these type of cases would be:
Koda v. Carnival Corp
http://www.unilex.info/case.cfm?pid=2&id=1528&do=case
Amanda Matthews v. Princess Cruise Lines, Ltd
http://www.unilex.info/case.cfm?pid=2&id=1631&do=case

42 *Fougerolles (France) v. Banque de Proche Orient (Lebanon)*, Cour de Cassation, 9/12 1981 [1982] Revue de l'Arbitrage183 and [1982] Journal Droit International (Clunet) 931.

the general principles of law applicable in international trade and awarded partial damages to the claimant. The respondents opposed enforcement on the ground that in applying general principles of law the arbitral tribunal had acted as amiable compositeur and thus exceeded its mission according to article 1028-1 of the then applicable procedural code. This argument was rejected by the Court of Cassation, which said that by applying general principles of international trade the arbitrators had complied with the duty imposed on them to define the applicable law.[43] This is thus recognition of the legal authority of non-state rules as the applicable law in arbitration.

This decision is reflected even more clearly in the 1991 *Valenciana* Case.[44] The respondent objected to the enforcement of an award based on the lex mercatoria by arguing that the arbitrator had acted as amiable compositeur without authorisation. Again, the Court of Cassation stated that the arbitrator had not overstepped its mission and rendered a decision in law. The court decided that the applicable law was the usages of international commerce also known as the lex mercatoria thereby equating the lex mercatoria with trade usages.[45] This decision is an important recognition of the lex mercatoria as a valid choice of law and greatly validates the claim that the lex mercatoria is a real body of law. These decisions recognize the lex mercatoria, trade usages, and general principles as possessing the legal authority of law (in the context of arbitral proceedings.)

Another example is *Norsolor S.A. (France) v Pabalk Ticaret Ltd. (Turkey)*.[46] A dispute arose between the French company Norsolor and its Turkish agent Pabalk over the cancellation of a marketing contract. Pabalk claimed lost commissions and other costs before the ICC tribunal. The tribunal awarded damages to Pabalk. The contract contained no choice of law clause and the tribunal applied the lex mercatoria, and especially the principles of good faith and fair dealing. Pabalk initiated legal action in France to have the award enforced whereas Norsolor sought legal action in Austria (where the arbitral tribunal was located) to have the award set aside.

The trial court in Paris granted execution of the award. Norsolor appealed on the basis that the arbitral tribunal had exceeded the scope of its mission by acting as amiable compositeur without a mandate to do so.[47] The court ruled that the arbitrators had conformed with the rules applicable to

43 Ibid.

44 *Valenciana de Cementos Portland SA v. Primary Coal Inc, Cour de Cassation chambre civile, 1991 Bull. Civ. 1 No. 1354,* 22/10/1991.

45 Paul Lagarde 'Note Cassation Civil 1e 22/10/1991' [1992] Revue de l'Arbitrage 457

46 *Société Pabalk Ticaret Limited Sirkeli v. Norsolor S.A.* 26/10/1979.

47 This specific article of the civil procedure code was abolished in 1980 and was then absorbed in a new version of the Code de Procédure Civil. In the current version this is article 1497

Philippe Kahn, 'Note Norsolor c/Pabalk Ticaret Ltd Sirketi' (1981) 108 Revue de l'Arbitrage.

the arbitration (Article 13 of ICC Rules) in choosing and applying a law.[48] This was under the older version of the ICC rules which did not distinguish between rules of law and law like the current version does. The court therefore considered the lex mercatoria to be law. The Court of Appeal in Paris decided to stay the enforcement of the award because of the simultaneous procedure in Vienna and after the Vienna Court of Appeal had set the award partly aside, decided that this should preclude enforcement in France. The question of the applicable law was not discussed in the appeal. The case went to the Court of Cassation, which stated that the Court of Appeal should have considered whether French law allowed for the enforcement of the award.[49]

The Austrian trial court upheld the award. The Vienna Court of Appeal reversed the decision with regards to damages and held that the lex mercatoria was a worldwide law of uncertain validity with no connection to any national legal order. The reference to the lex mercatoria could be seen as a violation of ICC rule 13(3). Thus, the Vienna Court decided the exact opposite of the Parisian Court. This decision was reversed by highest court in Austria on the grounds that the invocation of the lex mercatoria resulted in the application of the principle of good faith which is inherent to civil law systems, and which is not contradictory to any mandatory provisions in France or Turkey.[50]

Several issues came into play in this case. In France only the trial court ruled on the question of whether the lex mercatoria can be considered law (and decided that it is). The Vienna Court of Appeal evidently questioned the validity of the lex mercatoria as law. The Austrian Supreme Court revoked this decision but said nothing substantial about the lex mercatoria. It only stated that the legal principles invoked were reflective of the same principles that exist in France and Turkey and these could thus be applied. It consequently does not recognise or denounce the lex mercatoria as a law. In short of these six decisions only two say intrinsically something about the status of the lex mercatoria: The French trial court and the Vienna Court of Appeal (which hold contradictory views). The above demonstrates that even when the question of non-state rules comes up in enforcements/appeals of arbitral awards the exact legal status of these is not always considered.

French courts thus recognise the application of the lex mercatoria as law. This does not entail that it could be applied as law outside of arbitration. In France in litigation an international contract should always be attached to a state law and this invalidates the lex mercatoria and non-state rules in general

48 ICC Rules of Conciliation and Arbitration 1975 13 (3);

> The parties shall be free to determine the law to be applied by the arbitrator to the merits of the dispute. In the absence of any indication by the parties as to the applicable law, the arbitrator shall apply the law designated as the proper law by the rule of conflict, which he deems appropriate.

49 *Société Pabalk Ticaret Limited Sirkeli v. Norsolor S.A* 83-11.355 Cour d Cassation 09/10/1984.

50 Recht der Internationalen Wirtschaft 29, 86, Supreme Court, 18/11/1982.

as a choice of law in court proceedings.[51] However, the French cases show that the lex mercatoria is recognised as possessing the quality and authority of law. As arbitrators and state courts are in different legal orders the recognition of non-state rules as a valid choice of law in arbitration has no effect on whether state courts can apply non-state rules as the applicable law.

The above decisions are older cases and most of these fell under arbitral laws/rules that did not distinguish between law and rules of law. Therefore, courts needed to decide whether the lex mercatoria or other non-state rules could be considered as law. If they can be considered as law, then the grounds to challenge the award on the basis for non-respect of procedure would not apply. Nowadays, most arbitration laws and rules explicitly state that tribunals can choose the law or the rules of law it wishes to apply in the absence of a choice of law clause. This means that courts are even less likely to stay an award that is based on non-state rules for non-respect of procedure. They no longer must consider whether specific non-state rules possess the quality of law because they would fall under the broader concept of rules of law.

A recent case in France shows this. In a case before the ICC the Tribunal applied the UPICC as the applicable law.[52] The seller appealed the decision and among the reasons for appeal listed that the tribunal had exceeded its mandate by applying the UPICC as this means it had rendered the award in equity and not in law. The Parisian Court of Appeal rejected this as by applying the UPICC the tribunal had not acted as amiable compositeur but had rendered a decision according to the rules of law and subsequently confirmed the award.[53]

7.6 Conclusion: determining legal authority of non-state rules in arbitration

Several conclusions can be drawn based on the above discussion. National arbitration law and international arbitration rules usually allow parties to choose non-state rules and therefore enhance the freedom of the parties. Many arbitration laws (but not all) also allow the tribunal to choose non-state rules in the absence of a choice of law clause.

If an arbitrator is stating as amiable compositeur the legal authority of non-state rules does not matter, as the arbitrator does not have to follow any law. If the arbitrator is rendering a decision in law, then courts usually enforce an award where non-state rules are the applicable law.

51 *Messageries Maritimes*, Cour De Cassation, (Ch. Civ., Sect. Civ.), Henri Battifol, 'Note sur Arrêt Messageries Maritimes' [1950] Revue Critique Droit International Privé 609 *'Tout contrat international est nécessairement rattaché à la loi d'un Etat'.*

52 ICC Arbitral Award 13-06-2017.

53 Cour d'Appel Paris 17/18001, 25-02-2020 http://www.unilex.info/principles/case/2196

The application of non-state rules can only be challenged on limited grounds and the only real option would usually be non-respect of arbitral procedure. If the arbitrator were applying non-state rules at the request of the parties, it would be difficult to challenge an award on non-respect of arbitral procedure on this particular point. Therefore, the application of non-state rules could be challenged on this ground if these were applied in absence of a choice of law clause. That is not to say that such a challenge will be successful. Arbitral laws and rules can allow for non-state rules to be applied in absence of a choice of law clause and courts have enforced awards where this was challenged.

If the arbitral rules allow for the application of rules of law or differentiate between law and rules of law, then this allows non-state rules to be applied. The legal nature of non-state rules is recognised, but on different grounds than a state law. Occasionally decisions of courts go further than this. This has especially been the case in France where through the precedents of *Norsolor*, *Fougerolles*, and *Valenciana* it can be concluded that the lex mercatoria has the authority of law and not just of rules of law.

This chapter alongside the two previous chapters focused on when non-state rules can be applied. These chapters analysed the agency of the parties to choose non-state rules as the applicable law and whether the court/tribunal can apply non-state rules in the absence of a choice of law clause. The conclusion is that in litigation there are only limited possibilities for non-state rules to be used as the law of the contract whereas in arbitration it is possible for the parties to choose non-state rules as the law of the contract and in most cases even for the tribunal to apply these in the absence of a choice of law clause.

This is not to say that state courts do not apply non-state rules. Whilst non-state rules are seldom applied as the law governing the contract in litigation they are applied as part of the applicable law. This can be because the parties have included them by reference as contractual rules. It can also be at the initiative of the court. Courts apply non-state rules as sources of the applicable domestic law, to interpret the law, and to interpret the contract. The next part of this book analyses more closely how courts apply non-state rules, by focusing on the application of trade usages, general principles and accepted practices of commercial law, and codified non- state rules. In other words, this next part analyses the agency of the courts to apply non-state rules outside of private international law and clarifies further how the legal authority of non-state rules develops through their application.

Part 3

How courts apply non-state rules

8 Applying non-state rules as a source of domestic law

8.1 Introduction

This chapter focuses on the application of non-state rules as a source of domestic law: that is to say when non-state rules are a source of the applicable law to the contract. As an example, this chapter examines how trade usages are applied to understand how non-state rules function as part of domestic law and how courts interpret them.

Trade usages are usually recognised as sources of domestic law. For example, the Spanish Civil Code lists general principles and customs as a source of law.[1] In France the Civil Code states that contracts are not only binding in what is expressly included, but are also binding in all that follows from the contract: equity, trade usages, and law.[2] English common law treats usages as implied terms of the contract.[3] It should be noted that when non-state rules are recognised as a source in domestic law, they are also applicable to domestic contracts (unless the law makes a distinction between the two.) The specific trade usages and general principles that are applicable can vary between domestic contracts and international contracts.

This chapter uses two examples of how trade usages are applied as a source of law. The first is the UCC and the second the CISG.[4] Both of these pieces of legislation give an important place to trade usages and as such contribute to the development of non-state rules. This chapter demonstrates how domestic law gives legal authority to non-state rules by acknowledging their importance as a source of law. Codified non-state rules are regularly

1 Código Civil de España Artículo 3.

2 Art. 1194.- Les contrats obligent non seulement à ce qui y est exprimé, mais encore à toutes les suites que leur donnent l'équité, l'usage ou la loi.

3 See for instance: *Cunliffe-Owen v Teather & Greenwood* [1967] 1 WLR 1421.

4 Note that the UCC and the CISG are also non-state rules in origin. If parties were to choose either of these instruments directly as the governing law such a choice would likely not be honoured in states that do not accept a choice of law for non-state rules. Yet if parties choose the French law (which has ratified the CISG) as the applicable law or Californian Law (where both the UCC and the CISG are part of positive law) these would be applied.

See for this also: Olugbenga Bamodu, 'The Rome I Regulation and the Relevance of Non-State Law' in Peter Stone and Youseph Farah (Editors), *Research Handbook in EU Private International Law* (2015 Edward Elgar Publishing) 221.

applied as an expression of these trade usages and as such gain legal authority through their assimilation with a recognised source of law.

8.2 The application of non-state rules as a source of domestic law: trade usages & the UCC

UCC §1-103 (a) (2) states that *'The Uniform Commercial Code must be liberally construed and applied to promote its underlying purposes and policies, which are....to permit the continued expansion of commercial practices* **through custom, usage,** *and agreement of the parties.'*[5] Paragraph b of the same article states that the principles of law and equity, including the law merchant, must be taken into account, unless other provisions of the UCC displace these.[6] In article §1-201 an agreement is defined as '*the bargain of the parties in fact, as found in their language or inferred from other circumstances, including course of performance and course of dealing, or usage of trade.*' These articles indicate that trade usages are an important source of law under the UCC.

Article §1-205 on Course of Dealing and Usage of Trade defines the concept of trade usages.[7] It clarifies that a trade usage is any practice that occurs with such regularity in a place, vocation, or trade that the expectation that it will be adhered to is justified. The term regularity implies that usages do not have to be followed perfectly, but only to such a degree that there is a clear observable pattern. It is only necessary for parties to know the usages of their own trade and not those that are common in other trades, even when they have cross-dealings with these other trades.[8] §1-205 is also reflected in article §221 of the Restatement (Second) of the Law of Contracts:

5 UCC §1-103 (a) (2) https://www.law.cornell.edu/ucc/1/1-103.

6 See also: *Swift v. Tyson 41 U.S. 1* (1842): the law respecting negotiable instruments may be truly declared... to be in a great measure, not the law of a single country only, but of the commercial world.

And contrast with: *Erie Railroad Co. v. Tompkins*, 304 U.S. 64 (1938) where the Supreme Court rejects the general law concept of *Swift v Tyson.*

7 §1-205 (2) A usage of trade is any practice or method of dealing having such regularity of observance in a place, vocation or trade as to justify an expectation that it will be observed with respect to the transaction in question. The existence and scope of such a usage are to be proved as facts. If it is established that such a usage is embodied in a written trade code or similar writing the interpretation of the writing is for the court.

8 *JH Rayner and Company, LTD. v. Hambros Bank LTD*, Court of Appeal, [1943] 1 K.B. 37; This case concerned a company in Denmark, which asked the defendant to open a line of credit. The bank refused to pay because the invoice did not match the letter of credit. The name of the product was different in each document (machine shelled groundnut kernels versus Cormandel groundnuts.) The plaintiff claimed that these are the same and that the letters C.R.S in the invoice were short for Coros or Cormandel and that how these terms are used interchangeably is a trade usage. The court held that the bank did not have to honour the invoice or the bill of lading because the terms used were different and the bank not being in this particular trade was not expected to know that trade usage.

'A banker is not affected with knowledge of the customs... of every one of the thousands of trades for whose dealings he may issue letters of credit.'

(1) An agreement is supplemented or qualified by a reasonable usage with respect to agreements of the same type if each party knows or has reason to know of the usage and neither party knows or has reason to know that the other party has an intention inconsistent with the usage.

Article §219 of the Restatement defines usage as 'habitual or customary practice.[9]

The UCC does not clarify if a trade usage can only be used to interpret an agreement or whether it can add new terms to the contract.[10] In the case of *Barnard v. Kellogg*, which predates the UCC, it was argued that usages can only be used to interpret any ambiguities in the contract and that they cannot be applied when they contradict an express term of the contract.[11] Nevertheless, in other cases trade usages were applied that contradicted express terms of the contract.[12] The UCC tried to reconcile these cases by stating that if a trade usage and an express term seem to contradict each other they should be constructed as to be consistent, and only if that is not possible the express term should trump the trade usage.[13] From this it can be extrapolated that trade usages can add new terms to the contract. The importance of trade usages is such that they have been applied to vary express terms of a written contract, even if according to the UCC they should not.[14] Courts

9 §219. Usage is habitual or customary practice.
(1) A usage of trade is a usage having such regularity of observance in a place, vocation, or trade as to justify an expectation that it will be observed with respect to a particular agreement. It may include a system of rules regularly observed even though particular rules are changed from time to time.

10 Joseph H Levie, 'Trade Usage and Custom under the Common Law and the Uniform Commercial Code' (1965) 40 New York University Law Review 1101, 1109.

11 *Barnard v. Kellogg* 77 U.S. 10 Wall. 383 (1869);
'The proper office of a custom or usage in trade is to ascertain and explain the meaning and intention of the parties to a contract, whether written or in parol, which could not be done without the aid of this extrinsic evidence. It does not go beyond this and is used as a mode of interpretation on the theory that the parties knew of its existence and contracted with reference to it. It is often employed to explain words or phrases in a contract of doubtful signification, or which may be understood in different senses, according to the subject matter to which they are applied. But if it be inconsistent with the contract, or expressly or by necessary implication contradicts it, it cannot be received in evidence to affect it. Usage, says Lord Lyndhurst, 'may be admissible to explain what is doubtful; it is never admissible to contradict what is plain.' And it is well settled that usage cannot be allowed to subvert the settled rules of law.'

12 Roger W Kirst, 'Usage of Trade and Course of Dealing: Subversion of the UCC Theory' [1977] University of Illinois Law Review 811, 819.

13 § 2-208. Course of Performance or Practical Construction (2).

14 Lisa Bernstein, 'Merchant Law in a Merchant Court: Rethinking the Code's Search for Immanent Business Norms' (1996) 144 University of Pennsylvania Law Review 1765, 1784
An example of a case is *Columbia Nitrogen Corp v Royster Co 451 F2d 3, 8-11 (4th Cir 1971)* where a usage of trade was admitted as evidence to show that the express terms with regard to quantity were actually not terms and conditions but instead represented options for the buyer.

justify this on the grounds that the usages clarify or supplement the contract terms.[15] Trade usages are therefore considered implied terms of the contract.[16] Usages can be contracted out of by expressly excluding them.[17] Even if the parties include a general clause to exclude trade usages the court searches for the intent of the parties. For instance, if the clause is a boilerplate clause, the exclusion might not express the actual intent of the parties, as they might not have given conscious thought to whether they wished to exclude any trade usages.[18] The exclusion clause should thus be drafted in a precise and explicit manner. This favourable approach to trade usages can present difficulties if parties are not aware of the trade usage or if they are not aware that they need to contract out of them.[19] Seeking the intent of the parties is not always straightforward, especially when there are conflicting opinions between the contracting parties on whether they have excluded the trade usage.

The UCC presumes that the parties are aware of the relevant trade usages. This could seem unfair on those who are new to the trade as the importance of unwritten usages makes it more daunting for newcomers to enter the field. However, if pleading ignorance would be a reasonable defence for newcomers, this would hamper trade, as it would decrease legal certainty and discourage established traders from contracting with newcomers. In the long run this would not be practical, as it would prevent fledging competition from

15 Ibid;

See also: Joseph H Levie, 'Trade Usage and Custom under the Common Law and the Uniform Commercial Code' (1965) 40 New York University Law Review 1101, 1112.

16 See for a pre UCC example: *Dixons Irmaos & Cia v Chase National Bank* 53 F. Supp. 933 (S.D.N.Y. 1943) which concerned a conflict between a usage and a written term that was sometimes ignored in favour of the usage. The defendant confirmed a letter of credit issued by a Belgian bank for a Brazilian shipper. A provision in this letter required a full set of bills of lading. The bills of lading that were presented to the bank only contained one set instead of two sets. In lieu of the second set a letter of indemnity was issued. The bank rejected this and refused to pay. The issue was whether the express term of requiring a full set of bills of lading could be contradicted by a usage of trade, which accepted an indemnity letter in lieu of the full set. The trial court ruled that the defendant was not required to accept the letter of indemnity even though the usage did exist. The court of appeal ruled that the defendant was required to follow the usage because there was not a single instance to be found when the usage was not followed, and this therefore indicated it was not a discretionary matter.

For a thorough expose of this case see:

Dana Backus and Henry Harfield, 'Custom and Letters of Credit: The Dixon, Irmaos Case' (1952) 52 Colombia Law Review 589

John Honnold, 'Letters of Credit, Custom, Missing Documents and the Dixon Case: A Reply to Backus and Harfield' (1953) 53 Columbia Law Review 504.

17 See for instance: *Nanakuli Paving & Rock Co. v. Shell Oil Co.*, 664 F.2d 772 (9th Cir. 1981) which stated that under the UCC trade usages can explain or supplement the express terms of a written contract.

18 Roger W Kirst, 'Usage of Trade and Course of Dealing: Subversion of the UCC Theory' [1977] University of Illinois Law Review 811, 866.

19 David V Snyder, 'Private Law-making' (2003) 64 Ohio State Journal 371,417.

growing, and thus prevent the existence of a healthy, competitive market.[20] Furthermore, it would prevent trade usages from having any legal authority if a statement of ignorance by one of the parties would be enough for courts not to apply them. Taking the above into consideration it is unmistakable that under the UCC trade usages are a primary source of law and will always be applied, unless the intent of the parties that they should be excluded is clearly made manifest.

The UCC favours the word usage over custom. Under the common law the party seeking to establish custom should prove that this custom is legal, notorious, reasonable, certain, universal, obligatory, and ancient or immemorial. The UCC distinguishes between usage and custom by stating in the official commentary that usage is not bound by the common law test of custom.[21] Usages do not have to be universal, but can exist only in a specific location.[22] Usages do not have to be ancient or immemorial. There is no minimum amount of time that needs to elapse before a practice can be considered a trade usage.

The change from custom to usage under the UCC is significant. Under custom the perceived legal obligation of the participants is a vital component. This is not important for trade usages. This change represents a power shift from the business community to the court. Under the traditional understanding of what custom is, the business community could choose which customs they considered binding whereas under the UCC it is the court that declares which usages are binding. Courts declare a practice binding based on observation. Custom and usages are thus recognised in different ways: subjectively (opinio iuris) and objectively (observance).[23] It takes away legal authority from the merchant community to declare whether they should be bound by a rule.[24] Merchants can be required to follow a trade usage regardless of whether they consider this practice binding. Usages will continue to develop independently from the courts, but the courts have the power to declare these binding.[25]

20 Jim C Chen, 'Code, Custom, and Contract: The Uniform Commercial Code as Law Merchant' (1992) 27 Texas International Journal 91, 126.

21 Official commentary article §1-205 Course of Dealing and Usage of Trade:

> A usage of trade under subsection (2) must have the "regularity of observance" specified. The ancient English tests for "custom" are abandoned in this connection. Therefore, it is not required that a usage of trade be "ancient or immemorial', "universal' or the like. Under the requirement of subsection (2) full recognition is thus available for new usages and for usages currently observed by the great majority of decent dealers, even though dissidents ready to cut corners do not agree. There is room also for proper recognition of usage agreed upon by merchants in trade codes

This is also reflected in the Restatement (Second) of Contracts in the official comments of Article §222:

> *A usage of trade need not be "ancient or immemorial," "universal," or the like.*

22 See for instance the decision in *Ebasco Services Inc. v. Pennsylvania Power & L. Co.*, 402 F. Supp. 421 (E.D. Pa. 1975).

23 Jim C Chen, 'Code, Custom, and Contract: The Uniform Commercial Code as Law Merchant' (1992) 27 Texas International Journal 91, 118.

24 Joseph H Levie, 'Trade Usage and Custom under the Common Law and the Uniform Commercial Code' (1965) 40 New York University Law Review 1101, 1104.

25 Jim C Chen, 'Code, Custom, and Contract: The Uniform Commercial Code as Law Merchant' (1992) 27 Texas International Journal 91, 121.

There are several reasons why trade usages have an extensive place in the UCC. Firstly, the drafters consider the lex mercatoria as predecessor to the UCC. They were therefore sympathetic to the argument that merchants should have the possibility to self-organise. The UCC recognises that merchants operate in a community framework that can make collective decisions, which are imposed on individuals.[26] The drafters considered that trade usages better express the intention of the parties than the contract itself does as these usages are internalised so their inclusion should be presumed.[27] It makes the law more flexible and adaptable to the needs of trade. It can also reduce legal costs as not every single eventuality would need to be included in the contract and thus less time is needed for negotiations.[28] Consequently, trade usages allow merchants to operate within a flexible and low-cost environment: '*without freedom, individuals could not develop rational business practices in the pursuit of profit. When one looks at business practices, one sees the reflection, the echo of individual choices made over time. Business practices, as the products of liberty, have an inherent moral legitimacy.*'[29]

Bernstein questions whether when given the choice the parties would opt to be bound by trade usages or whether they would prefer to be solely bound by the contract and statutory law.[30] That merchants follow certain trade usages does not necessarily mean that they wish to be legally obliged to observe these as for reasons of trust, friendship, reputation, and/or long

26 Amy H Kastely, 'Stock Equipment for the Bargain in Fact: Trade Usage, Express Terms, and Consistency under § 1-205 of the Uniform Commercial Code' (1986) 64 North Carolina Law Review 777, 813.

27 *Urbana Farmers Union Elevator Co. v Schock* 351 N.W.2d 88 (1984) – *established practices and usages within a particular trade can more reliably reveal the parties' intent than the sometimes imperfect and often incomplete language of the contract.*

28 Lisa Bernstein, 'Merchant Law in a Merchant Court: Rethinking the Code's Search for Immanent Business Norms' (1996) 144 University of Pennsylvania Law Review 1765, 1769.

29 Kerry Lynn Mackintosh, 'Liberty, Trade, and the Uniform Commercial Code, When Should Default Rules Be Based on Business Practices?' (1996) 38 William & Mary Law Review 1465, 1478.

30 Lisa Bernstein, 'Merchant Law in a Merchant Court: Rethinking the Code's Search for Immanent Business Norms' (1996) 144 University of Pennsylvania Law Review 1765, 1769

In this article the author is critical of this approach by the UCC and analyses how it actually countermands the flexibility of the UCC.

She uses a case study of the National Grain and Feed Association (NGFA) tribunal which very rarely uses commercial practices and usages in their awards and instead relies upon their own trade rules. Bernstein notes that the arbitrators seem to be reluctant to use general trade practices and signal their dislike of these in the awards. Bernstein does note several uses of trade usages and practices: they are used as additional justification, to assess credibility of evidence, to signal whether the contract is out of sync with standard trade practices, and when they believe a standard trade practice should be incorporated in the Trade Rules. Despite this the arbitrators do not rely on trade usages as terms of the contract. Bernstein considers whether this stricter approach, which is initiated by the merchant community itself might not be more reflective of the wishes of the community than the approach of the UCC which prioritises trade usages as terms of the contract.

term gain, parties might make concessions on issues such as delivery, quantity, price, time, or other. They do not do so because they consider these concessions as trade usages, but because they value the longer-term contractual relationship and therefore want to be flexible with their trading partner. An example is warranties on software, which are limited in the contract, but are applied more generously in practice.[31] This is to the satisfaction of both parties: the software provider who limits his liability & the buyer who gets a cheaper product (as the warranty provisions are less extensive and thus less costly) but will enjoy a more generous practice.[32] If this is considered a trade usage this could lead to the provider restricting this practice or raising his prices. This would ultimately be a loss for both the buyer and the seller.

When the parties wish to end the contractual relationship, they do not necessarily wish to be held to the practices they established when preserving the relationship was the goal. Therefore, they do not perceive these practices as binding. As the binding value of usages under the UCC does not come from a sense of obligation, but from observance of the pattern this perception would have no effect on the legal obligations of the parties. Courts do not always distinguish between practices done out of courtesy, and trade usages. The parties can follow trade usages because they allocate authoritative value to them or because they wish to give space to informal practices that solidify the contractual relationship. Within business relationships reputation is key, this is especially so in more closed trades where the number of participants is smaller and entry costs are higher.

The official comments to §1-205 specify that the articles on unconscionable contracts and clauses should be used to deal with any unreasonable usage.[33] This article suggests three ways an unconscionable clause should be dealt with:

- Refuse to enforce the contract
- Enforce the contract without the clause
- Limit the application of the clause to avoid injustice[34]

An unreasonable trade usage could thus be dealt with by not enforcing the contract, enforcing the contract without taking the trade usage into account, or limiting the application of the trade usage. It is difficult to see why a valid contract would not be enforced just because a trade usage is unreasonable, except if the whole contract rests upon this usage. Limiting the application of the trade usage or simply not enforcing this would in most cases be the proper way to deal with this issue.

31 Ibid, 1790.

32 Ibid.

33 The policy of this Act controlling explicit unconscionable contracts and clauses …applies to implicit clauses which rest on usage of trade and carries forward the policy underlying the ancient requirement that a custom or usage must be "reasonable".

34 § 2-302 Unconscionable Contract or Clause.

What would the case be for codified non-state rules? Could these be applied as trade usages under the UCC? The Incoterms and the UCP are mainly considered contractual terms as discussed in chapter 4. This would also be the case for rules promulgated by trade branch associations. The UCC has its own trade terms which closely resemble the Incoterms, but which define them differently. Several Incoterms (such as DDP and CFR) do not appear in the UCC but others like FOB and CIF do. FOB is defined slightly differently under the UCC and can be used for any mode of transportation and not just transport by ship so this impacts when risk transfers between the buyer and the seller as this depends on the type of transportation.[35] The Incoterms should be included by name if that is the intent of the parties. If FOB is included without any additional information the court could apply FOB as defined in the UCC. The court could also decide that the intention of the parties was to include the Incoterms if the contract is international. This would thus cause some uncertainty for the parties.

The UCC has its own article on letters of credits, which is constructed to be consistent with the UCP.[36] The importance of the UCP in documentary credits is such that the drafters of the UCC wanted to ensure compatibility between the two. Nonetheless, the UCP would have no effect if they are not included in the contract as they are considered contractual rules.

The status of international restatements of law as trade usages is not clear. The official commentary on the UCC gives room to 'usage agreed upon by merchants in trade codes.'[37] Of course, merchants did not necessarily develop the international restatements, but the formulation is such that if merchants would use them then they could become trade usages. The Preamble of the UPICC states that they can be applied if parties have used a formula such as 'usages and customs of international trade' in their contract. It would thus be possible for the court to apply parts of the UPICC as trade usages. Whether they would do so in practice is a different question.

In a survey done in Florida on the application of the UPICC there was no indication that courts would apply these without the parties requesting this.[38] The same survey indicated that most judges did not feel they were

35 § 2-319. F.O.B. and F.A.S. Terms.

36 For a thorough expose on this see: Kerry Lynn Mackintosh, 'Liberty, Trade, and the Uniform Commercial Code, When Should Default Rules Be Based on Business Practices?' (1996) 38 William & Mary Law Review 1465

The drafters stated that: *'to facilitate its [article 5] usefulness it is essential that US law be in harmony with international rules and practices.'* and *'They [the rules] need to be substantively and procedurally consistent with international practices.'*

(American Law Institute, UCC Revised Article 5, Final Draft).

37 Official commentary article §1-205 Course of Dealing and Usage of Trade:

38 Michael Wallace Gordon, 'Part II Some Thoughts on the Receptiveness of Contract Rules in the CISG and the UNIDROIT Principles as Reflected in One State's (Florida) Experience of (1) Law School Faculty, (2) Members of the Bar with an International Practice, and (3) Judges' (1998) 46 American Journal of Comparative Law Supplement 361,369.

familiar with the UPICC.[39] This supports the argument that they would not be applied as trade usages. Although this survey concerned the application of the UPICC as the law of the contract it is reasonable to conclude from this that the UPICC are not established enough to be considered trade usages by American courts. A follow-up survey was conducted in 2007 among practitioners, academics, and judges from several different US states.[40] 88% of judges declared they were unfamiliar with the UPICC.[41] The results also indicate that the judiciary would only consider applying the UPICC if these are referenced in the contract.[42] If the UPICC or a single Principle is considered a trade usage then there is no reason why they could not be applied under the UCC. The lack of familiarity with the UPICC and their infrequent application would suggest that this is currently not the case although this can of course change in the future.[43]

8.3 The application of non-state rules as part of the applicable law: the example of the CISG

Article 9 of the CISG states:

(1) The parties are bound by any usage to which they have agreed and by any practices, which they have established between themselves.
(2) The parties are considered, unless otherwise agreed, to have impliedly made applicable to their contract or its formation a usage of which the parties knew or ought to have known and which in international trade is widely known to, and regularly observed by, parties to contracts of the type involved in the particular trade concerned.

This is supplemented by article 8(3) which reads that to determine the intentions of the contracting parties due consideration should be given to all relevant circumstances, including trade usages. The CISG does not lay out a hierarchy for established practices and trade usages the way the UCC does. Based on article 8(3) which gives primacy to the intentions of the parties it could be assumed that course of dealing is more important than trade usages as this more closely expresses the will of the parties. However, there is no clear rule, and this is left to the interpretation of the courts.

The CISG is silent on what happens if trade usages are conflicting, but scholarly commentary states that these should then be mutually exclusive,

39 Ibid.

40 Peter L Fitzgerald, 'The International Contracting Practices Survey Project: An Empirical Study of the Value and Utility of the CISG and the UNIDROIT Principles of International Commercial Contracts to Practitioners, Jurists, and Legal Academics in the United States' (2008) 27 Journal of Law and Commerce 1.

41 Ibid, 43.

42 Ibid, 80.

43 This is confirmed by the UNILEX case law database on use of the UPICC where none of the cases from the US have applied these as trade usages.

and if the contract gives no further indication the issue should be solved per the gap filling rules of the CISG.[44]

The CISG is silent on what happens in case there is a conflict between a trade usage and an article of the CISG. Commentary agrees that in such cases the trade usage should take precedence.[45] Article 6 states that the parties can opt out of the entire CISG or its individual provisions. As the rules of the CISG are thus variable rules, trade usages should take precedence over the CISG. Trade usages are considered implied terms of the contract and therefore reflect more closely the intentions of the parties than statutory law does.

For trade usages to be recognised they should be widely known and regularly observed in the specific trade. They do not necessarily need to be international in origin; they need only to be observed in international trade. Local usages could be applicable, provided these are either commonly used in trade with foreign parties, or that the foreign merchant has been doing business in that location regularly so it can be assumed that he has knowledge of the usage.[46] The wording 'ought to have known' indicates that pleading ignorance would not be sufficient defence for non-compliance.[47]

44 Cesare Massimo Bianca and Michael Joachim Bonell, 'Commentary on Usages and Practices' in Cesare Massimo Bianca and Michael Joachim Bonell (editors), *Commentary on the International Sales Law - The 1980 Vienna Sales Convention* (Giuffrè 1987) 110.

45 Ibid;

An example of a case dealing with this issue:

Bermatex s.r.l. v. Valentin Rius Clapers S.A. v. Sbrojovka Vsetin S.A, Juzgado Nacional Cortade Primera Instancia en lo Comercial No. 10, October 1994;

On the issue of determining the interest rate on a credit the court stated:

'Since CISG does not determine the interest rate, reference should be made to international trade usages which are assigned by CISG itself a hierarchical position higher than the very same CISG provisions (Art. 9 CISG)'.

46 See for instance: *Parties Unknown*, Oberlandesgericht Graz, Austria, November 1995,

Text available at: http://cisgw3.law.pace.edu/cases/951109a3.html#cx

'The wording of Art. 9(2) CISG does not mean that, in the future, purely national or local usages can find no application for the interpretation and supplementation of contracts without an explicit reference by the parties. One can still presume an exception for usages that are in force at certain stock markets, trade fairs or deposit sites, as long as the usage is also regularly observed there in the trade with foreigners. Furthermore, the possibility does not seem to be excluded that a foreign tradesman, who is constantly active in another country and has already formed a number of transactions there, is bound by possible national usages.'

But see also: *Parties Unknown*, Oberlandesgericht Frankfurt am Main (Germany)

Text available at: http://www.unilex.info/case.cfm?pid=1&do=case&id=169&step=Abstract

'CISG requires a trade usage to be international in order to be applicable to the contract, absent an agreement by the parties.'

(in this case the German usage of concluding a contract through a letter of confirmation was not an international usage and was therefore not applicable).

47 Zivilgericht Kanton Basel-Stadt (Switzerland), Dec. 12, 1992

Tekst available at: http://www.unilex.info/case.cfm?pid=1&do=case&id=104&step=Abstract

See also: Clayton P Gillette, 'Harmony and Stasis in Trade Usages for International Sale' (1998–1999) 39 Virginia Journal of International Law 707.

The historic importance of trade usages meant that these were given a prominent place in the CISG. The UCC considers the lex mercatoria an important fundament of commercial law and this is reflected in the CISG, although in contrast to the UCC the CISG does not mention the lex mercatoria by name as its inspiration. It can be added that the UCC was a source of inspiration for the CISG.[48] The strong position of trade usages under the UCC is reflected in the CISG. The scope that trade usages should be given was a matter of contention during the drafting process as anecdotal evidence from delegates suggests.[49] The participating socialist and developing countries viewed trade usages more negatively than the free-market economy countries and wanted to limit their role in the contract.[50]

The main division was between the objective and subjective theory on trade usages.[51] Per the subjective theory usages are only applicable if the parties have consented to using them. Therefore, a trade usage of which the parties were not aware is not part of the contract. This was the viewpoint of many of the participating socialist countries. The objective theory considers that trade usages exist independently from the contract and that they have the legal authority to bind the parties without their explicit consent. The participating liberal market states leaned more towards this theory. This theory reflects the concept of trade usages under the UCC more closely. After deliberations, the article was accepted in its current form, which is closer to the objective theory.[52]

The difficult negotiations explain why several key matters regarding trades usages were not resolved and left to the interpretation of the court. These include:

48 Franco Ferrari, 'The Relationship between the UCC and the CISG and the Construction of Uniform Law' (1996) 29 Loyola of Los Angeles Law Review 1021, 1023

Michael Joachim Bonell, 'The UNIDROIT Principles of International Commercial Contracts and CISG – Alternatives or Complementary Instruments?' (1996) 1 Uniform Law Review 26, 28.

49 Stephen Bainbridge, 'Trade Usages in International Sales of Goods: An Analysis of the 1964 and 1980 Sales Conventions' (1983–1984) 24 Virginia Journal of International Law 619, 636–637.

50 Ibid, 636–638

As the author himself notes these are of course generalisations and it could not be said that every developing and/or socialist state held the exact same view.

51 See for instance:

Clayton P Gillette, 'Harmony and Stasis in Trade Usages for International Sale' (1998–1999) 39 Virginia Journal of International Law 707

Ch Pamboukis, 'The Concept and Function of Usages in the United Nations Convention for the International Sales of Goods' (2005–2006) 25 Journal of Law and Commerce 107.

52 Stephen Bainbridge, 'Trade Usages in International Sales of Goods: An Analysis of the 1964 and 1980 Sales Conventions' (1983–1984) 24 Virginia Journal of International Law 619,641

Cesare Massimo Bianca and Michael Joachim Bonell, 'Commentary on Usages and Practices' in Massimo Bianca and Michael Joachim Bonell (editors), *Commentary on the International Sales Law - The 1980 Vienna Sales Convention* (Giuffrè 1987) 110.

- A definition of the concept of trade usages
- Whether there is a time requirement before a practice can be considered a trade usage
- The hierarchy between course of dealing and trade usages.
- Whether trade usages can contradict express terms of the contract.[53]
- Whether a usage should be reasonable, when it is reasonable, and what should happen if a trade usage is not reasonable.[54] Although this issue is not dealt with explicitly Article 7 states that regard should be had to the observance of good faith in international trade.[55] From this it can be inferred that a trade usage that does not meet the standard of good faith should be considered unreasonable.[56]

Determining whether a practice is a trade usage is left to the courts.[57] If courts apply trade usages in line with the underlying principles of the CISG a uniform definition of trade usages would emerge in the longer term.[58] Whether this actually happens is another matter. In practice there is a tendency for courts to use domestic law to define trade usages.[59] Courts liken international usages to local usages and interpret these accordingly.[60] Gillette analysed arbitral awards that applied usages in the context of the CISG and found that arbitrators generally are conservative and only apply those usages that can be proven easily and with certainty.[61] Furthermore,

53 Jim C Chen, 'Code, Custom, and Contract: The Uniform Commercial Code as Law Merchant' (1992) 27 Texas International Journal 91, 104.

54 This is different from the UNIDROIT Principles, which state that usages are not binding if they are not reasonable (Art 1.8 (2) – in specific cases a known trade usage might not be applied if it can be considered as unreasonable in this situation.)

Gillette discusses that during the drafting of the CISG Chines trade delegates made an unsuccessful proposal that only reasonable trade usages should be applied: Clayton P Gillette, 'The Law Merchant in the Modern Age: Institutional Design and International Usages under the CISG' (2004–2005) 5 Chicago Journal of International Law 157,169.

55 Article 7 (1) In the interpretation of this Convention, regard is to be had to its international character and to the need to promote uniformity in its application and the observance of good faith in international trade.

56 Cesare Massimo Bianca and Michael Joachim Bonell, 'Commentary on Usages and Practices' in Cesare Massimo Bianca and Michael Joachim Bonell (editors), *Commentary on the International Sales Law - The 1980 Vienna Sales Convention* (Giuffrè 1987) 113.

57 Article 4 CISG

This Convention governs only the formation of the contract of sale and the rights and obligations of the seller and the buyer arising from such a contract. In particular, except as otherwise expressly provided in this Convention, it is not concerned with:

(a) the validity of the contract or of any of its provisions or of any usage;

58 Ch Pamboukis, 'The Concept and Function of Usages in the United Nations Convention for the International Sales of Goods' (2005–2006) 25 Journal of Law and Commerce 107,111.

59 Franco Ferrari, 'Homeward Trend and Lex Forism in International Sales Law' [2009] International Business Law Journal 333.

60 Franco Ferrari, 'Uniform Interpretation of the 1980 Uniform Sales Law' (1994) 24 Georgia Journal of International and Comparative Law 183,197.

61 Clayton P Gillette, 'The Law Merchant in the Modern Age: Institutional Design and International Usages under the CISG' (2004–2005) 5 Chicago Journal of International Law 157,179.

arbitrators do not seem to use trade usages to change express terms of the contract.[62]

Would it be possible to apply codified non-state rules as trade usages under the CISG? Under article 9 (2) the knowledge of the trade usage needs to be widespread and regularly observed. If codified non-state rules adhere to these criteria, then there is no reason why they should not be accepted as trade usages. Courts at times have accepted the Incoterms as trade usages under the CISG.[63] The parties could incorporate a trade term without specifying that this should be interpreted as an Incoterm. As discussed previously trade terms do not only exist as Incoterms, but also exist in domestic legislation. Therefore, if a court were to apply a trade term it would have to decide the intention of the parties if this intention was not specified further. In a case that concerned the sale of gasoline between BP Oil International and an Ecuadorian oil company the court stated that: *'Incoterms are incorporated into the CISG through article 9(2)'* and *'even if the usage of Incoterms is not global, the fact that they are well known in international trade means that they are incorporated through article 9(2).'*[64] The court thus applied the Incoterms as trade usages. Knowledge of the Incoterms is widespread, and this could justify their application as trade terms.[65] This collaborates with the tendency to interpret trade terms internationally.[66] There are cases where it is questionable what the intentions of the parties are. If for instance the law of New York is the applicable law, then perhaps the intention of the parties would be for the trade term to be interpreted according to the UCC as applicable in the state of New York. At the same time the CISG is also applicable in New York per federal law. The intention of the parties should decide how the trade term is interpreted and this intention cannot always be determined in a straightforward manner. Scholarship and case law do point to the possibility of using the Incoterms as trade usages under the CISG.[67]

62 Ibid.

63 For a comprehensive analysis of cases that have arisen about this subject see: Ch Pamboukis, 'The Concept and Function of Usages in the United Nations Convention for the International Sales of Goods' (2005–2006) 25 Journal of Law and Commerce 107,126–129.

64 *BP Oil International v. Empresa Estatal Petroleos de Ecuador*, United States 11 June 2003 Federal Appellate Court [5th Circuit], http://cisgw3.law.pace.edu/cases/030611u1.html
See also: Cedar Petrochemicals, Inc v Dongbu Hannong Chemical Co Ltd: 'it is worth noting at the outset that the entire body of INCOTERMS, 'FOB' Included – is incorporated into the CISG under Article 9 of the CISG.'
And in China: N. Chem.Indus Corp v Bestom Chem. Corp (S.D. Text 2006)
'Incoterms is the dominant source of definitions for commercial delivery terms used by parties to international sale contracts.'

65 Cesare Massimo Bianca and Michael Joachim Bonell, 'Commentary on Usages and Practices' in Cesare Massimo Bianca and Michael Joachim Bonell (editors), *Commentary on the International Sales Law - The 1980 Vienna Sales Convention* (Giuffrè 1987) 110.

66 Ch Pamboukis, 'The Concept and Function of Usages in the United Nations Convention for the International Sales of Goods' (2005–2006) 25 Journal of Law and Commerce 107,126–129.

67 The UCP would not be considered usages under the CISG because their field of application is different from that of the CISG.

Could the UNIDROIT Principles be applied as usages under the CISG? The pre-amble suggests that they take on the role of trade usages but of course a self-declaration does not make them trade usages. There is some case law that seems to imply at least tacitly a strong connection between the Principles and trade usages. In 1998 a court of appeal in Paris enforced an arbitral award based on trade usages and referenced the UPICC and concluded that the *'arbitral tribunal is entitled to base its decision on the rules of law it considers most appropriate and to refer to trade usages'*[68] In 2003, in a dispute before the ICC, the parties requested that the decision should be based on '*international trade usages.*'[69] The Tribunal pointed out that this reference can be criticised for its vagueness and found that '*consideration of a specific codification, as the UNIDROIT Principles may provide a more precise set of rules.*' It is not clear from this formulation whether the Tribunal considers the UPICC as trade usages or whether it found the choice of law clause too impractical. In a case in the Netherlands the court stated expressly that the UPICC can be used to fill any gaps in the CISG but this does not necessarily qualify them as trade usages.[70] There is nothing in the CISG to suggest that the UPICC would not be able to be considered trade usages but it depends on how frequently and consistently the Principles are used by the merchant community and subsequently applied by courts/tribunals. Given that the use of the UPICC by merchants is still limited as of now it would be difficult to consider the Principles as trade usages.

Several conclusions can be made with regards to trade usages under the CISG. First of all, trade usages have an important place in the CISG, but key aspects are not resolved in the convention itself and left to the discretion of the courts. This hampers uniform interpretation and leads to unpredictability. Second, courts tend to fall back on domestic legislation to interpret trade usages. As the exact nature of trade usages under the CISG has not been defined the fall back on domestic legislation surrounding trade usages is understandable. Third, despite this there is some evidence that courts do try to use a more international interpretation through, for instance, the use of the Incoterms as trade usages.

8.4 Conclusion: applying and interpreting trade usages

Trade usages are applied regularly by courts and arbitral tribunals as a source of domestic law and therefore play an important part in international commerce.

68 *Société FORASOL v. Société mixte Franco-Kazakh CISTM*, Cour d'appel de Paris (1er Chambre Civile) (1998) http://www.unilex.info/case.cfm?pid=2&id=1034&do=case.

69 ICC Award No. 12040 (2003) http://www.unilex.info/case.cfm?id=1418.

70 *Parties Unknown*, Hof 'S-Hertogenbosch, 16-02-2002, English language abstract available at: http://www.unilex.info/case.cfm?pid=2&do=case&id=959&step=Abstract

For an arbitral award dealing with the same issue see:

Tribunal of International Commercial Arbitration at the Russian Federation Chamber of Commerce and Industry, 5 June 1997, 229/1996, English language abstract available at: http://cisgw3.law.pace.edu/cases/970605r1.html

The Tribunal applied the UNIDROIT Principles of International Commercial Contracts as an international usage on the basis of article 9.2 of the CISG.

Trade usages are implied contractual terms and therefore need to be explicitly contracted out of. There is a presumption that the parties wish to adhere to trade usages.

Trade usages demonstrate the agency of the merchant community to develop their own rules. They show that the merchant community has the legitimacy and the authority to make law. Within that process there is an important role for the courts (and tribunals.) Courts affirm the practices that were started by the merchant community. It is the court that decides whether a practice is a trade usage, usually based on observation. A sense of obligation is not required, and this is the main difference between trade usages and custom. This diminishes the authority of the merchant community to decide what is law as it blurs the differences between those practices done for relational reasons and those practices that the parties would acknowledge as having force of law. If it is left to the courts to decide through observation whether a practice is a usage, then the rights of the merchant community to make this distinction are diminished.

The place of trade usages in transnational commercial law shows that if we move away from the confines of private international law there is an important role for non-state rules. Non-state rules can be applied as part of the applicable law and as such fulfil an important role in the contract. They derive their legal authority from their status in domestic law.

Codified non-state rules can be applied as trade usages, this can especially be observed with the Incoterms. There is some evidence that this also happens with the UPICC, although this is more limited. This is for several reasons, first, the UPICC are a relatively recent work and second, whilst trade usages formed one of the sources of inspiration for the UPICC, they were not the only one which therefore makes it more difficult to claim that the UPICC are trade usages or are fully representative of existing trade usages. The UPICC are applied more frequently as usages under the CISG than under the UCC. The reasons for this are likely that the CISG and UPICC are both transnational commercial law instruments, the unfamiliarity of the US courts with the UPICC, and that the CISG and the UPICC are close in spirit. When codified non-state rules are applied as trade usages, they have legal authority through the status that trade usages have as a source of domestic law. Therefore, if they are applied in this way their legal authority comes from their assimilation with trade usages and does not stand on its own; it hinges on their application by the courts as trade usages.

Overall, it is clear that trade usages are an important source of law; they can displace variable rules of international commercial law, interpret contractual terms, and add terms to the contract. Courts recognise the key role that trade usages have in international commerce and as such apply them in an authoritative way. The legal authority of trade usages is enhanced through their application as courts give them a central place in international commercial law. The following chapter focuses on how courts use non-state rules to *interpret* the law and the contract.

9 The application of non-state rules to interpret the law

9.1 Introduction

This chapter examines how courts use non-state rules to interpret the law, as general principles of law, and accepted international commercial practices. The previous chapter focused on the use of non-state rules as a source of domestic law. This current chapter focuses on how non-state rules are applied to interpret the law or the contract. This is regardless of whether the parties have referenced/included non-state rules in their contract. This means that non-state rules are seen by courts to be representative of transnational commercial law doctrine. Courts thus attribute legal authority to non-state rules by applying these to interpret the law and the contract.

The first part of this chapter examines how non-state rules are applied to interpret conventional law and uses the CISG as the main example. The second part of this chapter examines how courts use non-state rules to interpret domestic law, and the third part analyses how non-state rules are used as transnational commercial law doctrine. This mainly focuses on case law from the UK and how this has built a narrative whereby accepted international commercial law practices are used as a reference in discussions on points of domestic law.

This chapter demonstrates that non-state rules play a key role in the interpretation of both the law and the contract. Courts use non-state rules to give further legitimacy to their decisions. By linking their reasoning to non-state rules courts clarify that their decision not only has legitimacy in the domestic sphere but also in the transnational sphere. Courts thus attach legal authority to non-state rules and treat them as accepted principles/practices of transnational commercial law.

9.2 The application of non-state rules as part of international conventional law

The 1964 Convention for a Uniform Law on the International Sale of Goods (ULIS) excluded the use of domestic law to interpret the convention.[1] This

1 Article 17 ULIS:

Questions concerning matters governed by the present Law, which are not expressly settled therein shall be settled in conformity with the general principles on which the present Law is based.

was to ensure a more uniform interpretation and to do justice to the international character of the instrument. As ULIS and its sister convention, the Uniform Law on the Formation of Contracts for the International Sale of Goods (ULFIS), were only ratified by eight states this interpretation never materialised in practice.[2]

As ULIS/ULFIS failed to attract ratifications UNCITRAL made the decision to develop a new convention, which would become the CISG. De Ly seeks the failure of ULIS/ULFIS in their complete exclusion of domestic law which was too radical for many states as well as in the predominantly civil law approach of the conventions.[3] It is therefore not surprising that the CISG took a different approach. The CISG does not exclude the use of domestic law to interpret the convention but relegates this to a secondary place:

Article 7

(1) In the interpretation of this Convention, regard is to be had to its international character and to the need to promote uniformity in its application and the observance of good faith in international trade.
(2) Questions concerning matters governed by this Convention which are not expressly settled in it are to be settled in conformity with the general principles on which it is based or, in the absence of such principles, in conformity with the law applicable by virtue of the rules of private international law.

The underlying principles the convention specifically mentions are internationality, uniformity, and good faith. The CISG does not specify how these principles should be applied or whether these are the only underlying principles. If no underlying principles can be found, the court can apply domestic law.

In practice courts frequently fall back on domestic law, even when this is not in accordance with Article 7. Article 7 does not specify that the Convention can be interpreted through domestic law. It only specifies that domestic law can be used to interpret matters governed by the convention. There is a tendency for courts to use the lex fori to interpret the CISG and contracts governed by the CISG.[4] This is known as the homeward

2 Belgium. Germany, Gambia, Israel, Italy, Luxembourg, San Marino, the Netherlands, and the United Kingdom (opt in).

Most of these have now denounced the convention. ULIS and ULFIS are still in force in San Marino, the UK, and the Gambia.

See for the current status:

http://www.unidroit.org/status-ulis-1964;

http://www.unidroit.org/status-ulfc-1964;

It is rarely applied. An example is ICC Case No. 8547 where the parties chose ULIS as the governing law (which was then supplemented by the UPICC and ULFIS to fill in the gaps).

3 Filip de Ly, 'Sources of International Sales Law: An eclectic model' (2005) 25 Journal of Law and Commerce 1,2.

4 Franco Ferrari, 'Homeward Trend and Lex Forism in International Sales Law' [2009] International Business Law Journal 333.

trend.[5] This is also not in accordance with article 7, which specifies that the applicable law should be used and this is necessarily the lex fori. For courts it is easier to apply the lex fori than to discover the underlying principles of the Convention. These principles are not well defined nor does the convention give concrete guidance on how these should be applied. Courts have a better understanding of the legal principles of the lex fori. It is thus easier to interpret the CISG by relying on domestic law. This is especially the case if the rules contained in the CISG are closely reflected in domestic law and lead to an easy analogy. Of course, there are also many examples where the CISG or matters underlying it are interpreted with respect to its international character.[6] It is however a worrying tendency that undermines the purpose and uniformity of the convention.

If the CISG should be interpreted in accordance with the underlying principles this immediately leads to the question of how these principles can be discovered and how they can be applied. The CISG mentions three principles explicitly: internationality, uniformity, and good faith. The interpretation of the CISG should thus be done in a manner to promote uniformity, with respect to the internationality of the Convention, and uphold good faith in international trade. Other principles that are implied by the convention through a holistic reading of its articles are freedom of contract, due diligence, favor contractus, and pacta sunt servanda.

To discover other underlying principles one possibility would be to use general principles of law as defined by article 38 of the ICJ and distil from these the principles that have a bearing on private law, but as discussed before this is not particularly practical because these principles are intended for state-state relations and are of a very general nature that makes their direct applicability to commercial contracts difficult. Courts could also use (international) key cases of the CISG or compare the private law principles of different legal systems to understand the majoritarian approach. These methods are time consuming and do not lead to predictable results. They

5 The term homeward trend originates with John Honnold who used it in his work *Documentary History of the Uniform Law for International Sales: The Studies, Deliberations, and Decisions that Led to the 1980 United Nations Convention with Introductions and Explanations* (Kluwer Law International 1989) 298–299

'The Convention, faute de mieux, will often be applied by tribunals (judges or arbitrators) who will be intimately familiar only with their own domestic law. The tribunals, regardless of their merit, will be subject to a natural tendency to read the international rules in light of the legal ideas that have been imbedded at the core of their intellectual formation. The mind sees what the mind has means of seeing.'

See also: John Honnold, 'The Sales Convention in Action- Uniform International Words: Uniform Application?' (1988) 8 Journal of Law and Communication 207

For a practical example see Angela M Romito, 'CISG: Italian Court and Homeward Trend - Queen Mary Case Translation Programme Corte d'Appello di Milano 20 March 1998 Italdecor s.a.s. Yiu's Industries (H.K.) Limited (default)' (2002) 14 Pace International Law Review 179.

6 Franco Ferrari, 'Homeward Trend and Lex Forism in International Sales Law' [2009] International Business Law Journal 333, 339.

are therefore not necessarily in the interests of the parties, as they do not provide certainty.

Another method to discover and interpret the principles underlying the CISG that courts have developed is to use codified non-state rules. This happens especially with the UPICC. When the UNIDROIT Principles were published the possibility of using these to interpret the CISG was raised immediately.[7] The advantages are self-evident. The UPICC are a concrete instrument that courts can consult easily which makes it a more attractive option than going through a longer process with an uncertain outcome of comparative discovery to find the underlying principles of the CISG. A less utilitarian argument would be that the UNIDROIT Principles were drafted with the CISG in mind and the instruments are close in spirit.[8] Furthermore, the Principles are a thorough and comparative work of research. Yet, it should be recognised that the UPICC are not just a restatement but are also a work of innovation and therefore not all the content would necessarily reflect globally accepted principles of commercial law (if such a thing even exists.)

It could be argued that the UPICC were drafted much later than the CISG and that therefore they should not be used to interpret the CISG, as the underlying principles the latter refers to cannot be the UPICC.[9] This depends on how the convention is interpreted. This can be in a narrow way which confines these principles to the space and time when the CISG was drafted or by adopting a wider view whereby these principles can change over time as circumstances and context change.[10] The ICJ stated that a treaty should be interpreted according to the context at the moment of

7 Michael Joachim Bonell, 'The UNIDROIT Principles of International Commercial Contracts and CISG – Alternatives or Complementary Instruments?' (1996) 1 Uniform Law Review 26, 35–37;

Professor Bonell gives several examples on how the UNIDROIT Principles could accomplish this. One of these is for instance that the criteria used to determine whether there is a fundamental breach of contract contained in article 7.3.1 of the Principles could be used to define the concept of fundamental breach under CISG article 25 further.

Alejandro M Garro, The Gap-Filling Role of the UNIDROIT Principles in International Sales Law: Some Comments on the Interplay between the Principles and the CISG, [1994–1995] 69 Tulane Law Review, 1149

Jürgen Basedow, 'Uniform Law Conventions and the UNIDROIT Principles of International Commercial Contracts' (2000) 5 Uniform Law Review 129

François Dessemontet, 'Use of the UNIDROIT Principles to Interpret and Supplement Domestic Law' (2002) Supplément Spécial Bulletin de la Cour Internationale d'Arbitrage de la CCI 1, 18

This possibility was also raised for the Principles of European Contract Law.

8 Michael Joachim Bonell, 'The UNIDROIT Principles of International Commercial Contracts and CISG – Alternatives or Complementary Instruments?' (1996) 1 Uniform Law Review 26.

9 Michael Joachim Bonell, 'The UNIDROIT Principles and Transnational Law' (2000) 5 Uniform Law Review, 199, 210.

10 Herbert Kronke, 'The UN Sales Convention, the UNIDROIT Contract, Principles and the Way Beyond' (2005–2006) 25 Journal of Law and Commerce 451, 457.

interpretation and not the moment of creation or ratification.[11] This decision supports the legitimacy to use the UPICC to interpret the CISG.

Courts started to use the UPICC to interpret the CISG shortly after they were first published. In October 1996 the Court of Appeal of Grenoble referenced the UNIDROIT Principles as support for the CISG and consequently made a connection between both instruments.[12] A French buyer and a German seller concluded a contract for the sale of machinery. The buyer claimed restitution of part of the excess purchase price paid. French law was the applicable law and through this the CISG. The court ruled that restitution should be made at the seller's place of business. The court pointed out that this rule is an interpretation of the general principle that payment takes place at the domicile of the creditor and that this principle is found in article 6.1.6 of the UNIDROIT Principles. The UPICC were accordingly used as support for an underlying principle of the CISG. In 1997 an ICC arbitration award went further and stated that the general principles of the CISG are contained in the UNIDROIT Principles.[13] The Court of Cassation in Belgium stated that gap filling in the CISG should take place per the underlying principles of the Convention, which can especially be found in the UPICC.[14]

An example of how the UPICC are used concretely is to determine the interest rate: Article 78 of the CISG states that the party in breach of its obligations should pay interest but does not say how the interest rate should be calculated. The UNIDROIT Principles contain guidelines on establishing the interest rate.[15] Several arbitral awards used the UPICC to interpret

11 Jürgen Basedow, 'Uniform Law Conventions and the UNIDROIT Principles of International Commercial Contracts' (2000) 5 Uniform Law Review 129, 133/136 quoting: International Court of Justice 21-06-71, ICI Rep. (1971), 31 (Legal consequences for States of the continued presence of South Africa in Namibia).

12 *SCEA GAEC Des Beauches Bernard Bruno v. Société Teso Ten Elsen GmbH & COKG*, Cour d'Appel de Grenoble, October 1996, http://www.unilex.info/case.cfm?pid=2&id=638&do=case.

13 ICC Award No. 8817 (1995)
http://www.unilex.info/case.cfm?pid=2&do=case&id=659&step=FullText;
A court decision in the Netherlands that same year confirmed this:
Cooperative Maritime Etaploise v. Bos Fishproducts District Court Zwolle 5 March 1997.

14 *Scafom International BV vs Lorraine Tubes s.a.s*, Cour de Cassation, 19/06/2009
http://www.unilex.info/case.cfm?pid=2&do=case&id=1456&step=Abstract.

15 Article 7.4.9(2) The rate of interest shall be the average bank short-term lending rate to prime borrowers prevailing for the currency of payment at the place for payment, or where no such rate exists at that place, then the same rate in the State of the currency of payment. In the absence of such a rate at either place the rate of interest shall be the appropriate rate fixed by the law of the State of the currency of payment.

interest rates under the CISG.[16] State courts have followed, for instance the Supreme Economic Court of Belarus used the UPICC to determine the interest rate.[17] The UPICC are thus used both to materialise the underlying principles of the CISG and to find the concrete rules that the court can apply.

Other non-state instruments could be used to interpret the CISG. The PECL have been used in this fashion, but not as regularly. As the PECL represent a European regional approach whereas the CISG is a global instrument it is not surprising that this does not happen regularly. The PLACL would have the same issue. The Incoterms are often used in conjunction with the CISG to regulate passage of risk. If an Incoterm is included in the contract it displaces the articles on the passage of risk in the CISG as express contract terms take precedent over the CISG. This is not the same as interpreting the passage of risk in the CISG through the lens of the Incoterms. The Incoterms do not contain general principles of interpretation. It would of course be possible to construct an Incoterm and the CISG rules on the passage of risk together if the contract asks for this. It would be difficult to use the Incoterms to interpret the CISG without the contract making any reference to the Incoterms.

Trade association rules are usually not neutral and universal enough to interpret the principles underlying the CISG. It is thus not surprising that mainly the UPICC are used in this fashion.

Courts can also use principles arising from case law to interpret the CISG. UNCITRAL maintains a database with CISG case law although some countries are overrepresented or underrepresented depending on available published cases.[18] Based on this database UNCITRAL publishes a case law digest.[19] This greatly facilitates the interpretation of the CISG as it arranges key cases per article of the CISG. Under the article 7 headline different

16 Michael Joachim Bonell, 'The UNIDROIT Principles and Transnational Law' (2000) 5 Uniform Law Review 199, 210

Two arbitral awards made by the International Court of Arbitration of Federal Chamber of Commerce in Vienna

And one made by the ICC: ICC Award No. 8128 (1995)

Text available at: http://www.unilex.info/case.cfm?pid=2&do=case&id=637&step=Abstract

This award also referred to article Art. 4.507 of the Principles of European Contract Law:

'L'arbitre considère justifié d'appliquer au litige les règles identiques contenues dans les principes UNIDROIT et les principes du droit européen des contrats en tant que principes généraux au sens de l'article 7(2) de la Convention.'

17 Parties Unknown, Supreme Economic Court of the Republic of Belarus, 03/01/2003

http://www.unilex.info/case.cfm?pid=2&do=case&id=1389&step=Abstract

Holzimpex Inc. v. Republican Agricultural Unitary Enterprise, Supreme Economic Court of the Republic of Belarus, 20/05/2003 http://www.unilex.info/case.cfm?pid=2&id=1007&do=case.

18 http://www.uncitral.org/uncitral/en/case_law.html

Pace Law School & Unilex also maintain case law collections on the CISG.

19 UNCITRAL Digest of Case Law on the United Nations Convention on Contracts for the International Sale of Goods

http://www.uncitral.org/pdf/english/clout/CISG-digest-2012-e.pdf.

principles are found that have been extracted from case law. These principles include party autonomy, favor contractus, mitigation of damage, and informality among others. The digest is not binding on ratifying states, but it has persuasive value and is an important tool that contributes towards a more uniform interpretation of the CISG.[20]

Another initiative that should be mentioned is the CISG Advisory Council, which was founded in 2001 and publishes opinions on aspects of the CISG to come to a uniform interpretation of the Convention.[21] The Advisory Council lacks any authoritative force and is a private initiative of a group of scholars. Nonetheless, their work is of significant value in aiding courts in interpreting the CISG and the Advisory Council has observer status at both UNIDROIT and UNCITRAL. If these opinions are used with regularity to interpret the CISG, they become more persuasive and gain legal authority. Currently there are 21 opinions published. These have all been translated in French, English, German, and Spanish. A number of the opinions are also translated in Russian, Arabic, Chinese, Portuguese, and Japanese.

Codified non-state rules and case law are thus used to discover the Principles underlying the CISG and to find concrete rules to interpret these principles. Good faith, uniformity, and internationality are all three generic principles of which a myriad of different meanings and interpretations can be found. Courts resort to domestic law to interpret the CISG and find the concrete rules. Although the Convention does allow for this it should only be done in the absence of any underlying principles. Furthermore, courts should resort in that case to the lex contractus and not to the lex fori.

The publication of the UPICC and to a smaller degree the PECL led to courts using these to find the principles underlying the CISG. Other international initiatives that aid in the interpretation of the CISG are the opinions issued by the CISG Advisory Council and the UNCITRAL case law digests. Concluding, courts apply non-state rules like restatements of law, case digests, and authoritative guidelines to interpret the CISG and find both the principles underlying the convention as well as concrete rules that can be applied to solve the contractual dispute and fill the gaps in the convention.

20 Another initiative is the trans-lex database, which is focused on transnational commercial law in general. This database has extracted principles on transnational commercial law from case law and other materials.

These principles can be found on the website:

http://www.trans-lex.org/principles/.

21 These opinions are published on their website:

http://www.cisgac.com/;

The Advisory Council is a private initiative that consists of scholars from different cultures and backgrounds and '*is guided by the mandate of Article 7 of the Convention as far as its interpretation and application are concerned: the paramount regard to international character of the convention and the need to promote uniformity.*'.

9.3 The use of non-state rules as guidelines for the interpretation of national law

Codified non-state rules are used to interpret and supplement domestic law, often as general principles of law or accepted commercial law doctrine. On the UNILEX database there are 198 cases where the UPICC are applied as means for supplementing or interpreting domestic law and 92 cases where they are applied to confirm that the solution in domestic law is in conformity with international standards.[22] As there are 476 cases in total on UNILEX it is clear the leading usage of the UPICC is to interpret the applicable domestic law. This is even more striking as the pre-amble to the 1994 edition of the UNIDROIT Principles did not anticipate this way of using the UPICC and makes no mention of it. The 2004 version of the pre-amble was updated to include that *they may be used to interpret or supplement domestic law*. The initiative for using the UPICC in this way started in courts and arbitral tribunals. The majority of the cases where the UPICC are used to interpret domestic law stem from Russia (35 cases), Spain (20), the Ukraine (16), Paraguay (16), Lithuania (14), and Australia (13).[23]

The Court of appeal of Grenoble in *Société Harper Robinson v Société Internationale de Maintenance et de Réalisations Industrielle* applied French law and supplemented its considerations with reference to the UNIDROIT Principles.[24] An American company and a French company entered into a contract regarding the transportation of machinery from the US to France. The packaging was faulty and damaged the equipment. The contract contained a liability clause, which read that the carrier would compensate any loss owning to defective performance. The incorporated standard term specified that the liability of the carrier was limited to $50 per shipment and thus conflicted with the liability clause. The court stated that in case of such contradiction a principle of international commercial law is that the term which is not the standard term should prevail and it then quoted the UPICC art 2.21 as evidence of this principle and that furthermore the clause should be constructed against who is relying on it (art. 4.6.)[25] The court thus used the UPICC as general principles of international commercial law. Even though French law was applicable to the contract, the fact that it was an international dispute compelled the court to rely on the UPICC.

22 http://www.unilex.info/principles/cases/article/102#article_102; Numbers date from June 2020.

23 There should not be a great value attached to the concrete numbers as the Unilex database is incomplete and the numbers will be higher in practice, especially given that arbitral awards are usually not published.

24 *Société Harper Robinson v. Société internationale de maintenance et de réalisations industrielles*, Cour d'Appel de Grenoble, January 1996.

25 *'Qu'il est de principe, en droit du commerce international, que "en cas d'incompatibilité entre une clause qui ne l'est pas, cette dernière l'emporte" (Principes d'Unidroit, article 2.21) et que "en cas d'ambiguïté, les clauses d'un contrat s'interprètent de préférence contre celui qui les a proposées' (Principes d'Unidroit, art. 4.6)'* http://www.unilex.info/case.cfm?id=633.

Codified non-state rules can be used for gap filling purposes. In a domestic dispute the Paraguayan judge referred to the UPICC as a 'complementary law' and applied among others Art. 5.1.3, which establishes a duty of cooperation between the parties.[26] The court stated that Paraguayan law does not officially recognise a duty of cooperation but this falls within the good faith principle that is recognised in Paraguayan law

The UPICC are also used and show that domestic law and international commercial law principles propagate the same solution.[27] In a case before the ICC the tribunal referred to the UNIDROIT Principles as *'a useful source for establishing general rules for international commercial contracts'* and consequently used the UPICC to demonstrate that these and the applicable New York law came to the same conclusion.[28] The court used the UPICC to show that national and international legal practices are aligned.[29] The Supreme Court of Paraguay used Articles 5.1.1 and 5.1.2 of the UPICC (on implied and express contractual terms) to confirm similar principles in the applicable domestic Paraguayan law.[30] When the law offers several possible interpretations the court might use the UPICC to justify why they picked a particular solution.

26 Tribunal de Apelación en lo Civil y Comercial de Asunción, Compañía de Petroleo y Asfalto (Compasa) c/ Petrobras Distribuidora S.A, 09-05-2016.
Available at: http://www.unilex.info/principles/case/1958.

27 Michael Joachim Bonell and Ole Lando, 'Future Prospects of the Unification of Contract Law in Europe and Worldwide' (2013) 18 Uniform Law Review 17,21.

28 ICC Award No. 8540 1996
http://www.unilex.info/principles/case/644.

29 See also: François Dessemontet, 'Use of the UNIDROIT Principles to Interpret and Supplement Domestic Law' (2002) Supplément Spécial Bulletin de la Cour Internationale d'Arbitrage de la CCI 1,22 who notes *'A consistent feature of most of the arbitral awards examined is that the arbitrators go to great lengths to show that the applicable domestic law and the Principles provide for identical solutions'* This article quotes several awards (a selection: Partial award of 4 September 1996 in ICC case 8540, UNIDROIT Cases No. 6; award of 17 December 1996, Court of Arbitration affiliated to the Economic Chamber and Agrarian Chamber of the Czech
Republic, UNIDROIT Cases No. 8; award in an ad hoc arbitration in Helsinki, 1998, UNIDROIT Cases No. 15; preliminary award of 25 November 1994, Zurich Chamber of Commerce, UNIDROIT Cases No.16; award in ad hoc arbitration in Auckland, New Zealand, 1995, UNIDROIT Cases No. 17; final awarding ICC case 8240, (1999) 10:2 ICC ICArb. Bull. 60)
Dessemontet notes: *'Only a minority of the decisions studied (approximately 10 out of 40) mention that the Principles embody a solution divergent from the (sometimes unclear) domestic law.'*

30 Corte Suprema de Justicia, Engracia Marina Haywood de Balbuena y otro v. Empresa de Transporte Nueva Asunción S.A. y otro, 1074/2016, 04-08-2016
Available at: http://www.unilex.info/principles/case/2140.

Are other codified non-state rules used for this purpose? The PECL have been applied in this way; often in conjunction with the UPICC.[31] The UPICC and the PECL were first published within a year of each other and in those earlier years they are often used together. Later cases refer more frequently solely to the UNIDROIT Principles. This is a logical consequence of how the PECL have developed into a work that is used more by scholars and legislators than by practitioners. Nevertheless, there are examples of cases where the PECL are used to interpret domestic contract law, especially in the European context.[32] They are sometimes even cited outside Europe, for instance by a court in Paraguay alongside the UPICC.[33]

In 2008 the High Commercial Court of Ukraine issued an Official Note stating that the Incoterms, the UCP, and the 1994 edition of the UNIDROIT Principles enshrine trade customs under Ukrainian law.[34] Since the publication of this note multiple cases in the Ukraine have referred to these instruments (especially the UPICC) as international trade usages, customary law, and general principles of commercial law.[35] Most of the cases concern domestic con-

31 The Unilex database does not keep track of PECL cases specifically but does mention cases where the PECL are used alongside the UNIDROIT Principles to supplement or interpret domestic law. There is no similar database for solely the PECL so it is difficult to determine how often these are used independently from the UPICC.

32 See for instance, Carlos Vendrell Cervantes, 'Application of the Principles of European Contract Law' (2008) 16 Zeitschrift für Europäisches Privatrecht 534, where the author analyses a number of decisions of Spanish courts that used the PECL to interpret domestic contract law, as a doctrinal authoritative guide, or as point of comparison.

See also Danny Bush, 'The Principles of European Contract Law before the Supreme Court of the Netherlands' (2008) 16 Zeitschrift für Europäisches Privatrecht 549, which analyses the use of the PECL in courts in the Netherlands.

33 Tribunal de Apelación en lo Civil y Comercial de Asunción, Sindulfo Ruiz Pavetti v. Maria Esther Recalde de Aliendre y Policarpo Ramón Aliendre, 17-10-2016.

Available at: http://www.unilex.info/principles/case/2105

34 Ralf Michaels, 'The UNIDROIT Principles as Global Background Law,' (2014) 19 Uniform Law Review 643; Official Note of the High Commercial Court of Ukraine No.01-8/211, 07.04.2008.

35 For instance:

Specialized foreign trade company Progress, subsidiary company of the State Company Ukrspecexport v. Ministry of Economy of Ukraine Kyiv District Administrative Court 8/311

Cherkassy Branch of OJSC Kredobank v. Individual entrepreneur 2 Cherkasy Regional Commercial Court 02/2625;

Dnipropetrovsk company Dnepryanka v. Inter-state Tax Administration of Dnipropetrovsk city and Department, Dnipropetrovsk Regional Administrative Court, 2-a-10084/09/0470;

TOV Ukrainian commercial vehicles v. Department of Transport and Communications of Chernihiv City Council High Commercial Court of Ukraine, 7/72;

Arcada PP v. Hobotovske enterprise Krahmaloprodukt High Commercial Court of Ukraine 42/90-10;

Public utility company Housing Management of Kyiv city v. TOV Kyiv Telecommunication Networks Kyiv Commercial Court 5011-7/3803-2012;

OJSC Druzhkovskaya factory of metal products v. TOV Company Light-Tech High Commercial Court of Ukraine 5023/4701/12;

Poltava oblavtodor v. TOV Kontakt-K, Dnipropetrovsk Regional Commercial Court 904/4611/13 (abstracts can all be found on UNIILEX).

tracts rather than international ones, and the UPICC, Incoterms, and UCP are used to interpret the applicable domestic (Ukrainian) law. As an example, a regional commercial court in a dispute between two Ukrainian companies referred to the applicable articles of the Ukrainian Civil Code, and noted that these were of a general nature, and that as the High Commercial Court of Ukraine officially endorsed the UPICC it would apply these to interpret the law.[36] This is one of several cases in which courts in the Ukraine apply the UPICC to interpret domestic law.[37]

In an appeal to the Supreme Court regarding a decision where the UPICC were applied the respondent pointed out that the UPICC do not have binding force in Paraguay and therefore their application violated Paraguayan law. The Supreme Court stated that as the UPICC were applied as a complementary law and the rights of the parties under Paraguayan law had not been infringed the Court of Appeal had been correct in its application of the UPICC.[38] The Supreme Court therefore recognised that transnational commercial law instruments can be used to interpret the law or to fill in gaps.

Codified non-state rules are thus used to interpret the law in both domestic and international contracts. The usage of codified non-state rules for this purpose is a new practice that mainly emerged with the publication of the UNIDROIT Principles. The CISG, the PECL, the UCP, and the Incoterms are all used for this purpose but the UPICC take the lead. They are used as general principles of transnational commercial law or as accepted international commercial law practices.

9.4 Non-state rules as a point of reference

Non-state rules are also used as a point of reference and evidence of international commercial law practice within discussions on domestic law. An example is whether pre-contractual negotiations should be admitted as evidence under English law.[39] English law has always been reticent on this issue although it recognizes that there are exceptions to this general rule. *Chartbrook Limited (Respondents) v Persimmon Homes Limited and Others (Appellants)* concerned a dispute between two construction companies with

36 *FG Alpha v. TOV NVF Sintal*, Kharkiv Regional Commercial Court 35/118-08, 23 September 2009
http://www.unilex.info/case.cfm?id=1739.

37 See also:
TOV Ukrainian commercial vehicles v. Department of Transport and Communications of Chernihiv City Council
High Commercial Court of Ukraine 7/72, 24 November 2010
http://www.unilex.info/case.cfm?id=1707.

38 Corte Suprema de Justicia - Sala Civil y Comercial, Jorge Moises Etcheverry Alí v. Rosa María Ramona Etcheverry de Brizuela, 27-03-2017.

39 Parts of this discussion appeared before in Johanna Hoekstra, 'The Normative Influence of the UNIDROIT Principles of International Commercial Law on Courts' (2019) 23 The Vindobona Journal of International Commercial Law and Arbitration 54.

regards to a payment.[40] The Court of Appeal took a wider approach than usual to admissibility of evidence external to the contract, which included pre-contractual negotiations. Lawrence Collins LJ stated that the policy reasons for this exclusionary rule are not self-evident and compelling. He quoted the UNIDROIT Principles (article 4.3) and the CISG (article 8) as evidence that in international commercial practice this is acceptable.[41] The case was appealed to the House of Lords, which held that the payment clause should be constructed so that it was clear to a reasonable person what was meant by it, and that the pre-contractual negotiations should not be taken into account.

About the CISG, the PECL, and the UNIDROIT Principles Lord Hoffmann stated:

> Supporters of the admissibility of pre-contractual negotiations draw attention to the fact that Continental legal systems seem to have little difficulty in taking them into account. Both the Unidroit Principles of International Commercial Contracts (1994 and 2004 revision) and the Principles of European Contract Law (1999) provide that in ascertaining the "common intention of the parties", regard shall be had to prior negotiations: articles 4 [...] But these instruments reflect the French philosophy of contractual interpretation, which is altogether different from that of English law.[42]

The lower court thus used non-state rules to contrast international practice with domestic law, as part of its argument on why pre-contractual negotiations should be admissible. Domestic law is shown as out of sync with international practice. Lord Hoffmann is clearly doubtful of whether the UPICC, PECL, and CISG are truly representative of an accepted international contract law doctrine and considers these reflections of French contract

40 *Chartbrook Limited v. Persimmon Homes Limited* 2008 EWCA Civ 183 Court of Appeal (Civil Division).

The contract stipulated that Persimmon Homes would build apartments on land owned by Chartbrook and then sell these apartments. The payment Chartbrook would receive was broken down in two parts a) a minimum guaranteed residential value and b) a balancing additional residential payment. With regards to the latter the contract stated that this would be: '*23.4% of the price achieved for each residential unit in excess of the minimum guaranteed residential unit value less the costs and incentives.*' The dispute arose as Chartbrook believed that this payment would be net proceeds of the sale of each housing unit whereas Persimmon reasoned that Chartbrook would either receive this payment or the minimum guaranteed residential value; whichever one was greater. This was discussed in the pre-contractual negotiations.

41 '*Nor is the exclusionary principle accepted in international instruments dealing with private law contracts, such as the UNIDROIT Principles of International Commercial Contracts (Art 4(3)) and the UN Convention on Contracts for the International Sale of Goods (1980).*'

42 *Chartbrook Limited (Respondents) v Persimmon Homes Limited* [2009] UKHL 38 House of Lords.

philosophy. It is questionable whether he is correct on that account[43] and the view of Lord Hoffmann was both criticised and supported.[44] This case shows how non-state rules are used in domestic law cases to criticise, support, or broaden national legal practice.

The discussion continued in *Proforce Recruit Limited v. The Rugby Group Limited,* which concerned the interpretation of what a preferential supplier entails.[45] Lady Arden wrote that consideration should be given to the possibility of admitting evidence from pre-contractual negotiations and she mentioned the CISG and the UPICC in this context:

> The UNIDROIT Principles of International Commercial Contracts give primacy to the common intention of the parties and on questions of interpretation requires regard to be had to all the circumstances, including the pre-contractual negotiations of the parties (art 4.3). The UN Convention on Contracts for the International Sale of Goods (1980) provides that a party's intention is in certain circumstances relevant, and in determining that intention regard is to be had to all relevant circumstances, including preliminary negotiations.[46]

The Square Mile Partnership Ltd v Fitzmaurice McCall Ltd also discussed the issue of pre-contractual negotiations. Lady Arden quotes *Proforce Recruit Ltd v. The Rugby* as an example of when pre-contractual negotiations can be

43 Indeed, commentators hold that there are aspects of the CISG, which are much closer to the common law than to civil law. The CISG follows for instance the breach of contract law approach that comes from common law and not the cause orientated approach that is prevalent in civil law (Ingeborg Schwenzer, and Pascal Hachem, 'the CISG- Successes and Pitfalls' (2009) 57 The American Journal of Comparative Law 457, 462).

44 For support of Lord Hofffmann's point see: Lord Hope of Craighead, 'The Role of the Judge in Developing Contract Law' (2011) 15 Jersey and Guernsey Law Review 6 which supports that the UNIDROIT Principles in the matter of pre-contractual negotiations run contrary to the common law for practical reasons (Lord Hoffman argued that it would be difficult to separate pre-contractual negotiation from statements of consensus and aspiration) as well as because of the fundamental matter of the absence of a general theory of good faith in English contract law.

Professor Eric Clive criticised Lord Hoffmann's position in a blog entry made on the University of Edinburgh blog on European Private News which is available at:

http://www.epln.law.ed.ac.uk/2010/04/22/interpretation-and-pre-contractual-negotiations-is-english-law-genetically-incompatible-with-european-private-law/ (2015);

Professor Clive argues that these instruments are not contrary to the common law because the roots of the ideology underlying these are not inconsistent with English common law.

45 *Proforce Recruit Limited v. The Rugby Group Limited* 2006 EWCA Civ 69. The High Court made a summary judgment and stated that evidence with regards to pre-contractual negotiations could not be considered. The Court of Appeal held that pre-contractual negotiations can be used to interpret the clause and referred the case to trial. LJ Mummery said that the expression preferred supplier status has no obvious meaning and could therefore only be interpreted in the context of the whole agreement and all the surrounding circumstances.

46 *Proforce Recruit Limited v. The Rugby Group Limited* 2006 EWCA Civ 69.

admitted and she quotes several articles to demonstrate that the CISG and the UPICC are reflective of international commercial practice.[47] Although ultimately in this case the court rejects the use of pre-contractual negotiations to interpret the contract it declares that sometimes this could be admissible.

The UPICC, were also used by the Supreme Court of the UK to discuss whether an oral modification of a long-term contract is valid.[48] Two English companies entered into a licence agreement, which contained a no oral modification clause. During the contract the licensee proposed a revised payment schedule. Confusion ensued on whether this modification was accepted by the licensor. When the licensee stopped paying according to the original schedule the licensor terminated the agreement. The licensee then sued for damages. The licensor stated that the no oral modification clause meant that the revised schedule was not valid. The court of first instance agreed with the licensor whereas Court of Appeal reversed the decision and stated that the oral agreement effectively dispensed the no oral agreement clause.

The Supreme Court stated that whether an oral agreement could nullify a no oral modification clause is a controversial subject under English law. It then quoted Art. 29 of the CISG and Art. 2.1.18 of the UNIDROIT Principles which both state that if the contract is specific about the form of modification any deviation from this would make the modification void. The UPICC add that *'a party may be precluded by its conduct from asserting such a clause to the extent that the other party has acted in reliance on that conduct.'* The Supreme Court thus used the CISG and the UPICC as examples of how it is not contradictory to have a system that does not impose a specific format for the contract whilst at the same time adhering the parties to the agreement that they made on the format.[49]

In 2013 the Spanish court referred to the UPICC in support of the applicable Spanish law to show that these both used the same solution.[50] A Russian court referred to the UPICC to show that the use of the contra proferentem

47 *The Square Mile Partnership Ltd v Fitzmaurice McCall Ltd* [2006] EWCA Civ 1690 Court of Appeal (Civil Division), 18.12.2006

Lady Arden observed: '*The Proforce case has been the subject of academic discussion: see in particular A. Berg, Thrashing through the Undergrowth [2006] 122 LQR 354 and M.J. Bonell, The UNIDROIT Principles and CISG - Sources of Inspiration for English Courts? [2006] 11 Uniform Law Review 305. Mr Berg makes the important point that the meaning of commercial contracts needs to be clear, and that the admission of evidence as to pre-contractual negotiations (or post-contractual conduct) "will often make it more difficult and time-consuming for a party to a commercial contract to ascertain his legal position." Professor Bonell expresses the view that the approach in the UNIDROIT principles and the CISG reflect the trend at international level.*'

48 *Rock Advertising Limited v MWB Business Exchange Centres Limited* [2018] UKSC 24; See also: *Kabab-Ji S.A.L. v. Kout Food Group* [2020] EWCA Civ 6.

49 Lord Sumption: *'These widely used codes suggest that there is no conceptual inconsistency between a general rule allowing contracts to be made informally and a specific rule that effect will be given to a contract requiring writing for a variation.'*

50 *Grupo Santa Monica Sports v. Real Club Deportivo de la Coruña*, Audiencia Provincial de A. Coruña (Seccion 4), 18.02.2013.

rule under domestic Russian law was in line with international practice[51] and the Georgian Supreme Court referred to both the CISG and the UPICC in support of domestic Georgian law with regards to the good faith principle to show that domestic law is in line with international practice.[52]

These cases demonstrate that non-state rules are used as a point of reference for accepted international commercial law practice and doctrine and contrast this against domestic law. These cases did not concern international contracts, but domestic contracts. Therefore, non-state rules find a role in the debate on national laws where they are used to illustrate certain points or as a reference material. Non-state rules are used as internationally accepted practices, standards, or principles of transnational commercial law. They have persuasive value; they are used as legal opinion, scholarship, or doctrine in domestic courts.

9.5 Conclusion: non-state rules as a tool of interpretation

Non-state rules are used to interpret domestic law and international conventions. Codified non-state rules, mainly the UPICC, but also the CISG and PECL, and in very specific circumstances the Incoterms serve as general legal principles or are used to find the concrete rules underlying these principles. Scholarly opinions and case law are used as guidelines to discover and apply these principles to the contract or to interpret the law.

Non-state rules have been shown in this chapter to have legal authority through their application as a comparative reference point to demonstrate accepted international commercial law principles This is often done to show that the domestic law and non-state rules propagate the same solution. This shows that domestic law is in accordance with accepted international commercial practice and that therefore the proposed solution is an equitable one for disputes arising from (international) contracts. Non-state rules are used in courts with the purpose to further debates on (national) legal principles by providing a reference point for commonly accepted international principles. In this way non-state rules raise awareness and influence courts, legislators, and policy makers. They are applied as legal scholarship and doctrine.

Non-state rules are thus used to help interpret the applicable law or to fill any gaps in the applicable law. It is precisely in these functions that non-state rules are applied the most frequently. The courts attribute legal authority to non-state rules if they are applied in these ways. It shows that courts attach value to non-state rules. As non-state rules are perceived to emerge from

51 Commercial Court of the Moscow Region, Ministry of the Internal Affairs of the Russian Federation v. Sberbank, 28-12-2017
http://www.unilex.info/principles/case/2155.

52 Georgia Supreme Court, AS-668-668-2018, 2.07.2018
http://www.unilex.info/principles/case/2236;
The Georgian Supreme Court made the same reference in several other cases, including also to the PECL. See for instance: AS-559-2019, 04-12-2019 and AS-1548-2019, 14.02.2020.

within the transnational business community, linking the decision of the court with non-state rules gives further legitimacy to the ruling. Not only does the ruling now have legitimacy within the domestic legal system, it also has legitimacy in the transnational commercial law sphere because non-state rules have the support of the business community, although it should be kept in mind that the extent of such usage depends on the applicable law and the lex fori. Not just because the legislative systems are different in their recognition of non-state rules as sources of law, but also because legal scholarship and judicial reasoning differs between legislations. Overall, it is clear that non-state rules play a key role in defining accepted international commercial law principles and practices.

10 The application of codified non-state rules as lex mercatoria

10.1 Introduction

This chapter analyses how courts apply codified non-state rules as an expression or reflection of the lex mercatoria. The previous chapters demonstrated that courts apply uncodified non-state rules more frequently. This could be either as a source of law or to interpret the law or the contract. These are mainly trade usages and general principles of law, which are also the two pillars of the lex mercatoria. The difficulty for courts is in uncovering the concrete substance of the lex mercatoria. Courts frequently turn to codified non-state rules for this purpose.

If the court or arbitral tribunal decides to apply non-state rules, either as the law governing the contract, as sources of domestic law, to interpret the contract, or as accepted principles of international commerce, the question arises how the court should apply these.[1] The answer is relatively straightforward if the court or tribunal is applying codified non-state rules. These are written down and there is a substantive body of guidelines and scholarly work to assist with the interpretation of these rules. The answer is more difficult when the court or tribunal is applying uncodified non-state rules. Their content is difficult to establish, they are not written down, and conflicting opinions make it difficult to understand how they should be applied and interpreted. Yet, in practice courts and tribunals apply uncodified non-state rules more frequently. Not only are usages and general principles recognised as a source of law in many domestic laws, but choice of law clauses also include uncodified non-state rules more frequently.

It is rare for the parties to choose specific transnational commercial rules as the law governing the contract outside of the framework of trade associations where often the contract will contain a choice of law clause directly referencing the particular guidelines/rules of that association (usually in combination with a reference to an applicable domestic law such as English law.) Outside of trade associations, parties refer more often to uncodified non-state rules in the contract, sometimes in conjunction with a state law.

1 This chapter discusses application in both litigation and arbitration but for ease of language will mainly use the word court.

Choice of law clauses referencing uncodified non-state rules use different terminology. The terms that are used include lex mercatoria, general principles of law, principles of international commerce, principles of good faith and fair dealing, trade usages, and accepted trade practices. There is no clear distinction between these concepts, and it is also difficult to ascertain what the parties exactly have in mind when they include one of these terms in their contract. Applying uncodified non-state rules as the governing law can create difficulties because they are incomplete and uncertain, therefore courts/tribunals need to fill the gaps, by for instance referring to a state law or codified non-state rules.

This chapter examines how courts apply uncodified non-state rules and analyses the tendency for dispute resolution bodies, courts and arbitral tribunals, to apply codified non-state rules when the contract calls for the application of the lex mercatoria, trade usages, or general principles of law. Codified non-state rules are written down and their content is thus easier to establish. Restatements of law specifically also have the advantage of being almost complete and therefore can govern the dispute (almost) autonomously. Section 2.4 discussed how general principles of law and trade usages are the sources of the lex mercatoria. Therefore, this chapter uses the term lex mercatoria to refer to both the lex mercatoria and these sources.

This chapter has the aim of establishing how the legal authority of codified non-state rules is established when they are applied as lex mercatoria. This issue was already touched upon by the previous two chapters, which discussed that codified non-state rules are regularly applied as trade usages, as general principles of law, and as legal doctrine/scholarship. If they are applied as general principles of law or trade usages, then their legal authority comes from the status of general principles of law and trade usages as sources of domestic law. This chapter takes this discussion further and examines how codified non-state rules are applied as lex mercatoria, and how this increases the authority of these codified non-state rules because of their association with a recognised and established body of transnational commercial law.

10.2 The application of codified non-states rules as lex mercatoria

Before the court can apply the lex mercatoria it needs to decide the substance of the lex mercatoria; that is to say which legal norms and concrete rules it should apply to solve the dispute. There is no consensus on this, and this is largely due to the difficulties of pinpointing the substance of the lex mercatoria. According to Selden (1995), 'For problems with determining the existence of any purported principle of lex mercatoria, just look at its sources: practices followed since time immemorial, or at least since the Roman ius gentium; ancient cases in dusty tomes; writings of erudite scholars who passed away about the time the steam engine was revolutionising industry. There is also the current literature in law reviews and academic publications, in a variety of languages. As a collection of commercial practices, the content of lex mercatoria has not been discoverable in any one single place. Furthermore, those partial listings that did exist were not found in the normal places to which judges and arbitrators (and lawyers) turn. The occasional law review article is no substitute for a code or, in common law jurisdictions, line of judicial opinions.'[2]

Furthermore, there is a lack of available case law given that the lex mercatoria does not come up in state courts frequently and arbitral awards are usually not published or at least not in their entirety. If the court/tribunal applies the lex mercatoria it would thus need to decide what the lex mercatoria is, what its content is, and most importantly what concrete rules it should apply.

It is difficult for the court/tribunal to apply the lex mercatoria because it cannot be found in a single place. The amount of scholarly writing on this topic is significant and it is difficult to know which works should be prioritised. Courts could look at guidelines published by international organisations, at standard contract terms, and at websites and databases produced by international organisations, but this is a confusing and massive collection of information. For a court or tribunal which is limited by restraints of time and budget, it is a daunting task to come up with any concrete rules using these elements.

Case law can shed light on what the principles of the lex mercatoria are. For instance, ICC Case No 8365 held that the lex mercatoria consists of principles such as (1) pacta sunt servanda (2) good faith and (3) favour validitatis.[3] Such case law is helpful in interpreting the contract and the law. It is less useful in finding concrete rules to apply to solve the dispute.

Courts have a tendency to rely on familiar legal systems and the lex fori to guide the interpretation of the lex mercatoria.[4] This 'homeward trend' is also noted with the application of foreign law and the CISG.[5] This of course defeats the purpose of applying non-state rules. After all, usually a motive behind their application is the transnational nature of the lex mercatoria. This is different if courts apply general principles and trade usages as a source of domestic law as in that instance, they should interpret these according to the specific domestic law. Nevertheless, in international transactions a more transnational application is warranted. Regardless of whether these trade usages and principles are applied as part of domestic law their international nature should be respected through a more transnational application.

The above demonstrates the difficulty that courts face, when applying the lex mercatoria or its elements. The amount of case law is limited in most

2 Barton S Selden, 'Lex Mercatoria in European and US Trade Practice: Time to Take a Closer Look' (1995) 2 Annual Survey International and Comparative Law 111,119

3 ICC Award No. 8365, Clunet 1997, at 1078 et seq. Available at: https://www.trans-lex.org/208365/_/icc-award-no-8365-clunet-1997-at-1078-et-seq/.

4 Lord Justice Mustill, 'Contemporary Problems in International Commercial Arbitration: A Response' (1989) 17 International Business Lawyer 161,163.

5 See Section 9.2.

jurisdictions. Accessing foreign decisions can be time consuming, expensive if translations are needed, and thus often impractical Using arbitral awards to discover precedents is problematic. Even if some awards are published, not all awards are, and those that are published are not always published in their entirety.[6] Furthermore, the legal reasoning is often missing, and it can thus not be ascertained why the tribunal reached certain conclusions. Without having a substantial percentage of awards fully published creating an authoritative lex mercatoria case law based on arbitral awards is thus not possible. This is not to say that arbitral cases have no value. An example of a way to use case law to establish the lex mercatoria is the Trans-Lex project.[7] This database uses case law and scholarly writings to extract principles of the lex mercatoria with references to specific arbitral awards and court cases. This database is thus extremely useful to find the content of the lex mercatoria. It has no authoritative value beyond its persuasiveness, but as the work is (partly) based on case law this ensures a form of legitimacy.

What stands out from this discussion is that the exact content of uncodified non-state rules is not easy to uncover. Therefore, this would leave the court a certain conundrum on how to apply the lex mercatoria. A full research study would be impractical; applying domestic law is not desirable, and using case law difficult.

If the court/tribunal applies the lex mercatoria in addition to a state law, then applying trade usages and general principles of law would pose less of a problem. To find concrete rules the courts can rely on the applicable law to fill in any gaps. These rules can be interpreted through the transnational lens of the lex mercatoria and its established principles. The combination of a state law with the lex mercatoria gives the court flexibility in how to apply the law and certainty in how to fill the gaps. The situation is more complex if non-state rules are applied as the sole governing law. The court/tribunal should then ideally solely rely on the lex mercatoria to solve the dispute. In practice gaps are regularly filled by referring to a state law or by the tribunal relying on their own sense of justice.

Another important way to solve this conundrum is to apply codified non-state rules as lex mercatoria, general principles of commercial law, and trade usages. There are four ways codified non-state rules are applied in this fashion: they are used as a guide to finding the lex mercatoria (or its elements), as evidence for the unwritten lex mercatoria (or its elements), as an expression of the lex mercatoria (or its elements), or as being the lex mercatoria (or its elements).

6 See for instance Bernardo M Cremades and Steven L Plehn, 'The New Lex Mercatoria and the Harmonization of the laws of International Commercial Transactions' (1983–1984) 2 Boston University International Law Journal 317,336.

7 Translex is a research and codification platform for transnational law. The database was founded and developed by Professor Klaus Peter Berger. The list contains 1549 Principles as of February 2020.
http://www.trans-lex.org/.

In the first scenario codified non-state rules serve to uncover the lex mercatoria. In the second scenario they are used as evidence for the existence of specific uncodified non-state rules. The codified rules are not themselves a source of the lex mercatoria in these two scenarios. In the third scenario the codified non-state rules are considered a source of the lex mercatoria. In the fourth scenario the set of codified non-state rules is assimilated with the lex mercatoria or one of its elements.

The advantages for tribunals/courts in using codified non-state rules are clear. They are easy to locate. They are written down. They contain specific articles that can be referred to. A more substantive argument is that these rules are the result of comparative research and thus represent an accurate reflection of transnational commercial practices. This usage happens especially with the UNIDROIT Principles and the CISG and to a lesser extent with the PECL. These instruments can function as the governing law of the contract because they provide general principles as well as concrete rules. By applying these there is less need to fall back on state law for gap filling purposes.

The next two sections look at the application of the UPICC and the CISG in lieu of the lex mercatoria or one of its elements.

10.3 Using codified non-state rules as lex mercatoria: the UNIDROIT Principles

The Preamble to the UPICC considers their application as lex mercatoria:

2. They may be applied when the parties have agreed that their contract be governed by general principles of law, the *lex mercatoria*, or the like.[8]

There was thus from the moment that the Principles were created a deliberate push for them to be accepted as lex mercatoria. This is prescriptive, and was not descriptive of the current state of affairs in 1994. The UPICC can state that they may be applied as lex mercatoria but that of course does not mean that they are lex mercatoria. That acceptance can only come from usage by the merchant community. It is not clear from the pre-amble whether the UNIDROIT Principles should be applied as a guide to finding the lex mercatoria, a reflection of the lex mercatoria, or an expression of the lex mercatoria. They are used in all these ways.[9]

The UPICC are used as a guide to establish what the lex mercatoria is. A Canadian company (service provider) and the UN (buyer) agreed that the law governing their dispute should be the '*generally accepted principles of international commercial law.*' The arbitral tribunal decided that to define these generally accepted principles it would refer to the UPICC.[10] The published abstract does not mention the reasons of the tribunal to do so.

8 UNIDROIT Principles of International Commercial Contracts 2010, Pre-amble.

9 Unless otherwise specified all case abstracts come from the UNILEX database.

10 Ad hoc Arbitration, Parties Unknown, New York (Unpublished).

In a dispute between a French company and an Illinoisan company both parties argued that their own domestic law was applicable, but that as an alternative, general principles of law should be applied. The tribunal decided that there were not enough connecting factors to a specific domestic law and that it would base its decision on the general principles of law or the lex mercatoria. The tribunal then stated that several ICC cases had considered the UNIDROIT Principles as the best approach to understand what the general principles of law are.[11]

The UPICC were applied *'as a primary set of guidelines in determining international rules of law applicable to the parties' contract'*, but the tribunal would also '*duly consider the lex mercatoria in its two fundamental principles, i.e. the standards of good faith which the parties should observe when performing the contract and the rule of pacta sunt servanda.*' The tribunal thus distinguished between the UPICC and the lex mercatoria. The UPICC are used as a guide to determine the international rules of law, which the tribunal differentiated from the fundamental principles of the lex mercatoria.

The UPICC are used as a reflection of the lex mercatoria. In 2000 a Court of Appeal in New Zealand stated that the UPICC are a *'document, which is in the nature of a restatement of the commercial contract law of the world.'*[12] In another case an English company (BAE) dealing in anti-missile systems and the Iranian government concluded nine contracts for the supply of equipment. After the Islamic Revolution the contracts were terminated on the initiative of the new Iranian government. BAE decided to sue for damages while the Iranian Ministry of Defence requested restitution of advance payments. The contracts contained an arbitral clause, but the only reference to the applicable law was that settlement should be according to natural justice. The arbitral tribunal interpreted natural justice to '*exclude the application of any specific domestic law and to have their contracts governed by general principles and rules which, though not enshrined in any specific national legal system, are specially adapted to the needs of international transactions and enjoy wide international consensus.'*[13] In a first partial final award the Tribunal stated that '*the contracts should be interpreted in accordance to, the UNIDROIT*

11 ICC Award No. 13012 (2004).

12 *Hideo Yoshimoto v Canterbury Golf International Ltd* [2000] NZCA 350
The issue concerned the interpretation of a clause (literally or liberally). The Court stated that a liberal interpretation would be in accordance with Article 8 of the CISG (in force in New Zealand) and articles 4.1 to 4.3 of the UNIDROIT Principles [*which] refines and expands the principles contained in the United Nations Convention.'*). Despite this the Court chose the literal interpretation because the Privy Council would not allow for the more liberal interpretation on the grounds that a) the CISG is not adopted in England and b) English common law does not support this liberal interpretation.

13 ICC Award No.7110 (1999)
As quoted in Michael Joachim Bonell, 'UNIDROIT Principles: A Significant Recognition by a United States District Court' (1999) 4 Uniform Law Review 651, 653.

Principles with respect to all matters falling within the scope of such Principles.'[14] In subsequent partial awards the Tribunal applied the UPICC on several points.

In the final partial award four years later the tribunal referred to the UPICC, but did not consider them '*in all cases as the expression of generally accepted principles of law.*'[15] It is not clear from the judgment whether the tribunal meant something different by the word expression than by their earlier use of the word reflection. BAE sought the annulment of the four Partial Final Awards, but this was unsuccessful.[16] The tribunal thus distinguishes between, on the hand the UPICC, and on the other hand general principles of law whilst at the same time acknowledging there exists an overlap between the two.

In a contract between a Romanian seller and an English buyer the choice of law clause stated: '*this contract is governed by international law.*'[17] During the arbitration the parties disagreed on what this meant. The seller stated that it meant '*general principles of law and the lex mercatoria which meant in accordance with Article 1.101 (3) of the PECL and paragraph 3 of the Preamble of the UNIDROIT Principles that the dispute should be governed by the PECL to be interpreted in the light of the UNIDROIT Principles.*' The buyer stated that English law was applicable. The tribunal decided that by referring to international law the parties demonstrated that they wished to exclude the application of state law. The tribunal then decided that international law should be understood as the lex mercatoria and general principles of law, which are reflected in the UPICC. Although international law and the lex mercatoria are not the same it is clear why the tribunal took this decision. If by international law is meant public international law, then this cannot be practically applied to a commercial law dispute. The lex mercatoria is

14 *Bae Systems Plc, U.K. Vs Ministry of Defence and Support for Armed Forces of the Islamic Republic of Iran*, ICC Award No.7110 (1995).

15 Michael Joachim Bonell, 'UNIDROIT Principles: 'A Significant Recognition by a United States District Court' (1999) 4 Uniform Law Review 651, 654;

As an example with regards to question of the whether it was excusable for the claimant to not pay for reasons amounting to force majeure/hardship the corresponding articles of the UNIDROIT Principles (6.2.1-6.2.3) were mentioned and the tribunal said that '*changed circumstances are not part of widely recognised and generally accepted legal principles.*'

16 *Bae Systems Plc, U.K. Vs Ministry of Defence and Support for Armed Forces of the Islamic Republic of Iran*, Rechtbank 'S Gravenhage, 2011,

One of these grounds was that the Arbitral Tribunal had exceeded its mission by not referring to the limitation periods as included in the UNIDROIT Principles 2004. The Iranian government stated that the 2004 Principles should not be applied retroactively which the courts agreed with. It was thus not the actual application of the UPICC, which was objected to, but the specific version of the Principles.

(The case went to the High Council in the Netherlands in the end. See: *Bae Systems Plc V Ministry of Defence and Support for Armed Forces of the Islamic Republic of Iran*, Hoge Raad 22 May 2015, ECLI:NL:HR:2015:1272. See: http://deeplink.rechtspraak.nl/uitspraak?id=ECLI:NL:HR:2015:1272).

17 ICC Award No. 12111 (2003).

considered the international law of commerce. Of course, whether the lex mercatoria can be equated with the UPICC and the PECL based on these instruments' self-declaration is another matter.

In an ICSID arbitration the Tribunal cited the UPICC in support of the ILC Draft Articles on Responsibility of States for Internationally Wrongful Acts and justified this reference by stating that '*it would be possible to illustrate these general principles from several other national systems (both common law and civilian), but it is unnecessary to do so here because, first, such principles are broadly re-stated in the UNIDROIT Principles* and, *second, the Tribunal is in no doubt that similar principles form part of international law, as expressed in the ILC Articles.*[18] The UPICC are thus used as a reflection of general principles of law.

In an ICC case, the UPICC were used to supplement the applicable state law.[19] This case concerned the enforcement of an arbitral award based on Iranian law supplemented by '*general principles of international law, including the lex mercatoria and trade usages.*' The arbitral tribunal decided on the UPICC to guide them: '*as to the contents of such rules, the Tribunal shall be guided by the Principles of International Commercial Contracts.*' The tribunal referred to the Principles on most points when it rendered the award except from the timing that interest should be awarded. The tribunal doubted that the solution provided for by the UPICC formed part of general accepted legal principles.[20]

The award was disputed in court by Cubic Defense systems on the grounds that the tribunal had exceeded its mission by referring to the UPICC.[21] Cubic Defense systems did not object to the application of general principles of international law and trade usages, but specifically objected to the use of the UNIDROIT Principles.[22] Therefore, one of the questions in dispute was whether the UPICC are a reflection/expression of these general principles and trade usages. The court enforced the award and thereby confirmed the

18 *Gemplus&Talsud v Mexico*, International Centre for Settlement of Investment Disputes (2010)
http://www.italaw.com/sites/default/files/case-documents/ita0357.pdf
In at least seven more cases between 2007 and 2020 ICSID referred to the UNIDROIT Principles as reflections or expressions of principles of law
(See www.unilex.com).

19 *The Ministry of Defence and Support for the Armed Forces of the Islamic Republic of Iran v Cubic Defense Systems* ICC Award No. 7365 (1997).

20 Another reason for the tribunal to make this decision was that the solution provided by the UPICC ran counter to the corresponding article 721 of the Iranian Code of Civil Procedure.
Michael Joachim Bonell, 'UNIDROIT Principles: A Significant Recognition by a United States District Court' (1999) 4 Uniform Law Review 651, 662.

21 *The Ministry of Defence and Support for the Armed Forces of the Islamic Republic of Iran v Cubic Defense Systems, Inc*, United States District Court, S D. California, 7 December 1998.

22 Michael Joachim Bonell, 'UNIDROIT Principles: a Significant Recognition by a United States District Court' (1999) 4 Uniform Law Review 651, 662.

assumption of the tribunal that the UPICC are indeed a reflection of general principles of law.

In a dispute between a Chinese and Indonesian company before the China International Economic and Trade Arbitration Commission (CIETAC), the contract referred to Singaporean law. Neither of the parties could provide sufficient evidence of how Singaporean law dealt with the concerned issues. Therefore, CIETAC decided on settling the dispute through international practices and that for this purpose it would refer to the UPICC which represent, '*the general principles of contract laws*' unless the parties could prove these ran contrary to Singaporean law, which they could not.[23]

The UNIDROIT Principles are used as an expression of the lex mercatoria. The UN Compensation Commission referred to the UPICC as '*principles of international commercial contract law*' and when deciding an issue in '*conformity with general principles of law*' referred to the UPICC.[24] In a case between an Italian company and a governmental agency of a Middle Eastern country the tribunal decided that, in the absence of a choice of law clause, it would base its decision on '*terms of the contract, supplemented by general principles of trade as embodied in the lex mercatoria.*' In the final award the tribunal referred to the provisions of the UNIDROIT Principles as a source of the lex mercatoria.[25]

In a contract between a French company and a Costa Rican company the parties agreed that any dispute should be resolved '*on the basis of good faith and fair usages and with regard to the soundest commercial practices and friendly terms.*'[26] The tribunal applied the UNIDROIT Principles as it considered these '*the central component of the general rules and principles regulating international contractual obligations and enjoying wide international consensus.*'

A dispute arose between a Russian company and a German company after they concluded a contract for the marketing of goods produced by the respondent.[27] The contract stipulated that disputes should be settled in accordance with the general principles of the lex mercatoria. There was a further provision that all terms were subject to the legislation of both Germany and the Russian Federation. The tribunal stated that by making both legal systems applicable this was tantamount to the absence of a choice of law. The tribunal decided to apply the UPICC as an expression of the general principles of the lex mercatoria.

23 China International Economic and Trade Arbitration Commission (CIETAC), 31-10-2016.

24 United Nations Compensation Commission, Panel of the Commissioners, Panel F1, Recommendation S/AC.26;

The Commission was set up to '*process claims and pay compensation for losses and damage suffered as a direct result of Iraq's unlawful invasion and occupation of Kuwait in 1990–91*'

25 ICC Award No. 8261 (1996).

26 Parties Unknown, Ad Hoc Arbitration (Costa Rica), 30.04.2001.

27 Parties Unknown, International Arbitration Court at the Chamber of Commerce and Industry of the Russian Federation, 11/2002.

The Civil Chamber of the Venezuelan Supreme Court ruled in a case between a Venezuelan and a Dutch company that international contracts are governed by the closest connected law and that to determine this law all objective and subjective elements of the contract should be taken into account on top of '*the general principles of international commercial law recognised by international organisations.*'[28] The Court specifically mentioned the UPICC as an example of these general principles. In a Paraguayan case the court referred to the UPICC as '*widely recognised principles in international commercial law.*'[29]

Other tribunals have been more cautious in linking the UNIDROIT Principles to the lex mercatoria or its elements. In a dispute the ICC Tribunal decided to apply the general principles of law in absence of a choice of law clause.[30] The tribunal stated that '*those general principles and rules of law applicable to international contractual obligations which qualify as rules of law and which have earned a wide acceptance and international consensus in the international business community, including notions which are said to form part of a lex mercatoria, also taking into account any relevant trade usages as well as the UNIDROIT Principles, as far as they can be considered to reflect generally accepted principles and rules.*' The tribunal justified this choice by stating the UPICC '*contain in essence a restatement of those principes directeurs that have enjoyed universal acceptance and, moreover, are at the heart of those most fundamental notions which have consistently been applied in arbitral practice.*'[31] The tribunal followed this by stating that the UPICC had not '*yet stood the test of detailed scrutiny in all their aspects, some of their individual provisions might not reflect international consensus.*' This award was rendered only two years after the UPICC were first published which would account for the reluctance of the tribunal.

A dispute arose from a contract containing a choice of law clause for Spanish law.[32] The contractor argued that the contract should be renegotiated for reasons of hardship in accordance with UNIDROIT Principles articles 6.2.2 and 6.2.3 and that these were applicable because they are trade usages, which the tribunal should take into account under the applicable ICC Arbitration Rules. The tribunal decided that the UPICC were not applicable because they should only be applied when the parties have expressly agreed to do so or where the contract refers to the lex mercatoria, general principles of law, or similar formulation in accordance with the pre-amble of the UPICC. As in this case Spanish law was applicable and

28 *Banque Artesia Nederland, N.V., V. Corp Banca, Banco Universal C.A V*, Civil Chamber of the Venezuelan Supreme Court, 02/21/2004.
http://www.tsj.gov.ve/decisiones/scc/diciembre/172223-RC.000738-21214-2014-14-257.HTML.

29 Tribunal de Apelación en lo Civil y Comercial de Asunción, Edgar Alberto Ayala Zalazar v. Carlos Tomas Gonzalez Figueredo, 31-05-2016.

30 ICC Award No. 7375 (1996).

31 Ibid.

32 ICC Award No. 8873 (1997).

the parties had made no reference to any non-state rules in the contract the UPICC should not be applied. Furthermore, the tribunal argued, the provisions of the UNIDROIT Principles on hardship are not the current practice in international trade. This decision recognises that the UPICC can be applied as lex mercatoria or general principles of law but did not consider them trade usages.

A Brazilian court applied the CISG and the UPICC to an international contract in absence of a choice of law clause. Whilst Brazilian private international law pointed to the application of Danish law the court stated that the new lex mercatoria, as expressed by the UPICC and the CISG should be applied. The court saw the content of the UNIDROIT Principles as coinciding to a large extent with the new lex mercatoria. The court defined the latter as *'the principles and rules, model contracts and clauses, usages and customs, which have been developed independently from the States by international trade practice and may therefore be considered "an authentic transnational commercial law*[33]*.'*

These cases demonstrate that there are several ways in which the UPICC are linked to the lex mercatoria and its two main components: general principles of laws and trade usages. The UPICC are a guide, a reflection, a primary reflection, and an expression of the lex mercatoria. The weakest of these criteria is a guide. If the UNIDROIT Principles are used as a guide, this can mean different things. A guide could be something someone refers to on occasion or it could be a strong guiding force. It also means that the UNIDROIT Principles themselves, are not a source of the lex mercatoria, but that they merely serve as aid to discover what the lex mercatoria is. The second strongest usage is that of a reflection. If they are the primary reflection it means that they are the key text that reflects the lex mercatoria. They are therefore the most important piece of evidence of the substance of the lex mercatoria or its elements. If they are a reflection, they are just one of more pieces of evidence. As a reflection of the lex mercatoria the UPICC themselves are not lex mercatoria. They are evidence of the lex mercatoria, but they are not a source.

The UNIDROIT Principles are also applied as an expression of the lex mercatoria. They are a source of the lex mercatoria. Their authority does not derive from other sources, but they are the authority in their own right. Finally, in some cases the lex mercatoria and the UPICC are likened without any further explanation and it almost seems as if the UPICC are just equated with the lex mercatoria. It is doubtful this is intentional and it is likely meant that they are a reflection or expression of the lex mercatoria.

If the UPICC are a source of the lex mercatoria, then this could mean that case law that recognises the lex mercatoria as law (such as *Valenciana de Cementos Portland SA v Primary Coal Inc)* also indirectly recognises the UPICC as law. Section 2.4 established that codified non-state rules are not

33 Court of Appeal of Rio Grande do Sul, Noridane Foods S.A. v. Anexo Comercial Importação e Distribuição Ltda. 14.02.2017.

part of the lex mercatoria under the most acceptable definition of the latter. Yet, the trend that emerges here links the UPICC to the lex mercatoria and considers that the UPICC are part of the lex mercatoria. The results also show that the UPICC were used as lex mercatoria very soon after their initial publication and that they continue to be applied in this fashion. The earlier cases show more reticence when referring to the UPICC as general principles of law, which demonstrates a gradually furthering acceptance of the UPICC as lex mercatoria.

10.4 Using the CISG as lex mercatoria

The CISG is ratified by 94 states, which means that it is the applicable law to the international sale of goods in almost two thirds of the world. The application of the CISG as lex mercatoria could only occur in sale of goods contracts. The CISG does not contain general contract principles (contrary to the UPICC) and this hampers its application as lex mercatoria. Despite this the CISG is regularly applied as a reflection or expression of the lex mercatoria. The assimilation of a convention with the lex mercatoria is problematic as it introduces the limits that conventions have into the lex mercatoria. Conventions are defined by existing state legislation and are the result of compromises between states. The influence of the business community on the drafting differs (less so with the CISG and the Hamburg Rules and more influential in the Cape Town Convention for instance.) Even if the business community has influence, conventions still do not originate within the business community and are more shaped by state interests. It is difficult to consider a convention as lex mercatoria, in origin, in form, and in application. Regardless of these objections in practice we can observe a linkage between the CISG and the lex mercatoria.[34]

In a case before the Iran-US Claims Tribunal the CISG was found to reflect the *'recognised international law of commercial contracts.'*[35] In this case the buyer (Iran) and the seller (a US company) concluded a contract for a sale of electronic communication equipment. The choice of law was for Iranian and US law. The buyer did not pay the agreed price. To mitigate the damage, the seller sold some of the equipment on to a third party, after having informed the buyer of this intention. On mitigation of damages American law and Iranian law differed. The tribunal ruled that the seller did have the right to do so under the UCC and that this right was '*consistent with recognized international law of commercial contracts*' as observed from

34 Below case abstracts are all taken from the UNILEX database unless otherwise specified.

35 *Watkins-Johnson Co. & Watkins-Johnson Ltd. v. The Islamic Republic of Iran & Bank Saderat Iran* 28.07.1989 Iran-United States Claims Tribunal, number 370 (429-370-1),

The CISG is applicable in the USA and came in force there in 1988. However, due to the article 1.1(b) reservation the US made under article 95 the CISG would not have been applicable in this case. Iran has not (yet) joined the CISG. Furthermore, events occurred before the CISG entered into force.

CISG article 88 and thereby acknowledges the CISG as the recognised international law of commercial contracts.

In an ICC Arbitration, the seller claimed that, despite the CISG not being applicable by law, it should be applied as lex mercatoria. This claim was rejected mainly on grounds that the issues raised in the case would not be covered by the CISG, but the court did state that *'[Seller] points out that the application of the lex mercatoria would be tantamount to the application of the Vienna Convention, (…). This is certainly true.'*[36] The court notes that in this particular case the application of the lex mercatoria might not stand up to the scrutiny of the court, because an earlier interim award decided that all arbitral proceedings in this case should be governed by one and the same law. At the same time the tribunal confirms the claim of the seller that applying the lex mercatoria would result in the application of the CISG. Therefore, the tribunal sees the CISG as an important (even defining) expression or reflection of the lex mercatoria.

The CISG is applied as a reflection of the lex mercatoria. In an arbitral award the contract did not contain a choice of law clause, but the parties referred to the INCOTERMS and the UCP.[37] Based on this, the tribunal concluded that the wish of the parties was for the contract to be governed by trade usages and accepted principles of international trade. In its decision the tribunal referred to the CISG and the UPICC as evidence for admitted practices in international trade for any issues not regulated by the INCOTERMS and the UCP. In a 1998 arbitral award where Italian law was applied the tribunal referred to the CISG and the UPICC as *'normative texts that can be considered helpful in the interpretation of foreign contracts.'*[38]

In a 1989 ICC Arbitration, regarding the conformity of goods, the applicable law was the law of the country of the seller.[39] In accordance with the ICC Arbitration Rules the tribunal took into account the relevant trade usages and stated that *'there is no better source to determine the prevailing trade usages than the terms of the United Nations Convention on the International Sales of Goods'* and that *'the Vienna Convention, which has been given effect to in 17 countries* [at the time], *may be fairly taken to reflect the generally recognized usages regarding the matter of the non-conformity of goods in international sales.'* The CISG was not ratified in the countries of the seller and the buyer and was applied as a reflection of current trade usages on the non-conformity of goods.

The CISG is applied as an expression of the lex mercatoria or one of its elements. In a 1999 arbitral award the tribunal applied general standards and rules of international contracting.[40] The tribunal held that the CISG

36 ICC Award No. 6149 (1990).
37 ICC Award No. 8052 (1996).
38 ICC Award No. 8909 (1998).
39 ICC Award No. 5713 (1989).
40 ICC Award No. 9474 (1999).

embodies the universal principles of contract law and that it should therefore be applied.[41]

In a 1994 ICC Arbitration concerning lack of conformity of goods, where the contract did not contain a choice of law clause, the tribunal decided that the dispute would be governed by general principles of international commercial practice. The tribunal stated that for the present case those principles are '*most aptly contained in the United Nations Convention for the International Sale of Goods*.'[42] The court argued that: '*the dominant theme of the Vienna Convention is the role of the contract construed in the light of commercial practice and usage, which was produced by agreement among States resulting from collaboration sustained for over a decade*.' The narrative is thus that as the CISG is the result of a reflective long-term cooperation between states it is as an adequate expression of the general principles of international commercial practice. This is problematic, as international commercial practices should emerge from cooperation between merchants and not necessarily cooperation between states.

Recently in a Brazilian case the CISG was applied alongside the UPICC as an expression of the new lex mercatoria. Of the CISG the court stated that *its regular observance by business people worldwide, may be considered the expression of the most widespread "practice" in the international trade of goods and as such become relevant according to Article 113 of the Brazilian Civil Code which provides that the interpretation of legal transactions must be in accordance with usages and customs.*'[43]

The CISG is therefore applied as a reflection and an expression of the lex mercatoria. In one case the CISG is the recognised transnational commercial law and in another case the application of the lex mercatoria is described as tantamount with the application of the CISG. These two cases date from 1989 and 1990 and precede the publication of the UPICC and the PECL. It is questionable whether the tribunals would use the same wording with regards to the CISG now that the landscape of codified non-state rules is more diffuse than it was in 1990.

It is interesting to note that most of the newer cases refer to the UNIDROIT Principles more readily than they do to the CISG. Consequently, the UPICC have now taken the leading role in defining the lex mercatoria. Most of the cases using the CISG as lex mercatoria date from the period before the UNIDROIT Principles were published. In newer cases both the CISG and the UPICC are applied or the court refers solely to the UPICC.

41 Of the UNIDROIT Principles and the PECL the tribunal said it would apply these for any issues not covered by the CISG as these express general standards and rules of commercial law.

42 ICC Award No.7331 (1994).

43 Court of Appeal of Rio Grande do Sul, Noridane Foods S.A. v. Anexo Comercial Importação e Distribuição Ltda. 14.02.2017.

10.5 Interpreting the lex mercatoria through codified non-state rules

After reviewing these cases it can be asserted that there is a trend to assimilate the application of unwritten non-state rules with codified non-state rules. They are applied as a reflection and as an expression (source) of the lex mercatoria. This trend is mostly observed in arbitration as tribunals more frequently apply non-state rules as the applicable law. The available court cases follow this trend.

The assimilation of codified non-state rules and the lex mercatoria especially happens with the UPICC and the CISG. This can be explained by several factors. The PECL is comparable in scope, but for the reasons explained in Section 4.6 the PECL have not had the same recognition. The PECL have received significantly less acknowledgment than the UPICC, both in theory and in practice.[44] Furthermore, the PECL are a regional instrument so to consider them, as an expression/reflection of a global lex mercatoria would be problematic although they could be used as an expression/reflection of a regional lex mercatoria. These doubts about the position of the PECL are reflected in a ruling from an ICC Arbitral Tribunal where the applicable law was the lex mercatoria. The claimant argued that this meant the application of the UPICC and the PECL. The tribunal agreed with regards to the UNIDROIT Principles but stated with regards to the PECL: '*they constitute an academic research, at this stage not largely well-known to the international business community and are a preliminary step to the drafting of a future European Code of Contracts, not enacted yet.*'[45]

Nonetheless, the PECL are used in some cases as an expression/reflection of the lex mercatoria and its elements: often in conjunction with the UNIDROIT Principles. Courts and tribunals quote these instruments together to show that these propagate the same solution. Using several internationally recognised instruments that express the same solution adds legitimacy, for if different experts agree it is more likely that this is indeed a generally recognised principle of law.[46]

The PLACL were published very recently and therefore their potential impact is not yet clear. The Incoterms cover a limited area of the contract and the UCP only cover documentary credits, but in those areas they have been used as an expression or reflection of the lex mercatoria as some of the cases discussed above have shown. The Incoterms could stand up as trade usages and indeed, as Section 8.2 examines, they are used in this capacity.

Codified non-state rules are thus used as a reflection or as an expression of uncodified non-state rules. It is not clear whether tribunals and courts

44 Friedrich Blasé, 'Leaving the Shadow for the Test of Practice – On the Future of the Principles of European Contract Law' (1999) 3 Vindobona Journal of International Commercial Law and Arbitration 3,6.

45 ICC Award No. 12111 (2003).

46 Michael Joachim Bonell and Ole Lando, 'Future Prospects of the Unification of Contract Law in Europe and Worldwide' (2013) 18 Uniform Law Review 17, 23.

distinguish between the concepts of expression and reflection or that they use these words interchangeably without attaching any further meaning to it.

Whether the assimilation of the UPICC, the CISG, and similar instruments to the lex mercatoria is progress is debatable. By using codified non-state rules to define the lex mercatoria there is a risk that the lex mercatoria loses its flexibility and becomes assimilated to codified and conventional laws.[47] This would change the essence of the lex mercatoria and reduces it to written instruments that are drafted and modified by international organisations. It does not emerge spontaneously from within the merchant community. If the lex mercatoria is reduced to one or more instruments, even a qualitative instrument like the UPICC then there is no longer a real law merchant that draws from a plurality of principles and usages. Yet, this core quality of the lex mercatoria is also its weakness: it is difficult to apply the lex mercatoria in a consistent and clear manner if it comes from a vast array of sources that change over time, space, and trades. Using the UPICC gives the courts an almost complete restatement of law, including official commentary and examples on how the law should be applied. It makes it far more feasible to apply the lex mercatoria as the governing law, in a concrete, consistent, and coherent manner.

Tribunals apply codified non-state rules as a reflection/expression of the lex mercatoria because there is a need for a clear and concise lex mercatoria. In a 2003 arbitration case the tribunal stated that the UPICC were preferable to other transnational principles and rules because they are much more precise.[48] Parties seldom seem to object to the use of codified non-state rules as lex mercatoria even though they rarely include these codified non-state rules in a choice of law clause. When arbitrators/courts apply the lex mercatoria without reference to codified non-state rules it can be difficult to find the applicable rules and principles and this creates inconsistency. The lack of case law based on the lex mercatoria (and the lack of access to complete published awards) also contributes to the lack of predictability and uncertainty what to expect when the tribunal or the court applies the lex mercatoria.

When the court applies codified non-state rules as a reflection/expression of the lex mercatoria it is much easier to find the concrete rules. These rules are written down, coherent, and systematic. Another advantage of using codified non-state rules in lieu of the uncodified elements of the lex mercatoria is the enhanced predictability and certainty that they bring for both the courts and the parties.

47 Ralf Michaels, 'The True Lex Mercatoria: Law Beyond the State' (2007) 14 Indiana Journal of Global Studies 447, 462.

48 ICC Award No. 11575 (2003).

10.6 Conclusion: linking the lex mercatoria and codified non-state rules

An aspect that emerges from reviewing court cases and arbitral awards is that the terms lex mercatoria, general principles of law, principles of commercial law, trade usages, and commercial practices are used interchangeably. When a contract makes a reference to general principles of commercial law what is generally meant is the lex mercatoria.[49] There is thus an assimilation between the lex mercatoria and its elements (general principles and trade usages). This should be kept in mind when reading cases and arbitral awards.

Codified non-state rules are applied in lieu of non-codified non-state rules. They are applied as reflecting, expressing, or being the lex mercatoria, trade usages, and general principles of law. This can be observed with the UPICC and to a lesser extent the CISG and the PECL. The Incoterms are used as a reflection or expression of international trade usages. This usage facilitates the application of the lex mercatoria. Selden notes: '*the great importance of the* [UNIDROIT] *Principles is that the volume exists. It can be taken to court, it can be referred to page and article number, and persons who are referred to its provisions can locate and review them without difficulty.*'[50]

In cases where codified non-state rules are applied as lex mercatoria the court/tribunal does not necessarily justify this usage. Are these seen as a reflection of the lex mercatoria or as a guide to finding this? In that case they are the written evidence of the unwritten rules where the authority lies. Are they an expression of the lex mercatoria? In that case they are an intrinsic part of the lex mercatoria and derive their authority from being a source of this. These questions are usually not answered in the court's analyses.

There is thus a synergy where uncodified non-state rules feed into the elaboration of codified non-state rules. Through the application of codified non-state rules these gain in prominence and in turn become accepted trade usages and general principles of law. Uncodified trade usages and principles are gradually changed through applying codified-non state rules. The two categories are no longer easy to separate. Codified non-state rules are based partly on uncodified trade usages and principles. Part of their acceptance derives from a previous acceptance by the merchant community of these trade usages and general principles. As codified non-state rules can be used as evidence of uncodified non-state rules it becomes difficult to separate what is the (original) source and what is the evidence of this source.

An important objection to this development is that codified non-state rules are not based solely on existing trade usages and general principles of law. The UPICC and PECL are both based on comparative legal research. The drafters innovated on this research and followed the approach they

49 Philippe Kahn, 'Les Conventions Internationales de Droit Uniforme devant les Tribunaux Arbitraux' (2000) 5 Uniform Law Review 121, 125.

50 Barton S Selden, 'Lex Mercatoria in European and US Trade Practice: Time to Take a Closer Look' (1995) 2 Annual Survey International and Comparative Law 111, 122.

deemed most suitable for solving international disputes, rather than necessarily following the majoritarian approach.[51] These instruments therefore do not necessarily reflect the lex mercatoria. The CISG is a convention made along lowest common denominator policy lines, which reflects states' policies more than the practices of merchants. It furthermore was not intended to function as lex mercatoria but as part of a domestic legal system. Codified non-state rules and uncodified non-state rules have a different nature. Despite these differences they are intrinsically linked, and especially through their application in practice this linkage is strengthened.

Chapter 8, 9, and 10 together analysed how non-state rules are applied in courts. Chapter 8 concerned the application of trade usages as a source of (domestic) law, Chapter 9 analysed the application of non-state rules as general principles of international commercial law whereas chapter 10 examined how codified non-state rules are applied as lex mercatoria. These chapters thus provided a full overview of how non-state rules are applied other than as the governing law of the contract. These chapters have demonstrated that despite private international law usually not allowing for non-state rules to be used as the governing law of the contract, they are nonetheless pervasive as they are applied frequently in different ways. This application gives further legitimacy to non-state rules because it demonstrates the value that both courts and the business community attach to non-state rules. Therefore, through how courts apply these, non-state rules gain further legal authority.

51 Astreinte is part of the UNIDROIT Principles but cannot be seen as an international trade usage for example (Charles R Calleros, 'Towards Harmonization and Certainty in Choice of Law Rules for International Contracts: Should the U.S. Adopt the Equivalent of Rome I?' (2010) 28 Wisconsin International Law Journal 639, 649).

11 Ascertaining the legal authority of non-state rules

11.1 Introduction

The introductory chapter asked the key question of how the legal authority of non-state rules can be measured. To answer this question Chapters 2, 3 and 4 examined the nature of non-state rules through defining non-state rules, examining how their legal authority can be ascertained, how they contribute to the harmonisation of international commercial law, and analysing their status as a source of law. This first part of the book concluded that the legal authority of non-state rules could especially be understood through their usage in practice i.e. through their application. Thus, two other prominent questions that are key to understanding the legal authority of non-state rules arose. When are non-state rules applied? And how are they applied? These questions were answered in chapters 5, 6, 7, 8, 9, and 10. Chapters 5, 6, and 7 concentrated on when non-state rules can be applied and explored the agency of both the parties and the courts/tribunals to use non-state rules as the law governing the contract. Chapters 8, 9, and 10 analysed how courts apply non-state rules to interpret the law and the contract.

This concluding chapter examines the conclusions from the analyses in the preceding chapters and comes to some final thoughts and an overall conclusion. The first section examines the criteria against which the legal authority of non-state rules can be measured, the second section examines the application of non-state rules as the most important of these criteria, and the third section analyses how the application of non-state rules contributes to understanding their legal authority. A section discussing the wider place of non-state rules in international commercial law follows this. This chapter concludes that non-state rules play a key role in international commerce. Whilst they are not as regularly applied as the law governing the contract, they are applied frequently as sources of domestic law, to interpret the contract, and to interpret the law. This demonstrates the support that they have in the business community and among legal professionals. Non-state rules gain in legal authority through a more frequent application by courts/tribunals as this contributes to their development from social norms or contractual rules to law or rules of law. As non-state rules become more authoritative, they also contribute further to the harmonisation of international commercial law.

11.2 Categorising legal authority

Non-state rules in international commercial law can be divided into six categories:

- General principles of law. They exist in international commercial law, international public law, and domestic law. In international law general principles of law are defined as those principles, which are common to most legal systems as per Article 38 of the ICJ. These principles are intended for state relations, which is why they are not necessarily a good fit for private commercial relations. Whilst they can provide some guidance in understanding the principles underlying international commerce (such as the importance of pacta sunt servanda), they provide limited practical help in interpreting the contract. Domestic laws tend to recognise general principles of law as a source of law. These are not necessarily the same as general principles of international law, but they rather serve as the underlying principles of the law that provide an understanding of the foundations of the law. General principles of transnational commercial law find their inspiration in both international and domestic legal principles. These principles are developed by merchants, international organisations, arbitral tribunals, and courts to fit the needs of international commerce. They are uncodified, although can of course be written down or found in legal instruments (such as in the CISG.)
- Custom, trade usages, and practices. Practices have the weakest legal authority of these. There are two different types of trade practices. The first are those practices between two or more parties that regularly do business together and can thus be equated with course of dealing. These would not have any value beyond the specific contractual relationship. The second are practices that exist within a trade or locality. They would occur with some regularity, but not so often as to be considered trade usages. They would thus not be binding unless the parties regularly adhere to these (in which case they become a course of dealing).

Trade usages have stronger legal authority. Usages change between trades, ports, and regions. They can be binding even when the parties are not aware of them. It is usually only necessary that the parties ought to have known they existed. Trade usages do not require a sense of obligation. Only the regular observation of the practice as noted by the court/tribunal determines whether it is a binding trade usage. Their legal authority thus comes from the court's observations and the merchant's practices.

Custom is more universal and has older roots than trade usages. It takes more time for a custom to emerge. For a usage to be considered custom a sense of obligation is necessary. Traders do not follow the usage because it is convenient but because they believe it is obligatory.

It should be noted that the three terms are often used interchangeably by courts, practitioners, and in scholarly writing. There are many commonalities between the three and distinguishing trade usage from custom is difficult and it does not change how binding they are. Practices, trade usages, and custom are unwritten, flexible, and can change over time/sector/place. They can be a source of domestic and of conventional law.

- International conventions are elaborated by international organisations or delegates appointed by state governments. Once they are ratified by a state and enter into force, they become part of the domestic law of that specific state. If they are not ratified or have not entered into force, they would be considered non-state rules and their legal authority would be similar to that of a restatement of law (see below).
- Restatements of law in international contracts are mainly initiated by a group of private individuals, which can be connected to an international organisation. The main ones are the UNIDROIT Principles of International Commercial Law, the Principles of European Contract Law, and the Principles of Latin American Contract Law. These instruments represent a codification of existing principles of commercial law. The drafters did not merely codify existing principles and trade usages, but also innovated on these to ensure that the result represents the most appropriate solution for international trade. This category has transnational legal authority through their application in arbitration/litigation and their incorporation in contracts (either as the governing law or by reference). They have no standing in domestic legislation, unless they are considered general principles of law or trade usages.
- Model laws have limited authority on their own. They can be adopted by states and become part of domestic law. Differently from conventions, model laws can be adapted during adoption, and therefore the adopted law does not necessarily resemble the original model law. The newly adopted law becomes absorbed in the domestic law. The original model law remains as a non-state rule. The parties to the contract could use them in the same way as a restatement of law is used but as they are aimed at states rather than at the contracting parties, they are not used frequently in commercial law disputes.
- Model contracts and standard contract terms. These are developed by international organisations and by trade branch associations. The parties incorporate them in the contract. In some trades standard terms of contract are used habitually. In domestic law these are often considered contractual rules. Their legal authority mainly stems from their incorporation in the contract although they could develop into trade usages.
- Guidelines, travaux préparatoires, scholarly reflections, arbitral case law digests, and other similar works can be considered as part of international commercial law scholarship and doctrine. These documents are prepared by a myriad of stakeholders including international organisations, trade associations, domestic legislations, practitioners, scholars, and private working groups. Their legal authority is diffuse. Overall, it is considered

weak, but if the organisation behind the work is a prominent one this can increase their influence. Guidelines can have legal authority if they are incorporated in the contract or, if they are used by courts as scholarly doctrine (which is a (secondary) source of law in some jurisdictions.)

The expression lex mercatoria can be used to denominate all six of these categories or several of these. Under the most common understanding of the lex mercatoria, which represents a direct continuation of the medieval lex mercatoria, this should be restricted to trade usages and general principles of law. If codified non-state rules are included the debate would centre on whether all should be included or whether this should exclude those instruments (conventions and model laws) that are aimed at the legislator and only include those that are aimed at the parties (model contracts, standard terms, and restatements of law.)

Custom, usages, and principles can be recognised as sources of domestic law. Codified non-state rules usually have no direct standing in domestic law. They can have legal authority if they are incorporated in the contract (restatements, guidelines, conventions, and standard contract terms), they are ratified by a state (conventions), adopted by a state (model laws), or used by courts/tribunals to interpret or fill any gaps in the applicable law (all of these).

Non-state rules have authority in two spheres: national (domestic commercial law) and international (transnational commercial law). Non-state rules can have legal authority in domestic law when they are applied as contractual rules, sources of the applicable law, the applicable law itself, to interpret the applicable law, or as legal scholarship/doctrine. The specific authority depends on the legislation of a particular jurisdiction.

Non-state rules can have authority in the international community. This international community is a diffuse phenomenon. It consists of businesses, arbitrators, other legal professionals, and (international) organisations. The legal authority of non-state rules in that community differs from sector to sector and from region to region. It can be measured by looking at usage in contracts by businesses, the application by arbitrators, and the support from international organisations. The legal authority of non-state rules in the international community cannot be hierarchised easily. The above elements contribute to establishing the authority of non-state rules in the international community (and in transnational commercial law) and work together.

Non-state rules harmonise the law through a more bottom-up approach rather than a top down approach. They need to be contracted into (like a restatement of law) or can be contracted out off (like trade usages) and their usage is not mandatory. Therefore, when and how they are used is key to understanding their legal authority. This can be done by looking at the theory (what does the legislation say about when they can be used?) and the practice (when are they actually used?) The first can be understood by studying legislation (when can they be applied?) and the second by looking at the actual application (when are they applied? & how are they applied?) (Figure 11.1).

Authority of Non-State Rules in the International Business Community	Authority of Non-State Rules in the State
Incorporation in Contracts	Incorporation in Legislation
Application in Arbitration	Application in National Courts
Research and Publications (Both academic and non-academic)	Research and Publications (Both academic and non-academic)

Figure 11.1 Measuring the Legal Authority of Non-State Rules

To determine the legal authority of a specific non-state rule one can look at the promulgator of the rule (international organisation, business community, trade association), the support it has (incorporation in contracts, legalisation, scholarly writing, usage by legislators), the content (analysis by legal professionals and scholars), and the application of the rule (by courts and arbitrators).

Chapter 2 concluded that the most important factor to measure the legal authority of non-state rules is their application (when and how are non-state rules applied?) and through this one can understand the support they have (how are they perceived and used by the international business community?) This is because of the inherent nature of non-state rules: they are not imposed but are (at least initially) used without any coerciveness from the state. The origin and the content of the rule, whilst important, would thus take a back seat compared to their usage. This usage can be determined by studying the application of non-state rules in theory and in practice. This application measures both how courts apply non-state rules and how the parties to the contracts use them. By focusing on the application in state courts it is possible to analyse the legal authority of non-state rules in domestic law and through this understand their authority in the international community.

11.3 Understanding legal authority through application

As discussed in the previous section the legal authority of non-state rules is largely measured by their application in courts. Subsequently, it is important to analyse in which ways non-state rules can be applied and how this application measures their legal authority. In descending order of legal authority these are:

- Non-state rules are applied in the absence of a choice of law clause by the court. This would place non-state rules on par with (foreign) state law. Courts could apply non-state rules in this way if the private international law of the forum allows for this. This is very rare in litigation but happens with more regularity in arbitration.
- Non-state rules are included in a choice of law clause as the applicable law to the contract and they are applied in that capacity by the court.

Several jurisdictions allow for this, but they are in the minority. Non-state rules are applied independently as law. Non-state rules have a status grosso modo equal to foreign law in private international law.

- Non-state rules are applied by courts to interpret the applicable law or to fill any gaps in that law without being included in the contract. The court applies non-state rules in a subsidiary capacity through the applicable law. They are applied as general principles of law or as a filter through which the state law is applied and interpreted. This is what the Supreme Court in Paraguay has referred to as a 'complimentary law.' They have legal authority as accepted international commercial law principles and practices.
- Non-state rules are applied by the court as part of the applicable domestic law. The applicable domestic law recognises (certain) non-state rules as a source of law. Thus, when the court applies this law it has the possibility to apply non-state rules. Non-state rules are not applied independently, but through the applicable state law. Non-state rules have the authority of sources of law in domestic law. They could be considered as primary sources of law or secondary sources of law depending on the jurisdiction.
- Non-state rules are applied as evidence of accepted international commercial law practices and principles. Courts do not actually apply non-state rules but refer to them. This can be, for instance, to show that the applicable law and accepted international commercial practices would solve the contractual dispute in the same way. In that case non-state rules have the legal authority of scholarship/doctrine.
- Non-state rules are included in the contract by reference and replace variable rules of the law, but they are not the applicable law. Non-state rules are applied as contractual rules in a subsidiary capacity at the request of the parties. They have the legal authority of contractual terms.

A final application that should be mentioned is when the enforcement of an arbitral award, where non-state rules are the applicable law, is requested or challenged. In those cases, courts apply procedural arbitration law that could indicate whether under the specific circumstances the application of non-state rules was valid. The court hence does not apply non-state rules but merely validates their application. However, these decisions often say more about how the forum treats arbitration than how they treat non-state rules. If the exequatur of a foreign judgement based on non-state rules is requested the legal authority of non-state rules is based upon their acceptance by the private international law of the forum regarding enforcement of foreign court decisions.

Figure 11.2 explains how the legal authority of non-state rules can be perceived depending on the type of application.

When non-state rules are applied as the law of contract they are applied autonomously and directly as (transnational) law or rules of law. The legal authority comes from the instrument itself and from the private international

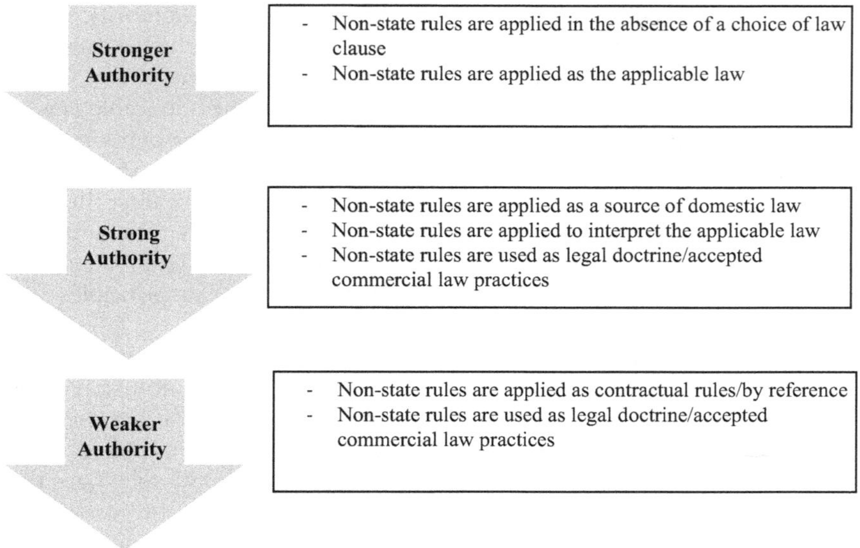

Figure 11.2 Degrees of Legal Authority of Non-State Rules

law or the lex arbitri that allows for their application. When non-state rules are applied to interpret the applicable law or as sources of domestic law they are applied in an indirect way as part of the applicable law. They derive their legal authority from their status in domestic law. Finally, when non-state rules are applied as contractual rules their legal authority comes from contract law. The law recognises that the parties have the freedom to shape their contract. Therefore, the legal authority can be considered weaker even if in practice the effect of these rules would be pivotal for the contract and any disputes

When courts use non-state rules as normative legal scholarship/doctrine the authority of the rules is more uncertain. The court is not applying non-state rules in a direct way, but cites the non-state rule as evidence, as a standard, as accepted practices, or common principles. They would have persuasive value that could be authoritative because they are used as a normative value against which domestic law is measured through furthering the legitimacy of domestic law to adequately solve the dispute. Although in general the legal authority of this usage is weaker this would depend on their status in the jurisdiction. In some jurisdictions legal scholarship/doctrine is applied more frequently than in others and it can be considered a primary or secondary source of law. This is the reason why it can be found in two categories in the above illustration.

The above relates to understanding the legal authority of non-state rules in the domestic sphere and provides criteria against which this legal authority can be measured. The application of non-state rules in domestic law can also help to understand the legal authority of non-state rules in the transnational sphere, although the order is different. It is more difficult to hierarchise this legal authority in the transnational sphere, as there is no existing legal framework against which this authority can be measured. A tentative classification in terms of legal authority is as follows:

- Non-state rules are used as the applicable law of the contract. The parties to the contract value the specific non-state rules to the extent that they believe these represent the best law for the transaction. Non-state rules have the value of law for the parties.
- Non-state rules are applied by arbitral tribunals in the absence of a choice of law clause. Non-state rules are applied on par with a state law. They are trusted to function as the best possible applicable law by the tribunal.
- Non-state rules are included in the contract by reference. Non-state rules are not the applicable law, but they shape the contract. They are thus valued by the contracting parties, as bringing something to the contract that state law does not do. It could be that the parties would have chosen non-state rules as the applicable law if the jurisdiction allowed for this. The parties trust non-state rules to provide the contractual terms or to guide the interpretation of the contract.
- Non-state rules are applied by arbitral tribunals in addition to the applicable state law. Non-state rules are used to fill gaps, to interpret, or as reference material. Non-state rules are considered accepted international commercial practices and principles.

(International) organisations and other groups contribute to understanding the legal authority of non-state rules in the international community in several ways:

- When (international) organisations draft or recognize non-state rules this demonstrates their support. The authoritative value of this increases if the organisation is more prominent. This contributes to understanding the place of non-state rules as internationally accepted commercial practices.
- The endorsement of non-state rules by (international) organisations through reference to these in their own legal instruments, recommending their use, or otherwise supporting the instrument (s). The strength of the endorsement and the prominence of the organisation would influence the authoritative value. This also works the other way around when an (international) organisation discourages the use of (certain) non-state rules this could carry persuasive value. An example of this is if trade associations actively discourage the application of the CISG through inserting a clause in their model contracts excluding its application. This contributes to understanding the role non-state rules play as internationally accepted commercial practices.

Most of the scholarly attention is given to the contributions that non-state rules make to legal harmonisation and the possibilities for the parties to choose non-state rules as the applicable law of the contract. This latter constitutes a direct application of non-state rules. Yet, in practice it can be concluded, as evidenced by the analysis in the previous chapters, that the number of cases where non-state rules are the applicable law is limited outside of arbitration. For instance, the UPICC have never been enforced as a direct choice of law before a state court as far as is known.[1] This is mainly because the number of jurisdictions that allow parties to choose non-state rules as the law of the contract is limited. Yet, even in the jurisdictions where this is allowed this choice does not appear to occur frequently as the lack of case law demonstrates. It can be concluded that non-state rules are most often applied to interpret the applicable law (mainly the UPICC), as contractual terms (Incoterms, UCP600 and related contract terms, contract terms of trade associations), or as a source of the applicable law (trade usages and general principles.) Consequently, their role in (international) contract law is greater than in private international law. The principles upon which private international law is based are strongly linked to territory and statehood. Therefore, the autonomy of the parties is defined within the context of the state. The parties can choose a state law, but they cannot choose a law that is detached from the state.

Freedom of contract is one of the foundations of contract law. The parties decide on the content of their contract and this freedom is usually only limited by the public policy and mandatory provisions of the applicable law (and the lex fori). The parties thus have the freedom to refer to non-state rules in their contract. The governing law will then be subsidiary to the express will of the parties as found in the contract, including the referred non-state rules, unless these infringe on mandatory laws and public policy. Arbitration delocalises the contract and therefore within that transnational sphere the freedom to shape proceedings and the applicable law is considerable, including allowing the arbitrator to apply non-state rules as the law of the contract. Therefore, whilst private international law places the connection with the state first, both contract law and arbitration law prioritise the freedom of the parties and this enhances the role of non-state rules.

11.4 The application of codified non-state rules as lex mercatoria

One of the important conclusions on how non-state rules are applied is that codified non-state rules are often applied as an expression or a reflection of uncodified non-state rules. Trade usages and general principles of law can be sources of domestic law. Codified non-state rules usually are not recognised as a source of domestic law. In practice, there is substantial interaction between codified non-state rules and uncodified non-state rules.

1 Ralf Michaels,'Non-State Law in The Hague Principles of Choice of Law in International Contracts' (2014) 6 http://papers.ssrn.com/sol3/papers.cfm?abstract_id=2386186.

When courts or arbitral tribunals apply the lex mercatoria or its elements (trade usages or general principles of law) there is a need to determine their actual substance. These uncodified non-state rules are imprecise. There are multiple possibilities of what these could entail and determining which of these possibilities should be used is difficult and time consuming. This flexibility is sometimes needed as it allows tribunals leeway to find an appropriate solution. To find the concrete rules the court/tribunal either uses the lex fori or another state law, their own sense of justice, or they turn to codified non-state rules. These codified instruments are easy to research and they are accompanied by material on how they should be applied and interpreted. This represents a substantial advantage for the court/tribunal.

There are four ways in which codified non-state rules are applied in this fashion.

- As a guide to finding the lex mercatoria. The court uses codified non-state rules to find underlying commercial law principles and trade usages.
- As a reflection of the lex mercatoria. Codified non-state rules are applied as evidence of the lex mercatoria. They are not a source of the lex mercatoria, but they reflect the lex mercatoria.
- As an expression of the lex mercatoria. Codified non-state rules form an intrinsic part of the lex mercatoria. They are a source of the lex mercatoria.
- As being the lex mercatoria. The specific instrument is applied as lex mercatoria without further indication that the lex mercatoria is more than just this specific instrument.

From the case analysis in chapter 10 it can be observed that in practice courts/tribunals do not always make the distinction between these four different ways of applying codified non-state rules. For instance, when a court applies the UPICC as the lex mercatoria it is doubtful whether the court/tribunal wants to imply that these constitute the whole of the lex mercatoria. Even if it is formulated in this fashion, this is most likely not what is meant. The most common application is that codified non-state rules are applied as a reflection or as an expression of the lex mercatoria. Most cases, as was seen in chapter 10, do not rationalise why the choice was made to apply codified non-state rules as the lex mercatoria. The court might state that general principles of law are the applicable law and that these are best reflected or expressed by the CISG or the UPICC. Yet, why this is the best reflection or expression is not explained. That leaves the question whether tribunals and courts make a conscientious distinction between expression and reflection.

Whilst not being the perfect solution, using codified non-state rules as lex mercatoria can be justified. Codified non-state rules use trade usages and principles as their starting point. Consequently, there is an intrinsic linkage between the lex mercatoria and codified non-state rules. Yet at the same time although unwritten usages and general principles of law are the starting point of these codifications the work also represents an innovation. This has several reasons. The first is that the exact content of uncodified non-state rules is difficult to uncover. There are diverging opinions on the substance. The second reason is that the drafters make choices during the process. They discover differing practices and norms and they innovate on these to find what they consider to be the most appropriate solution. So, whilst existing uncodified non-state rules have an impact on the codification the end result is still a different product. This therefore makes it unlikely that at the time of writing they are a true reflection of the lex mercatoria.

If codified non-state rules are not a precise reflection, then perhaps application of these as an expression of the lex mercatoria would be better. That brings up the question of whether codified non-state rules do not have a nature which is so different from the lex mercatoria that it would be difficult to justify that they are part of this. After all, the lex mercatoria is unwritten and spontaneous in origin. Two characteristics that codified non-state rules do not share. This makes it difficult to claim that codified non-state rules are a source of the lex mercatoria.

It should be asked what the expectation of the parties is in such cases. When parties choose non-state rules as the applicable law, they most commonly refer to general principles of law, international principles of law, lex mercatoria, or another such formula.[2] Therefore, the parties do not necessarily expect codified non-state rules to be applied. After all, if the parties wanted for instance the UPICC as the applicable law to the contract they could just have included that in their choice of law clause.

Yet, it could be countermanded that when tribunals/courts decide to apply codified non-state rules as a reflection or expression of the lex mercatoria this seems to be accepted by the parties judging from the limited number of appeals made on this specific point.

Another concern with applying codified non-state rules in lieu of the lex mercatoria is that this could lead to ossification of the lex mercatoria and loss of flexibility. Although codified non-state rules can be amended and updated (as can be observed with the UNIDROIT Principles) this does not always happen (as can be seen with the PECL as the commission that drafted those no longer exists and the CISG which is a convention and thus not amended easily.) The assimilation of the lex mercatoria and conventions could make the first more formalistic and this touches on the very core of what the lex mercatoria is.[3]

Despite these concerns there is a clear trend towards applying codified non-state rules in this way. One of the reasons why courts can be reluctant to apply non-state rules is that these are not clearly defined and uncertain, but the existence of codifications solves this issue. This is advantageous in terms of accessibility and unambiguity. Furthermore, they are more complete,

2 Michael Joachim Bonell, 'The UNIDROIT Principles and Transnational Law' [2000] 5 Uniform Law Review 199, 204.

3 Philippe Kahn, 'Les Conventions Internationales de Droit Uniforme devant les Tribunaux Arbitraux' (2000) 5 Uniform Law Review 121, 127.

concrete, and coherent. Applying trade usages and general principles of law leaves gaps and courts would usually fill this with reference to a domestic law. Especially if non-state rules are applied as the governing law then using the codifications ensures a more certain and predictable application which also benefits the parties to the contract. Uncodified non-state rules constitute a patchy landscape and to fill any gaps reference is often made to a state law. By applying codified non-state rules to either fill in these gaps or on their own, it is easier to solve the dispute without needing to refer to a state law.

If non-state rules truly gain legitimacy and authority through their application, then dissuading courts/tribunals from using codified non-state rules would also countermand the nature of the lex mercatoria. The risk of the arbitrator or court settling as amiable compositeur without authorisation is present when the content of the lex mercatoria is imprecise and unclear. This issue thus has different sides whereby there is need for both flexibility and certainty.

A solution presents itself. If courts and arbitral tribunals continue to apply non-state rules as elements of the lex mercatoria and if the parties accept this application, then this constitutes an acceptance of these codified non-state rules, which gain legal authority in the international community. As the lex mercatoria consists of unwritten rules these codified non-state rules could not be part of the lex mercatoria. Yet, if the codified non-state rules have shaped trade usages or general principles, they could be said to constitute an adequate reflection of the lex mercatoria. Thus, what was not true in origin becomes true through regular application over a longer period of time. It would be incorrect to name codified non-state rules as a source of the lex mercatoria, but individual non-state rules could develop into a reflection of the lex mercatoria and its elements.

In this usage the UNIDROIT Principles play a key role. When one reads through the preceding chapters it is noticeable that many of the cases use the UPICC as the primary example to interpret the lex mercatoria as does much scholarly research. Thus, rather than being chosen as the law of the contract, the UPICC are mainly used as an expression/reflexion of the elements of the lex mercatoria.[4] Other instruments that are used in this way are the CISG, the PECL, and the Incoterms. Although the CISG has the oldest papers of the three and is binding law in many countries, it is limited to international sales law and it does not contain general principles of contract law. Furthermore, the CISG dates from 1980 and has not been amended since. Therefore, it does not have the same flexibility as the UPICC provides. It also a convention and therefore drafted to function as part of the domestic legal system. The PECL and the PLACL are regional instruments, The Incoterms and the UCP are used as trade usages, but they only cover a limited area of law. The UPICC offers the most complete codification of transnational contract law. Hence, it is clear why the UPICC take the

4 The UNILEX database indicates that their most frequent usage is to interpret domestic law and the second most common usage is their application as lex mercatoria.

leading role in interpreting the lex mercatoria. Codified standard terms and conditions (either by the ICC or by trade associations) are especially popular as contractual terms and the parties frequently incorporate these in their contract. The international business community also plays a more important role in drafting these contractual terms. These thus have the support of the international business community and are chosen far more frequently by the parties than the UPICC. The initiative to use the UPICC often comes from the court/tribunal, rather than from the parties.

How often the UPICC are used is not clear. In 2011 UNILEX reported 107 decisions of domestic courts and 159 arbitral awards that made reference to the UNIDROIT Principles.[5] In February 2020 there are 254 decisions from domestic courts and 215 arbitral awards that make reference to the UNIDROIT Principles.[6] This indicates that especially the usage of the Principles in domestic courts has risen substantially.

Two remarks need to be made. UNILEX is not a complete database. UNIDROIT is dependent upon these cases being reported to them. Especially, from certain jurisdictions there might be underreporting because cases are not registered online. This means that the numbers in practice will be higher. The second issue is that UNILEX reports on every case where the UNIDROIT Principles are mentioned regardless of whether they played a deciding role in the case. In some cases, they are merely referenced by one of the parties. Nevertheless, it can be concluded that the usage of the UPICC (whilst modest) is on the rise.

Through the application of codified non-state rules as a reflection of uncodified non-state rules they both become more intrinsically linked. Trade practices can become usages. Usages may become custom. General principles might be distilled from trade usages and custom. General principles of law and trade usages form the basis for codified non-state rules.

Consequently, although non-state rules are not a coherent whole they are linked, there is interaction between rules, which leads to a strong mutual influence and co-dependency. They share a common objective: securing and facilitating international commercial relations. They share the same ways of measuring legal authority: support in the international community, support in domestic law, incorporation in contracts, and most importantly, application by state courts and arbitral tribunals.

11.5 Non-state rules, private international law, and legal harmonisation

Currently in most jurisdictions it is not possible to choose non-state rules as the governing law of the contract nor would it be possible for the court to apply these in absence of a choice of law. Is this something which is likely to

5 Eleonora Finazzi Agrò, 'The Impact of the UNIDROIT Principles in International Dispute Resolution in Figures' (2011) 16 Uniform Law Review 719, 720.

6 http://www.unilex.info/dynasite.cfm?dssid=2377&dsmid=13617.

change in the near future? In order for the court to apply non-state rules in the absence of a choice of law clause private international law would need to be overhauled, including the underlying principles This has as drawback that it would probably decrease certainty and predictability as to establishing the applicable law.

Enlarging party autonomy to include non-state rules as a choice of law has more potential. This is already possible in certain jurisdictions (Oregon, Louisiana, Venezuela, Paraguay, and Mexico are the examples mentioned throughout this work.) The publication of The Hague Principles on Choice of Law in International Contracts could also potentially be a positive development. So, although there are jurisdictions that allow for parties to choose non-state rules as the lex contractus there is no strong trend towards enlarging private international law to allow for this possibility.

As this research shows the issue of extending party autonomy is of subsidiary importance. The demand to have the possibility of choosing non-state rules as the applicable law in court litigation seems to be low although it is difficult to draw any real conclusions, as parties would not choose it in the first place if it were not permissible. In arbitration, this choice is made more regularly, but this cannot be equated one on one with the potential interest for this in litigation. Parties might choose non-state rules as the applicable law in arbitration because they wish to delocalise their dispute to the transnational sphere or to have more flexibility in the procedure.

So, should party autonomy be enlarged to include non-state rules? As was discussed in chapter 6 the objections raised against extending party autonomy to include non-state rules can be negated. The issue is of subsidiary importance as the demand seems to be limited so it is not recommended to re-draft legislative instruments just for this reason as the cost-benefit analysis would not be favourable. However, when private international law is updated it would be a sensible recommendation to consider this issue and enlarge party autonomy to allow a choice of law for non-state rules. The articles on choice of law in The Hague Principles could be taken as model. This would be advantageous as consistent usage of the Hague Principles on Choice of Law will, as intended, lead to a more harmonised concept of choice of law worldwide which would increase security and predictability for international commerce.

A few brief conclusions can be made on harmonisation and non-state rules. If non-state rules are applied to interpret a contract, they contribute to harmonising the underlying principles of international commercial law. This influences the development of international commercial law within domestic law and in the long-term leads to further transnational convergence. When non-state rules are applied as contractual terms or as the law governing the contract this influence is weaker as their authority comes from the contract (and the procedural laws of the forum) and not from their status as accepted international commercial principles.

The application of codified non-state rules as elements of the lex mercatoria contributes to harmonisation of transnational commercial law. If courts apply elements of the lex mercatoria without resorting to codified non-state rules there is a risk of greater divergence. If courts consistently apply codified non-state rules that are developed by international organisations as the lex mercatoria then this would lead to a more harmonised interpretation. Although as discussed there are disadvantages to applying codified non-state rules as lex mercatoria it does contribute further to the harmonisation of international commercial law as it allows for a more consistent and similar application of the lex mercatoria across countries.

As arbitral awards are confidential, their contribution to legal harmonisation is more diffuse than court decisions. Yet, they do contribute because abstracts from awards are regularly published (and collected on case law digest sites such as UNILEX) which influences future arbitrations and scholarly works and leads to increased acceptance of non-state rules. They shape what arbitrators consider accepted interpretations of non-state rules.

11.6 Concluding remarks

This book has shown that the legal authority of non-state rules does not fit into a traditional hierarchy of sources of law. The legal authority of non-state rules exists in the transnational sphere and in the domestic sphere. To determine whether non-state rules constitute a source of law we can look at the same criteria that establish what a source of law is: origin, process, reason, and substance. However, those criteria are not in itself enough to measure the legal authority of non-state rules. For that we need to study the framework that gives them legitimacy. That is the domestic law in the national framework and the support of the business community and their application in courts in the transnational framework. It is especially the last factor, which plays a deciding role. By studying the application of non-state rules in state courts their legal authority in domestic law can be understood. Through understanding this legal authority in domestic law conclusions can be drawn with regards to their legal authority in the international community and thus in transnational commercial law. The discussion of the ways that the application of non-state rules measure legal authority ensures a new focus and fills in the gap in the wider debate. The analysis in this book of the application of non-state rules as a way to measure legal authority is thus an important piece of the puzzle in understanding that legal authority.

As non-state rules cannot be chosen as the law of the contract in most jurisdictions this leads to an easy conclusion that non-state rules play a marginal role in international commerce. However, it has been shown here that this is misleading as non-state rules are applied frequently. They are applied with some regularity in arbitration as the governing law, especially in state-company contracts, which often do not include a choice of law for a state law. Arbitration is of course commercially extremely valuable and plays a key role in international trade.[7] More regularly arbitrators apply non-state rules in addition to the applicable law. The preference is often for the application of uncodified non-state rules (general principles of law and trade usages), but regularly tribunals choose the UPICC or other codified non-state rules to express these.

In addition, they are regularly applied as part of the applicable law. This happens first when non-state rules are used as contractual terms at the behest of the parties. The parties choose to include them in addition to the applicable state law. These can displace variable rules of commercial law and therefore take a leading role in defining the contractual obligations of the parties. Second, when they are applied as a source of the applicable law. Third, when they are applied to interpret the law or the contract This can be observed when there are gaps in the applicable law, when the applicable law proposes contradictory solutions, or even when the courts believe this to be necessary in order to facilitate international commerce. This happens regardless of whether they are included in the contract. As discussed, this way of using non-state rules is even observed with domestic contracts.

So, far from being marginal non-state rules occupy an important position in international commercial law and practice. When courts apply the lex mercatoria, they often resort to codified non-state rules to go from the general principle to the practical application. One can question whether this is the right development because of the intrinsic differences between these two types of rules, but practical reasons ensure that this usage of codified non-state rules will continue. In the end this means that codified non-state rules will become a reflection of the lex mercatoria.

It can be concluded that non-state rules are pervasive in international commercial law and are at the core of international contracting. This shows that non-state rules should be given a more prominent place in the theoretical study and in the practical application of international commercial law. This work has examined the legal authority of non-state rules through a new lens by demonstrating the importance of application to establish this legal authority. It has demonstrated the different ways that non-state rules have legal authority and how this is at least partly determined by their application. They can have legal authority as the applicable law to the contract, as sources of (domestic) law, as legal doctrine/scholarship, and as terms of the contract. They can be considered as law, rules of law, contractual rules, and/or normative practices.

7 The aggregate value of cases before the ICC solely already represented a value of $36 billion, an average of $45 million per case in 2018. (see: https://iccwbo.org/media-wall/news-speeches/icc-arbitration-figures-reveal-new-record-cases-awards-2018/).

Table of cases

Court cases

Allstate Insurance Co. v. Hague [1981] 449 U.S. 302,312-13.

Amanda Matthews v. Princess Cruise Lines, Ltd [2010] 728 F. Supp. 2d 1326 (S.D. Fla.).

American Trading Company, Cour de Cassation, Chambre Civil, 5 Décembre 1910.

Arcada PP v. Hobotovske enterprise Krahmaloprodukt, High Commercial Court of Ukraine [2001] 42/90-10.

Bae Systems Plc, U.K. vs Ministry of Defence and Support for Armed Forces of the Islamic Republic of Iran, Rechtbank 'S Gravenhage [2011].

Bae Systems Plc v. Ministry of Defence and Support for Armed Forces of the Islamic Republic of Iran ECLI:NL: HR:2015:1272.

Banco Union v. Banque Worms [1989] Corte Suprema de Justicia, 144 Gaceta Forense 507.

Bank of Conway v. Stary et al [1924] 51 N.D. 399, 200 N.W. 505.

Bank Mellat v. Helleiniki Techniki [1983] 3 WLR 783 (CA).

Banque Artesia Nederland, N.V., v. Corp Banca Banco Universal C.A V, Civil Chamber of the Venezuelan Supreme Court [2004].

Barnard v. Kellogg [1869] 77 U.S. 10 Wall. 383.

Bermatex s.r.l. v. Valentin Rius Clapers S.A. v. Sbrojovka Vsetin S.A, Juzgado Nacional de Primera Instancia en lo Comercial No. 10 [1994].

BP Oil International v. Empresa Estatal Petroleos de Ecuador, Federal Appellate Court [5th Circuit] [2003].

Bremen v. Zapata Off-Shore Co [1972] - 407 U.S. 1.

Brown Jenkinson & Co v. Percy Dalton [1957] 2 Lloyd's List L. R.1 (C.A.).

Chase Manhattan Bank v. Milton May 311 F.2d 117 (3d Cir. 1962).

Cooperative Maritime Etaploise v. Bos Fishproducts District Court Zwolle [5 March 1997].

Channel Tunnel Group Ltd and Another v. Balfour Beatty Construction Ltd and Others [1993] AC 334 CA.

Chartbrook Limited v. Persimmon Homes Limited 2008 EWCA Civ 183 Court of Appeal (Civil Division).

Chartbrook Limited (Respondents) v. Persimmon Homes Limited and others (Appellants) and another (Respondent) [2009] UKHL 38 House of Lords.
Cherkassy Branch of OJSC Kredobank v. Individual entrepreneur 2, Cherkasy Regional Commercial Court, 02/2625, 30 November 2009.
Columbia Nitrogen Corp v. Royster Co [1971] 451 F2d 3, 8-11 4th Cir.
Compañía de Petroleo y Asfalto (Compasa) c/ Petrobras, Distribuidora Tribunal de Apelación en lo Civil y Comercial de Asunción , S.A, 09-05-2016.
Cunliffe-Owen v. Teather & Greenwood [1967] 1 WLR 1421.
Curtis 1000, Inc. v. Suess 24 F.3d 941 (7th Cir. 1994).
Delchi Carrier SpA v. Rotorex Corp. 71 F.3d 1024 (2d Cir. 1995) (N.D. Ill. May 25, 2003).
Deutsche Schachtbau – und Tiefbohrgesellschaft mbH v. Ras Al Khaimah National Oil Co [1987] 3 WLR 1023 (CA) k.
Dixons Irmaos & Cia v. Chase National Bank 53 F. Supp. 933 (S.D.N.Y. 1943).
Dnipropetrovsk company Dnepryanka v. Inter-state Tax Administration of Dnipropetrovsk city and Department, Dnipropetrovsk Regional Administrative Court, 2-a-10084/09/0470, 21 June 2010.
Ebasco Services Inc. v. Pennsylvania Power & L. Co. 402 F. Supp. 421 (E.D. Pa. 1975).
Engracia Marina Haywood de Balbuena y otro v. Empresa de Transporte Nueva Asunción S.A. y otro, Corte Suprema de Justicia 1074/2016, 04 August 2016.
Erie Railroad Co. v. Tompkins [1938] 304 U.S. 64.
Exxon Mobil Corp. v. Drennen [2014] WL 4782974 (Tex. 2014).
FG Alpha v. TOV NVF Sintal, Kharkiv Regional Commercial Court, 35/118-08, 23 September 2009.
First National Bank of Mitchell v. Daggett [1993] 497 N.W.2d 358 (Nebraska).
Fougerolle (France) v. Banque de Proche Orient (Lebanon), Cour de Cassation, 9/12 [1981].
Fourrures Renel, Cour de Cassation, Chambre Civil, 6 Juillet 1959.
Grupo Santa Monica Sports v. Real Club Deportivo de la Coruña.
Halpern v. Halpern [2007] EWCA Civ 291.
Hideo Yoshimoto v. Canterbury Golf International Ltd [2000] Court of Appeal New Zealand, 2000 NZCA 350.
Holzimpex Inc. v. Republican Agricultural Unitary Enterprise, Supreme Economic Court of the Republic of Belarus [20 May 2003].
Italdecor s.a.s. v. Yiu's Industries (H.K.) Limited (default)' Corte d'Appello di Milano [2002].
Joe Buck E. Evans v. Harry Robinson Pontiac Buick, Inc [1999] 98-191 983 S.W.2d 946 Supreme Court of Arkansas.
JH Rayner and Company, LTD. v. Hambros Bank LTD, Court of Appeal [1943] 1 K.B. 37.
Jorge Moises Etcheverry Alí v. Rosa María Ramona Etcheverry de Brizuela, Corte Suprema de Justicia - Sala Civil y Comercial [27 March 2017].

Koda v. Carnival Corp, United States District Court, S.D. Florida [2007].
Manners v. Morosco [1919] 2 Cir., 258 F. 557, 560.
Messageries Maritimes, Cour De Cassation, Chambre Civile [1950].
The Ministry of Defence and Support for the Armed Forces of the Islamic Republic of Iran v. Cubic Defense Systems, Inc [1998] United States District Court, S.D. California.
Mitsubishi v. Soler Chrysler-Plymouth [1985] 473 U.S. 614.
Nanakuli Paving & Rock Co. v. Shell Oil Co. [1981] 664 F.2d 772 (9th Cir.).
Ninth circuit Arbitrazh Court of Appeal [23 June 2016] 09AP-24129/2016.
Noridane Foods S.A. v. Anexo Comercial Importação e Distribuição Ltda. [14 February 2017] Court of Appeal of Rio Grande do Sul.
OJSC Druzhkovskaya factory of metal products v. TOV Company Light-Tech [16 April 2013] High Commercial Court of Ukraine 5023/4701/12.
Parties Unknown, Hof 'S-Hertogenbosch [2002].
Parties Unknown, Oberlandesgericht Graz, Austria [1995].
Parties Unknown, Supreme Economic Court of the Republic of Belarus [2003].
Parties Unknown, Ninth circuit Arbitrazh Court of Appeal, 09AP-24129/2016 [23 June 2016].
Pillans v. van Mierop [1765] 3 Burr 1663.
Poltava oblavtodor v. TOV Kontakt-K, Dnipropetrovsk Regional Commercial Court [2013] 904/4611/13.
Pritchard v. Norton [1882] 106 U.S. 1224.
Proforce Recruit Limited v. The Rugby Group Limited 2006 EWCA Civ 69.
Prows v. Pinpoint Retail Sys. [1993] 868 P.2d 809 (Utah).
Public utility company Housing Managment of Kyiv city v. TOV Kyiv Telecommunication Networks, Kyiv Commercial Court, 5011-7/3803-2012.
Radioactive, J.V v. Manson [2001] 153 F. Supp. 2d 462 (S.D.N.Y).
Rafael Alberto Martínez Luna y María Mercedes Bernal Cancino v. Granbanco S.A, Corte Suprema de Justicia [21 February 2012].
Raw Materials, Inc. v. Manfred Forberich GmbH & Co. [2004] KG, No. 03 C 1154, U.S. District.
R. v. International Trustee for the Protection of Bondholders Aktiengesellschaft [1937] A.C. 500.
Republic of Nicaragua v. The United States of America [1986] ICJ.
Rock Advertising Limited v MWB Business Exchange Centres Limited [2018] UKSC 24.
Robinson v. Bland W. [1760] B1. 234, 96 E.R. 129.
Scafom International BV vs Lorraine Tubes s.a.s, Cour de Cassation [19 June 2009].
SCEA GAEC Des Beauches Bernard Bruno v. Société Teso Ten Elsen GmbH & COKG, Cour d'Appel de Grenoble [October 1996].
Seeman v. Philadelphia Warehouse [1927] 274 U.S. 403 (47 S.Ct. 626, 71 L.Ed. 1123).
Shamil Bank of Bahrain EC v. Beximico Pharmaceuticals Ltd. (2004) EWCA Civ. 19.

Shell International Petroleum Co. Ltd. (Sitco) (UK) v. Deutsche Schachtbaund Tiefbohrgesellschaft MbH (DST) (FR Germany) [1989] 2 A.C.375.
Société Forasol v. Société mixte Franco-Kazakh CISTM, Cour d'appel de Paris (1er Ch.C.) [1998].
Société Harper Robinson v. Société internationale de maintenance et de réalisations industrielles, Cour d'Appel de Grenoble [1996].
Société Nationale Industrielle Aerospatiale v. United States Dist. Court [1987] 482 U.S., 553.
Société Pabalk Ticaret Limited Sirkeli v. Norsclor S.A. [26 October 1979].
Société Pabalk Ticaret Limited Sirkeli v. Norsclor S.A 83-11.355 [09 October 1984] Cour d Cassation.
The Square Mile Partnership Ltd v. Fitzmaurice McCall Ltd [2006] EWCA Civ 1690.
Specialized foreign trade company Progres, subsidiary company of the State Company Ukrspecexport v. Ministry of Economy of Ukraine, Kyiv District Administrative Court, 8/311 [12 December 2008].
Swift v. Tyson [1842]41 U.S. 1.
TOV Ukrainian commercial vehicles v. Department of Transport and Communications of Chernihiv City Council, High Commercial Court of Ukraine [24 November 2010] 7/72.
Trans Meridian Trading Inc. v. Empresa Nacial de Comerzialicion de Insumo [1987] 829 F.2d 949, 953-54 (9th Cir).
Urbana Farmers Union Elevator Co. v. Schock [1984] 351 N.W.2d 88.
Valenciana de Cementos Portland SA v. Primary Coal Inc [22 October 1991] Cass civ. Ire, 1991 Bull. Civ. 1 No. 1354.
Valley Juice Ltd., Inc. v. Evian Watersof France, Inc. [1996] 87 F.3d 604, 608 (2d Cir.).
Vita Food Products, Inc. v. Unus Shipping Co., Ltd. [1939] A.C. 277.
Voges Metalurgia Ltda. v. Inversiones Metalmecanicas I.C.A. – IMETAL I.C.A. Court of Appeal of Rio Grande do Sul [30 03 2017].
Wayman v. Southard [1825] 10 Wheat. (23 U.S.) 1.
Zivilgericht Kanton Basel-Stadt (Switzerland) [12 December 1992].

Arbitral awards

Bae Systems Plc, U.K. v. Ministry of Defence and Support for Armed Forces of the Islamic Republic of Iran, ICC International Court of Arbitration 7110/1995.
China International Economic and Trade Arbitration Commission (CIETAC) [31 Ocober 2016].
Gemplus&Talsud v. Mexico, International Centre for Settlement of Investment Disputes [2010].
ICC Award No 5713 (1989).
ICC Award No. 6149 (1990).
ICC Award No. 7331 (1994).

ICC Award No. 7375 (1996).
ICC Award No. 8128 (1995).
ICC Award No. 8817 (1995).
ICC Award No. 8261 (1996).
ICC Award No. 8540 (1996).
ICC Award No. 7365 (1997).
ICC Award No. 8873 (1997).
ICC Award No 8909 (1998).
ICC Award No.7110 (1999).
ICC Award No. 8547 (1999).
ICC Award No. 9474 (1999).
ICC Award No. 11018 (2002).
ICC Award No. 11575 (2003).
ICC Award No. 12040 (2003).
ICC Award No.12111 (2003).
ICC Award No. 13012 (2004).
ICC Award No.8502 (1996).
Parties Unknown, Ad Hoc Arbitration (Costa Rica), 30.04.2001.
Parties Unknown, International Arbitration Court at the Chamber of Commerce and Industry of the Russian Federation, 11/2002.
Sapphire International Petroleums Ltd. v. National Iranian Oil Company, ad-hoc tribunal [1963].
Tribunal of International Commercial Arbitration at the Russian Federation Chamber of Commerce and Industry, 5 June 1997, 229/1996.
Watkins-Johnson Co. & Watkins-Johnson Ltd. v. The Islamic Republic of Iran & Bank Saderat Iran 28.07.1989 Iran-United States Claims Tribunal, number 370 (429-370-1).

Bibliography

Books and articles

Abbott K W and Snidal D 'Hard and Soft Law in International Governance' (2000) 54 *International Organization.*

Aguilar Viera I, 'The CISG and Party Autonomy in Brazilian International Contract Law' (2013) 1 *Panorama of Brazilian Law* 173.

Albornoz M M, 'Choice of Law in International Contracts in Latin American Systems' (2010) 6 *Journal of Private International Law* 23.

Araujo N and I Guedes de C. Saldanha F, 'Recent Developments and Current Trends on Brazilian Private International Law Concerning International Contracts' (2013) 1 *Panorama of Brazilian Law* 73.

Arnaldez J-J, Desrains Y and Hascher D, *Collection of ICC Arbitral Awards 1996–2000* (Wolters Kluwer 2009).

Arnold D G, 'Corporations and Human Rights Obligations' (2016) 1 *Business and Human Rights Journal* 255.

Baasch Andersen C, 'Uniformity in the CISG in the First Decade of its Application' in Fletcher I F, Mistelis L and Cremona M, (editors) *Foundations and Perspectives of International Trade Law,* (Sweet & Maxwell 2000).

Backus D and Harfield H, 'Custom and Letters of Credit: The Dixon, Irmaos Case' (1952) 52 *Colombia Law Review* 589.

Bainbridge S, 'Trade Usages in International Sales of Goods: An Analysis of the 1964 and 1980 Sales Conventions' (1983–1984) 24 *Virginia Journal of International Law* 619.

Bamodu O, 'Exploring the Interrelationships of Transnational Commercial Law 'the New Lex Mercatoria' and International Commercial Arbitration' (1998) 1 *African Journal of International and Comparative Law* 37.

Bamodu O, 'Extra-national Legal Principles in the Global Village: A Conceptual Examination of Transnational Law' (2001) 4 *International Arbitration Law Review* 14.

Bamodu O, 'The Rome I Regulation and the Relevance of Non-State Law' in Stone P, and Farah Y, (Editors), *Research Handbook in EU Private International Law* (2015 Edward Elgar Publishing) 221/222.

Basedow J, 'Uniform Law Conventions and the UNIDROIT Principles of International Commercial Contracts' (2000) 5 *Uniform Law Review* 129.

Battifol H, *Les Conflits de Lois en Matière des Contrats* (Librairie du Recueil Sirey 1938).

Battifol H, 'Note sur arrêt Messageries Maritimes' (1950) *Revue Critique Droit International Privé* 609.

Battifol H, 'Note sur arrêt Fourrures Renel' (1959) *Revue Critique du Droit International Privé* 708.

Beale J H, 'What Law Governs the Validity of a Contract?' (1910) 23 *Harvard Law Review*.

Beale J H, *A Treatise on the Conflicts of Laws Volume 2: Choice of Law* (Baker, Voorhis & Co 1935).

Bëhr V, 'Rome I Regulation, A Mostly Unified Private International Law of Contractual Relationships within most of the European Union' (2010) 29 *Journal of Law and Commerce* 233.

Benson B L, 'The Spontaneous Evolution of Commercial Law' (1989) 55 *Southern Economic Journal* 644.

Berger K P, '*Berthold Goldman and the Dijon School: The rebirth of the Lex Mercatoria*' http://www.trans-lex.org/000001.

Berger K P, 'Lex Mercatoria doctrine and the UNIDROIT principles of international commercial contracts' (1997) 28 *Law and Policy in International Business* 943.

Berger K P, *The Creeping Codification of the Lex Mercatoria* (Kluwer Law International 1999).

Berger K P, 'The New Law Merchant and the Global Market Place' (2000) 4 *International Arbitration Law Review* 92.

Berger K P, 'The New Law Merchant and The Global Market Place: A 21st Century View of Transnational Commercial Law' in Berger K P (Editor), *The Practice of Transnational Law* (Kluwer Law International 2001).

Berman H J, 'The Law of International Commercial Transactions (Lex Mercatoria)' (1987) 2 *Emory Journal of International Dispute Resolution* 235.

Berman H J, 'Towards an Integrative Jurisprudence: Politics, Morality, History' (1988) 76 *California Law Review* 779.

Bernstein L, 'Opting out of the Legal System: Extralegal Contractual Relations in the Diamond Industry' (1992) 21 *Journal for International Legal Studies* 115.

Bernstein L, 'Merchant Law in a Merchant Court: Rethinking the Code's Search for Immanent Business Norms' (1996) 144 *University of Pennsylvania Law Review* 1765.

Blasé F, 'Leaving the Shadow for the Test of Practice – On the Future of the Principles of European Contract Law' (1999) 3 *Vindobona Journal of International Commercial Law and Arbitration* 3.

Block-Lieb S, 'Soft and Hard Strategies: The Role of Business in the Crafting of International Commercial Law' (2019) 40 *Michigan Journal of International Law*.

Bianca C M and Bonell M J, 'Commentary on Usages and Practices' in Bianca C M and Bonell M J (editors), *Commentary on the International Sales Law - The 1980 Vienna Sales Convention* (Giuffrè 1987).

Bonell M J, 'The UNIDROIT Principles of International Commercial Contracts and CISG – Alternatives or Complementary Instruments?' (1996) 1 *Uniform Law Review* 26.

Bonell M J, *An International Restatement of Contract Law: The UNIDROIT Principles of International Commercial Contracts* (2nd edition, Transnational Publishers 1997a).

Bonell M J, 'The UNIDROIT Principles of International Commercial Contracts: Towards a new lex mercatoria?' (1997b) *International Business Law Journal* 145.

Bonell, 'UNIDROIT Principles: a Significant Recognition by a United States District Court' (1999) 4 *Uniform Law Review* 651.

Bonell M J, 'The UNIDROIT Principles and Transnational Law' (2000) 5 *Uniform Law Review* 199.

Bonell M J, 'The CISG, European Contract Law and the Development of a World Contract Law' (2008) 56 *American Journal of Comparative Law* 1.

Bonell M J, 'The New Provisions on Illegality in the UNIDROIT Principles 2010' (2011) 16 *Uniform Law Review* 517.

Bonell M J and Lando O, 'Future Prospects of the Unification of Contract Law in Europe and Worldwide' (2013) 18 *Uniform Law Review* 17.

Bonell M J, 'The Law Governing International Commercial Contracts and the Actual Role of the UNIDROIT Principles' (2018) 23 *Uniform Law Review* 15.

Bruch C S, 'Codifications of Conflicts Law: the Louisiana Draft' (1987) 35 *American Journal of Comparative Law* 255.

Bush D, 'The Principles of European Contract Law before the Supreme Court of the Netherlands' (2008) 16 *Zeitschrift für Europäisches Privatrecht* 549.

Busseuil G, 'L'Avenir des Principes Unidroit Relatifs aux Contrats de Commerce International et des Principes Européens du Droit du Contrat : du Droit Mou ou Droit Dur ?' (2004) *Centre de Droit Civil des Affaires et du Contentieux Economique* http://www.glose.org/CEDCACE4.pdf.

Calleros C R, 'Towards Harmonization and Certainty in Choice of Law Rules for International Contracts: Should the U.S. Adopt the Equivalent of Rome I?' (2010) 28 *Wisconsin International Law Journal* 639.

Cattaui L M, 'Harmonising Commercial Law: Keeping Pace with Business' in Fletcher I F, Mistelis L and Cremona (editors) *Foundations and Perspectives of International Trade Law* (Sweet & Maxwell 2000).

Chen J C, 'Code, Custom, and Contract: The Uniform Commercial Code as Law Merchant' (1992) 27 *Texas International Journal* 91, 98.

Chuah J C T, 'Impact of Islamic Law on Commercial Sale Contracts – A Private International Law Dimension in Europe' (2010) 4 *European Journal of Commercial Contract Law* 191.

Clarkson C M V and Hill J, *Jaffey on the Conflicts of Laws* (2nd edition, Oxford University Press 2002).

Clive E, 'Interpretation and pre-contractual negotiations: is English law genetically incompatible with European private law?' (2010) *European Private Law News Blog* http://www.epln.law.ed.ac.uk/2010/04/22/interpretation-and-pre-contractual-negotiations-is-english-law-genetically-incompatible-with-european-private-law/.

Collins H, *The European Civil Code: The Way Forward* (Cambridge University Press 2008).

Collins H, Cosmopolitanism and Transnational Private Law (2012) 8 *European Contract Law Review* 311.

Cordero Moss G, *Norwegian National Report to the XVII Congress of the International Academy of Comparative Law Contracts without a Proper Law in Private International Law and Non-State Law* (2006).

Cordero-Moss G, 'The Transnational Law of Contracts: What it Can and What it Cannot Achieve' in Weiler T and Baetens F (editors), *New Directions in International Economic Law: In Memoriam Thomas Wälde* (Martinus Nijhoff 2011).

Cranston R, '*A Theory for International Commercial Law?*' http://biblio.juridicas.unam.mx/libros/5/2332/18.pdf.

Cremades B M and Plehn S L, 'The New Lex Mercatoria and the Harmonization of the laws of International Commercial Transactions' (1983–1984) 2 *Boston University International Law Journal* 317.

Curtin K M, 'Contractual Expansion & Limitation of Judicial Review' (2000) 15 *Dispute Resolution Journal* 56.

Dalhuisen J H, *On Transnational and Comparative Commercial, Financial and Trade Law Volume - The New Lex Mercatoria and its Sources* (Hart Publishing 2001).

Dalhuisen J H, *On Transnational and Comparative Commercial, Financial and Trade Law* (3rd edition, Hart Publishing 2007).

De la Colette J, *Les Contrats de Commerce Internationaux* (3rd edition, De Boeck Université 1996).

Delaume G R, 'L'Autonomie de la Volonté en Droit International Privé' (1950) 39 *Revue Critique de Droit International Privé* 321.

De Ly F, *International Business Law and Lex Mercatoria* (T.M.C Asser Instituut 1992).

De Ly F, 'Sources of International Sales Law: An Eclectic Model' (2005) 25 *Journal of Law and Commerce* 1.

Dennis M J, 'Modernizing and Harmonizing International Contract Law: The CISG and the UNIDROIT Principles Continue to Provide the Best Way Forward' (2014) 19 *Uniform Law Review* 114.

Dessemontet F, 'Use of the UNIDROIT Principles to Interpret and Supplement Domestic Law' (2002) *Supplément Spécial Bulletin de la Cour Internationale d'Arbitrage de la CCI.*

Dicey, *Morris & Collins, the Conflicts of Law*, (14th edition, Sweet & Maxwell 2006).

DiMatteo L A, 'The Scholarly Response to the Harmonization of International Sales Law' (2012) 30 *Journal of Law & Commerce* 1.

DiMatteo L A, *International Contracting: Law and Practice* (Wolter Kluwer Law & Business 2013).

Drettmann A K, '*Would English law on trade usages benefit from adopting a more formal approach such as seen in other jurisdictions as well as in international conventions?*' (2009) http://www.cisg.law.pace.edu/cisg/biblio/drettmann.html.

Eberhard S, *Les Sanctions de L'Inexécution du Contrat et les Principes Unidroit* (Cedidac UNIL Centre du Droit Lausanne 2005) 7.

Edlund H H, 'The Concept of Unification and Harmonization' in Fogt M M (editor), *Unification and Harmonization of International Commercial Law: Interaction or Deharmonization?* (Wolters Kluwer Law & Business 2012).

Elod Cserep V, 'E Pluribus Unum - Out of Many, One Common European Sales Law' (2017) 29 *Pace International Law Review* 199.

Estrella Faria J A, Future Directions of Legal Harmonisation and Law Reform: Stormy Seas or Prosperous Voyage? (2009) 14 *Uniform Law Review* 5, 9.

Ferrari F, 'Uniform Interpretation of the 1980 Uniform Sales Law' (1994) 24 *Georgia Journal of International and Comparative Law* 183.

Ferrari F, 'Le Champ d'Application des << Principes pour les Contrats Commerciaux Internationaux>> élaborés par UNIDROIT' (1995) 47 *Revue Internationale de Droit Comparé* 985.

Ferrari F, 'The Relationship between the UCC and the CISG and the Construction of Uniform Law' (1996) 29 *Loyola of Los Angeles Law Review* 1021.

Ferrari F, *Le Contrat de Vente International, Applicabilité et Application de la Convention de Vienne sur les Contrats de Vente Internationale de Marchandises* (2nd edition, Helling & Lichtenhahn 2000).

Ferrari F, 'Homeward Trend and Lex Forism in International Sales Law' (2009) *International Business Law Journal* 333.

Finazzi Agrò E, 'The Impact of the UNIDROIT Principles in International Dispute Resolution in Figures' (2011) 16 *Uniform Law Review* 719.

Fitzgerald P L, 'The International Contracting Practices Survey Project: An Empirical Study of the Value and Utility of the CISG and the UNIDROIT Principles of International Commercial Contracts to Practitioners, Jurists, and Legal Academics in the United States' (2008) 27 *Journal of Law and Commerce* 1.

Fletcher I F, Mistelis L and Cremona (editors) *Foundations and Perspectives of International Trade Law* (Sweet & Maxwell 2000).

Foster N D H, 'Comparative Commercial Law: Rules or Context?' in Örucü E and Nelken D (Editors), *Comparative Law, A Handbook* (Hart Publishing 2007).

Fox E M, 'Harmonization of Law and Procedures in a Globalized world' (1991) 60 *Antitrust Law Journal* 593.

Fresnedo de Aguirre C, 'Party Autonomy - A Blank Cheque?' (2012) 17 *Uniform Law Review* 655.

Gabriel H D, 'The Advantages of Soft Law in International Commercial Law: the role of UNIDROIT, UNCITRAL, and The Hague Conference' (2008) 34 *Brooke Journal of International Law* 655.

Gabriel H D, 'The UNIDROIT Principles of International Commercial Contracts: an American Perspective on the Principles and Their Use' (2012) 17 *Uniform Law Review* 507.

Gabriel H D, 'The Use of Soft Law in the Creation of Legal Norms in International Commercial Law: How Successful Has it Been?' (2019) 40 *Michigan Journal of International Law* 413.

Gama Jr L, 'Prospects for the UNIDROIT Principles in Brazil' (2011) 16 *Uniform Law Review* 613.

Gama e Souza Jr L, 'The UNIDROIT Principles of International Commercial Contracts and their Applicability in the MERCOSUR Countries' (2012) 36 *Revue Juridique Thémis* 375.

Gannagé L, 'Le Contrat Sans Loi en Droit International Privé' (2007) 11 *Electronic Journal of Comparative Law* 1.

Garro A M, The Gap-Filling Role of the UNIDROIT Principles in International Sales Law: Some Comments on the Interplay between the Principles and the CISG (1994–1995) 69 *Tulane Law Review* 1149.

Garro A M 'Rule-Setting by Private Organisations, Standardisation of Contracts and the Harmonisation of International Sales Law' in Fletcher I F, Mistelis L and Cremona (editors) *Foundations and Perspectives of International Trade Law* (Sweet & Maxwell 2000).

Ghestin, J 'La notion de contrat' (1990) 12 *Periodicals Archive Online* 7, 10.

Gillette C P, 'Harmony and Stasis in Trade Usages for International Sale' (1998–1999) 39 *Virginia Journal of International Law* 707.

Gillette C P, 'The Law Merchant in the Modern Age: Institutional Design and International Usages under the CISG' (2004–2005) 5 *Chicago Journal of International Law* 157.

Gillette C P and Scott R E, 'The Political Economy of International Sales Law' (2005) *International Review of Law and Economics* 446, 467.

Giovannucci Orlandi C, 'Procedural Law Issues and Uniform Law Conventions' (2000) 5 *Uniform Law Review* 23.

Goldman B, 'Frontières du Droit et Lex Mercatoria' (1964) *Archives du Philosophie du Droit.*

Goldman B, '*Lex Mercatoria: Lecture' Forum Internationale 3* (Kluwer 1983).

Goldman B, 'The Applicable Law: General Principles of Law- the lex mercatoria' in Lew J D M (Editor) *Contemporary Problems in International Arbitration* (Springer 1987).

Goode R, *Commercial Law* (2nd edition, Penguin Books 1995).

Goode R, 'Usage and Its Reception in Transnational Commercial Law' (1997) 46 *International & Comparative Law Quarterly* 2.

Goode R, 'Usage and its Reception in Transnational Commercial Law' in Ziegel J S and Lerner S (editors), *New Developments in International Commercial and Consumer Law, proceedings of the 8th Bienal Conference of the International Academy of Commercial and Consumer Law* (Hart Publishing, Oxford 1998).

Goode R, Kronke H, Mckendrick E and Wool J, *Transnational Commercial Law: Text, Cases and Materials* (Oxford University Press 2007).

Goode R, 'Contract and Commercial Law: The Logic and Limits of Harmonisation' (2003) 7 *Electronic Journal of Comparative Law.*

Gordon M W, 'Part II Some Thoughts on the Receptiveness of Contract Rules in the CISG and the UNIDROIT Principles as Reflected in One State's (Florida) Experience of (1) Law School Faculty, (2) Members of the Bar with an International Practice, and (3) Judges' (1998) 46 *American Journal of Comparative Law Supplement* 361.

Gourion P A, Peyrard G and Soubeyrand N, *Droit du Commerce International,* (4th edition, L.G.D.J. Lextenso Editions 2008).

Greenstein R K, 'Is the Proposed UCC Choice of Law Provision Unconstitutional?' (2000) 73 *Temple Law Review* 1159.

Guniberti G, 'Le Nouvel Article 3.3.1 Des Principes Unidroit 2010 Sur le Contrat Violant une Règle Impérative: un Regard Critique du Point de Vue du Droit International Privé' (2013) 18 *Uniform Law Review* 490.

Günther K, '*Legal Pluralism or Uniform Concept of Law: Globalisation as a Problem of Legal Theory*' (2008) http://www.helsinki.fi/nofo/NoFo5Gunther.pdf.

Hadfield G K, Privatzing Commercial Law: Lessons from the Middle and Digital Ages, (2000) Working Paper No.195.

Hall R B and Biersteker T J, 'The emergence of private authority in the international system' in Hall R B and Biersteker T J, (editors) '*The Emergence of Private Authority in Global Governance* (CUP 2002) 5.

Hall P A, 'Policy Paradigms, Social Learning, and the State: The Case of Economic Policy Making in Britain' (1993) 25 *Comparative Politics* 275.

Halverson Cross K, 'Parol Evidence under the CISG: The 'Homeward Trend' Reconsidered' (2007) 68 *Ohio State Law Journal* 133.

Han S, 'Principles of Asian Contract Law: An Endeavor of Regional Harmonization of Contract Law in East Asia (2013) 58 *Villanova Law Review* 589.

Hoekstra J, 'The Normative Influence of the UNIDROIT Principles of International Commercial Law on Courts' (2019) 23 *The Vindobona Journal of International Commercial Law and Arbitration* 54.

Honnold J, 'Letters of Credit, Custom, Missing Documents and the Dixon Case: A Reply to Backus and Harfield' (1953) 53 *Columbia Law Review* 504.

Honnold J, 'The Sales Convention in Action- Uniform International Words: Uniform Application?' (1988) 8 *Journal of Law and Communication* 207.

Honnold J, *Documentary History of the Uniform Law for International Sales: the Studies, Deliberations, and Decisions that Led to the 1980 United Nations Convention with Introductions and Explanations* (Kluwer Law International 1989).

Hope D, 'The Role of the Judge in Developing Contract Law' (2011) 15 *Jersey and Guernsey Law Review* 6.

Horn N, 'The Use of Transnational Law in the Contract Law of International Trade and Finance' in Berger K P (Editor), *The Practice of Transnational Law* (Kluwer Law International 2001).

Howells G, 'European Contract Law Reform and European Consumer Law -- Two Related but Distinct Regimes' (2011) 7 *European Review of Contract Law* 173.

Jansen, N, *The Making of Legal Authority* (Oxford University Press 2010) 20.

Juenger F K, 'The Inter-American Convention on the Law Applicable to International Contracts Some Highlights and Comparisons' (1994) 42 *American Journal of Comparative Law* 381.

Juenger F K, 'American Conflicts Scholarship and the New Law Merchant' (1995) 28 *Vanderbilt Journal of Transnational Law* 487.

Juenger F K, 'The *lex mercatoria* and private international law' (2000) 60 *Louisiana Law Review* 1133.

Ka J, 'Introduction to PACL' in Angelo T, Castellani L and Sage Y-L (editors) *Contributions to the Study of International Trade/ADR in the South Pacific* (2010) 55.

Kabik M, 'Through the Looking-Glass: International Trade in the 'Wonderland' of the United Nations Conventions of the International Sales of Goods' (1992) 9 *International Tax and Business Lawyer* 408.

Kadens E, 'The Myth of the Customary Law Merchant' (2012) 90 *Texas Law Review* 1153.

Kahn P, 'Note Norsolor c/ Pabalk Ticaret Ltd Sirketi' (1981) 108 *Revue de l'Arbitrage* 386.

Kahn P, 'Les Conventions Internationales de Droit Uniforme devant les Tribunaux Arbitraux' (2000) 5 *Uniform Law Review* 121.

Kastely A H, 'Stock Equipment for the Bargain in Fact: Trade Usage, Express Terms, and Consistency under § 1-205 of the Uniform Commercial Code' (1986) 64 *North Carolina Law Review* 777.

Kirst R W, 'Usage of Trade and Course of Dealing: Subversion of the UCC Theory' (1977) *University of Illinois Law Review* 811.

Klabbers J, The Undesirability of Soft Law (1998) 67 *Nordic Journal of International Law* 381, 387/391.

Kröll S, 'Selected Problems Concerning the CISG's Scope of Application' (2005–2006) 25 *Journal of Law and Commerce* 39.

Kronke H, 'International Uniform Commercial Law Conventions: advantages, disadvantages, criteria for choice' (2000) 5 *Uniform Law Review* 13.

Kronke H, 'The UN Sales Convention, the UNIDROIT Contract, Principles and the Way Beyond' (2005–2006) 25 *Journal of Law and Commerce* 451.

Lagarde P, 'Note Cassation Civil 1e 22/10/1991' (1992) *Revue de l'Arbitrage* 457.

Lagarde P, 'Remarques sur la Proposition de Règlement de la Commission Européenne sur la Loi Applicable aux Obligations Contractuelles (Rome I)' (2006) 95 *Revue Critique de Droit International Privé* 33.

Lalive J-F, 'Contracts between a State or a State Agency and a Foreign Company' (1964) 13 *International and Comparative Law Quarterly* 987.

Lando O, 'New American Choice-of-Law Principles and the European Conflicts of Law of Contracts' (1982) 30 *American Journal of Comparative Law* 19.
Lando O, 'The Lex Mercatoria in International Commercial Arbitration' (1985) 34 *International & Comparative Law Quarterly* 747.
Lando O, 'The Common Core of European Private Law and the Principles of European Contract Law' (1998) 21 *Hastings International and Comparative Law Review* 809.
Lando O, 'Principles of European Contract Law and UNIDROIT Principles: Moving from Harmonisation to Unification' (2003) 8 *Uniform Law Review* 123.
Legrand G, 'La Notion de Droit en France au 19eme siècle' (1921) 23 *Revue Néo-Scolastique de Philosophie* 436.
Legrand P, 'Against a European Civil Code' (1997) 60 *Modern Law Review* 44.
Lehmann M, 'Liberating the Individual from Battles between States: Justifying Party Autonomy in Conflict of Laws' (2008) 41 *Vanderbilt Journal of Transnational Law* 381.
Levie J H, 'Trade Usage and Custom under the Common Law and the Uniform Commercial Code' (1965) 40 *New York University Law Review* 1101.
Levin M J, 'Party Autonomy: Choice-of-Law Clauses in Commercial Contracts' (1957–1958) 46 *Georgetown Law Journal* 260.
Loken K, 'A New Global Initiative on Contract Law in UNCITRAL: Right Project, Right Forum?' (2013) 58 *Villanova Law Review* 509.
Low H Y, UCP 600: the new rules on documentary compliance (2010) 52 *International Journal of Law and Management* 193.
Madrid Martínez C, 'Notas Sobre La Lex Mercatoria: entre el Silencio del Legislador Europeo y el Silencio de los Estados Americanos' in Rodríguez J M and Arroyo D F (editors) *Derecho internacional privado y Derecho de la Integración. Libro Homenaje a Roberto Díaz Labrano* (CEDEP 2003).
Mackintosh K L, 'Liberty, Trade, and the Uniform Commercial Code, When Should Default Rules be Based on Business Practices?' (1996) 38 *William & Mary Law Review* 1465.
Marques L, *International Uniform Commercial Law: towards a progressive consciousness* (Ashgate, Aldershot 2005) 11.
Matteucci M,' Prospects of International Unification of Law from a European Viewpoint' (1949) 10 *Louisiana Law Review* 15.
Mazzotta F G, 'Why Do Some American Courts Fail to get it Right?' (2005) 3 *Loyola University Chicago International Review* 85.
Methven O'Brien C and Dhanarajan S, 'The Corporate Responsibility to Respect Human Rights: A Status Review' (2015) National University of Singapore, Faculty of Law Working Paper Series, Working Paper 2015/005.
Michaels R, 'Globalizing Savigny? The State in Savigny's Private International Law and the Challenge of Europeanization and Globalization' (2005a) Duke Law School Legal Studies Research Paper Series, Research Paper N.74.
Michaels R, 'The Re-statement of Non-State Law: The State, Choice of Law, and the Challenge from Global Legal Pluralism' (2005b) 51 *Wayne Law Review* 1209.
Michaels R, 'The True Lex Mercatoria: Law Beyond the State' (2007) 14 *Indiana Journal of Global Studies* 447.
Michaels R, '*Non-State Law in The Hague Principles of Choice of Law in International Contracts*' (2014a) http://papers.ssrn.com/sol3/papers.cfm?abstract_id=2386186.

Michaels R, 'The UNIDROIT Principles as Global Background Law' (2014b) 19 *Uniform Law Review* 643.

Mistelis L, 'Is Harmonisation a Necessary Evil? The Future of Harmonisation and New Sources of International Trade' in Fletcher I F, Mistelis L and Cremona (editors) *Foundations and Perspectives of International Trade Law* (Sweet & Maxwell 2000).

Mitchell W, *An Essay on the Early History of the Law Merchant* (Cambridge University Press 1904).

Momberg R and Vogenauer S, The Principles of Latin American Contract Law: Text, Translation, and Introduction (2018) 23 *Uniform Law Review* 144, 153/154.

Montesquieu C-L, *De l'Esprit des Lois Livre XX, Chapitre 2. De l'Esprit du Commerce* (2008) http://classiques.uqac.ca/classiques/montesquieu/de_esprit_des_lois/partie_4/de_esprit_des_lois_4.html.

Moss S, 'Why the United Kingdom Has Not Ratified the CISG' (2005) 25 *Journal of Law and Commerce* 483.

Muir Watt H, 'Party Autonomy in international contracts: from the making of a myth to the requirements of global governance' (2010) 6 *European Review of Contract Law* 250.

Mustill M, 'The New Lex Mercatoria: the First Twenty-Five Years' (1998) 4 *Arbitration International* 86.

Mustill M, 'Contemporary Problems in International Commercial Arbitration: A Response' (1989) 17 *International Business Lawyer* 161.

Nafziger J A R, 'Oregon's conflicts law applicable to contracts' (2002) 38 *Willamette Law Review* 397.

Nordstrom R J and Ramerman D B, 'The Uniform Commercial Code and the Choice of Law' (1969) 4 *Duke Law Journal* 623.

Oppetit B, 'Le Droit International Privé, Droit Savant' (1992) 234 *Droit Savant recueil Cours de l'académie de DIP de la Haye* 331.

Örucü E and Nelken D (Editors), *Comparative Law, A Handbook* (Hart Publishing 2007).

Oser D, *The Unidroit Principles of International Commercial Contracts: A Governing Law* (Martinus Nijhoff 2008).

Pamboukis C, 'The Concept and Function of Usages in the United Nations Convention for the International Sales of Goods' (2005–2006) 25 *Journal of Law and Commerce* 107.

Ramberg J, 'Incoterms 1980' in Horn N and Schmitthoff C M (editors), *The Transnational Law of International Commercial Transactions* (Kluwer 1982).

Ramberg J, *International Commercial Transactions* (ICC Kluwer Law International Norstedts Juridik AB 1998).

Randall K C & Norris J E, 'A New Paradigm for International Business Transactions' (1993) 71 *Washington University Law Review* 599.

Ranouil V, *L'Autonomie de la Volonté: Naissance et Evolution d'un Concept* (Presses Universitaires de France 1980).

Reimann M, 'Savigny's Triumph? Choice of Law in Contracts Cases at the Close of the Twentieth Century' (1998–1999) 39 *Virginia Journal of International Law* 571.

Reimann M, 'Parochialism in American Conflicts Law' (2001) 49 *American Journal of Comparative Law* 369.

Romito A M, 'CISG: Italian Court and Homeward Trend - Queen Mary Case Translation Programme Corte d'Appello di Milano 20 March 1998 Italdecor s.a.s. Yiu's Industries (H.K.) Limited (default)' (2002) 14 *Pace International Law Review* 179.

Roosevelt III, K, 'Certainty vs. Flexibility in the Conflict of laws' (2018) Public Law and Legal Theory Research Paper Series Research Paper No.18-40, 7.

Rühl G, 'Party Autonomy in the Private International Law of Contracts: Transatlantic Convergence and Economic Efficiency' (2007) 3 Comparative Research in Law & Political Economy Research Paper http://digitalcommons.osgoode.yorku.ca/clpe/227.

Sack A.N., 'International Unification of Private Law Rules on Air Transportation and the Warsaw Convention' (1933) 4 *Air Law Review* 345.

Saumier G, 'The Hague Principles and Choice of Non-State Rules of Law to Govern an International Commercial Contract' (2014) *Brooke Journal of International Law*.

Schagen van E, 'The Proposal for a Common European Sales Law: How its Drafting Process Might Affect the Optional Instrument's Added Value for Contract Parties and its Success' in Keirse A and Loos M (editors), *Alternative Ways to Ius Commune* (Intersentia 2012).

Schaffer G C and Pollack M A, 'Hard vs. Soft Law: Alternatives, Complements and Antagonists in International Governance' (2010) 94 *Minnesota Law Review* 706.

Schmitthoff C M, 'International Business Law-A New Law Merchant' (1961) 2 *Current Law and Social Problem* 129.

Schmitthoff C M, 'The Unification of the Law of International Trade' in Schmitthoff C (editors), *The Sources of the Law of International Trade* (Frederick A. Praeger 1964).

Schmitthoff C M, 'The Unification of the Law of International Trade' (1964 Handelshögskolan Göteburg, Skrifter) reproduced in Cheng C and Schmitthoff C M, (editors), *Select Essays on International Trade* (Marinus Nijhoff Publishers 1988).

Schmitthoff C M, 'American and European Commercial Law' (1979) 6 *Journal of Legislation* 44.

Schmitthoff C M, 'The Unification or Harmonisation of Law by Means of Standard Contracts and General Conditions' (1986) 17 *International & Comparative Law Quarterly* 551.

Schultz T, *Transnational Legality: Stateless Law and International Arbitration* (Oxford University Press 2014) 16/17.

Schwenzer I, 'Who Needs a Uniform Contract Law, and why?' (2013) 58 *Villanova Law Review* 723.

Schwenzer I and Hachem P, 'The CISG- Successes and Pitfalls' (2009) 57 *American Journal of Comparative Law* 457.

Selden B S, 'Lex Mercatoria in European and US Trade Practice: Time to Take a Closer Look' (1995) 2 *Annual Survey International and Comparative Law* 111.

Shackleton S, 'The Applicable Law in International Arbitration under the New English Arbitration Act 1996' (1997) 13 *Arbitration International* 375.

Smits J M, 'European Private Law: A Plea for a Spontaneous Legal Order' in Curtin D M, Smits J M et al. (editors), *European Integration and Law: Four Contributions to Celebrate the 25th Anniversary of Maastricht University's Faculty of Law* (Antwerp-Oxford, 2006) 70.

Smits J M, 'Convergence of Private Law in Europe', in Örucü E and Nelken D (Editors) *Comparative Law, A Handbook* (Hart Publishing, 2007).

Snyder D V, 'Private Lawmaking' (2003) 64 *Ohio State Journal* 371.

Stringer D, 'Choice of Law and Choice of Forum in Brazilian International Commercial Contracts: Party Autonomy, International Jurisdiction and the Emerging Third Way' (2005–2006) 44 *Columbia Journal of Transnational Law* 959.

Symeonides S C, 'Les Grands Problèmes de Droit international Privé et la Nouvelle Codification de Louisiane' (1992) 81 *Revue Critique de Droit International Privé* 223.

Symeonides S C, 'Louisiana Conflicts Law: Two 'Surprises' (1994) 54 *Louisiana Law Review* 497.

Symeonides S C, 'Contracts subject to Non-State Norms' (2006a) 54 *American Journal of Comparative Law* 209.

Symeonides S C, 'Party Autonomy and Private-Law Making in Private Law: The Lex Mercatoria that Isn't' published in *Liber Amicorum Konstantinos D Kerameus* (Sakkoulas/Kluwer Press, 2006b).

Symeonides S C, 'Oregon's choice of law codification for contract conflicts: an exegesis' (2007) 44 *Willamette Law Review* 205.

Symeonides S C, 'The Conflicts Book of the Louisiana Civil Code: Civilian, American, or Original?' (2008) 83 *Tulane Law Review* 1041.

Symeonides S C, 'The Hague Principles on Choice of Law for International Contracts: Some Preliminary Comments' (2013) 61 *American Journal of Comparative Law* 873.

Symeonides S C, 'Party Autonomy in International Contracts and the Multiple Ways of Slicing the Apple' (2014a) 39 *Brooklyn Journal of International Law* 1123.

Symeonides S C, 'Choice of Law in the American Courts in 2013: Twenty-Seventh Annual Survey' (2014b) 62 *American Journal of Comparative Law* 223.

Symeonides S C, 'Choice of Law in the American Courts in 2014: Twenty-Eight Annual Survey' (2015a) 63 *American Journal of Comparative Law* 299.

Symeonides S C, 'The Choice-of-Law Revolution Fifty Years after Currie: An End and a Beginning' (2015b) 2 *University of Illinois Law Review* 1847.

Symeonides S C, 'Choice of Law in the American Courts in 2014: Twenty-Eight Annual Survey' (2015c) 63 *American Journal of Comparative Law* 299.

Symeonides S C, 'Choice of Law in the American Courts in 2015: Twenty-Ninth Annual Survey' (2016) 64 *American Journal of Comparative Law* 222.

Symeonides S C, 'Choice of Law in the American Courts in 2019: Thirty-Third Annual Survey' (2020) 68 *American Journal of Comparative Law*.

Talpis J, 'Retour Vers le Futur : Application en Droit Québécois des Principes d'Unidroit au Lieu d'une Loi Nationale' (2002) 36 *Revue Juridique Thémis* 609.

Teubner G, 'Global Bukowina: Legal Pluralism in the World Society' in Teubner G (editor), *Global Law without a State* (Brookfield 1997).

Teubner G, 'Breaking Frames: Economic Globalization and the Emergence of Lex Mercatoria' (2002) 5 *European Journal of Social Theory* 199.

Torsello M, 'Reservations to International Uniform Commercial Law Conventions' (2000) 5 *Uniform Law Review* 85.

van Houtte H, *The Laws of International Trade* (Sweet & Maxwell 1995).

Tiburcio C, 'Private International Law in Brazil: A Brief Overview' (2013) 1 *Panorama of Brazilian Law* 11.

Vendrell Cervantes C, 'Application of the Principles of European Contract Law' (2008) 16 *Zeitschrift für Europäisches Privatrecht* 534.

Weintraub R J, 'Functional Developments in Choice of Law for Contracts' (1984) 187 *Recueil des Cours Académie du Droit International* 271.

Weintraub R J, 'Courts Flailing in the Waters of the Louisiana Conflicts Code: Not Waving but Drowning' (2000) 60 *Louisiana Law Review* 4.

Yntema H E, 'Autonomy' in Choice of Law' (1952) 1 *The American Journal of Comparative Law* 341.

Xiao Y and Long W, 'Contractual Party Autonomy in Chinese Private International Law' (2009) 11 *Yearbook of Private International Law* 193.

Zweigert K and Kötz H, *An introduction to comparative law* (Weir T tr, 3rd edition, Oxford University Press 1998).

Other sources

Communication from the Commission to the Council and the European Parliament on European contract law, COM (2001) 398 - Official Journal C 255 of 13.9.2001.

Communication to the European Parliament and the Council – A more coherent European contract law- An action plan, (COM (2003) 68 of 12 February 2003.

Dickinson H, *Cargo Conventions: Comparing Hague, Hague/Visby, and Hamburg Rules, Shipping at a Glance, Guide 1* http://www.hilldickinson.com/pdf/Cargo%20conventions.pdf.

Directorate General for Research, The Private Law Systems in the EU: Discrimination on Grounds of Nationality and the Need for a European Civil Code, Working Paper, 3 http://www.europarl.europa.eu/workingpapers/juri/pdf/103_en.pdf.

European Commission, 'A Digital single market strategy for Europe' (2015) Com 192 of 6th May 2015.

ICC Position on the EC Proposal for Common European Sales Law, 12/07/2012 http://www.iccwbo.org/Advocacy-Codes-and-Rules/Document-centre/2012/ICC-Position-on-the-EC-proposal-for-a-Common-European-Sales-Law/.

Max Planck Institute for Comparative and International Private Law, Comments on the European Commission's Proposal for a Regulation of the European Parliament and the Council on the law applicable to contractual obligations (Rome I) (2007) 226 http://scholarship.law.duke.edu/cgi/viewcontent.cgi?article=2612&context=faculty_scholarship.

UNCITRAL, Coordination Committee for Australia, *North Korea joins the CISG* (14April2019a)https://uncca.org.au/2019/04/14/north-korea-joins-the-cisg/.

UNCITRAL, Liechtenstein accedes to the UN Convention on Contracts for the International Sale of Goods (7 May 2019b) https://uncitral.un.org/en/news/liechtenstein-accedes-un-convention-contracts-international-sale-goods-cisg.

United Nations Information Series, The Lao People's Democratic Republic accedes to United Nations Convention on Contracts for the International Sale of Goods (25 September 2019) http://www.unis.unvienna.org/unis/en/pressrels/2019/unisl280.html.

Index

For Product Safety Concerns and Information please contact our EU representative GPSR@taylorandfrancis.com
Taylor & Francis Verlag GmbH, Kaufingerstraße 24, 80331 München, Germany

www.ingramcontent.com/pod-product-compliance
Lightning Source LLC
LaVergne TN
LVHW011124300926
849160LV00008B/504
* 9 7 8 0 3 6 7 7 4 0 8 1 8 *